GW00361683

STOY HAYWARD GUIDE TO

PERSONAL FINANCIAL PLANNING

To my parents,
Babs and Monty Stillerman

STOY HAYWARD
Accountants and Business Advisers
A member of Horwath International

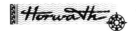

STOY HAYWARD GUIDE TO

PERSONAL FINANCIAL PLANNING

BARRY STILLERMAN

CENTURY
BUSINESS

First published in 1992 in Great Britain by
Century Business
An imprint of Random Century Limited
20 Vauxhall Bridge Road, London SW1V 2SA

Random Century Australia (Pty) Limited
20 Alfred Street, Milsons Point, Sydney
New South Wales 2061, Australia

Random Century New Zealand Limited
18 Poland Road, Glenfield
Auckland 10, New Zealand

Random Century South Africa (Pty) Limited
PO Box 337, Bergvlei, South Africa

Typeset in Bembo by SX Composing Ltd, Rayleigh, Essex
Printed and bound in Great Britain by
Mackays of Chatham PLC, Chatham, Kent

A catalogue record for this book is available from the British Library.

ISBN 0-7126-9817-5

CONTENTS

ACKNOWLEDGEMENTS

I would like to express my thanks to Zigurds Kronbergs who provided invaluable assistance on a number of chapters in this book. I would also like to thank Alan Page and Roger Allen of the Stoy Hayward Personal Financial Planning section and Anne Sheridan and Glen McKeown of Stoy Benefit Consulting who provided illustrations. My thanks also go to Jackie Smith, Julie Martin and Amanda Mulroy who worked so hard to ensure that the book was completed on time.

Most of all I would like to thank my wife, Beverley, and my two children Gemma and Olivia for putting up with the weekends and long evenings during which I was working on the book instead of being with them.

PREFACE

In recent years, the daily and weekend newspapers have devoted many pages to personal financial planning and I am pleased that more information is now provided to the public on this very important issue. Too often we spend long hours at the office earning money without thinking seriously about the way in which we can increase our income, reduce our tax, improve our wealth and, finally, pass wealth to our dependants rather than to the Inland Revenue.

This book takes you through the basic financial planning needs, examining the ways in which the tax system can be used for your benefit, and covers a whole range of important issues such as investments, pensions, and insurance cover. You may wish to read the book from beginning to end. Alternatively, you can select individual chapters and cover topics which may be of particular interest to you.

The book concludes with a chapter on independent advice. There are many reputable insurance brokers but alas there are too many who give that industry a bad name. I have come across many cases where the only person who appeared to benefit from financial advice was the broker. You should get the best advice before investing your money.

If you would like me to carry out an initial review of your own position, please complete and return the questionnaire at the back of the book and send it to me so that I can, at no initial charge, contact you to discuss your case.

I began writing this book early in 1992 and it was completed immediately after the General Election result was known. It is therefore based upon the tax regime of the continuing Conservative Government and includes details of the March 1992 Budget proposals. While a few of the proposals were enacted before 9 March, the remaining measures are likely to be considered by Parliament during the Summer of 1992.

Barry Stillerman
Personal Financial Planning Partner, Stoy Hayward

WARNING

This book is written as a general guide. As any course of action must depend upon your individual circumstances, as well as changes in the law and investment opportunities, you are strongly recommended to obtain specific professional advice before you proceed. Whilst every effort has been made to ensure that the facts and law in this book are correct, neither the author, Stoy Hayward nor the publisher accept any responsibility for any loss which may be sustained by any person as a result of having read this book.

1
INTRODUCTION

THE FINANCIAL MAZE

The last decade has seen an explosion in the 'personal financial planning' market. Direct evidence for this is easily obtained by glancing at the daily and Sunday newspapers. All the broadsheets, and even the less frivolous tabloids, now devote many pages per week to advising readers on how to manage their money. There was certainly not the same level of advice at the beginning of the 1980s.

The greatly increased flexibility and choice of pensions, the plethora of privatization issues fuelling the stock market boom of the 1980s, the introduction of several tax-efficient savings vehicles – PEPs, TESSAs, BES etc – and increased reliance on private schooling and private medicine have all contributed to a greater interest in and awareness of financial planning for individuals.

This is not a subject that should be limited to the seriously wealthy. The recent recession has illustrated a far more general need for prudent financial management. Personal financial planning includes making the best use of financial resources in order to produce the maximum financial security for yourself and your family in the most tax-efficient way. All of us, with even a modest disposable income, would benefit from good advice on negotiating our way through the maze of plans, products and tax traps waiting round every corner. Even if you find your income barely matching monthly expenses, vital pounds can be saved by shopping around between banks and building societies for the best accounts and by careful budgeting.

TAX PLANNING

The tax system has been radically restructured during the 1980s and it is important that you move with the times when planning your affairs. Income tax rates have fallen dramatically from a top marginal rate of 98 per cent on unearned income at the end of the 1970s to a top rate of 40 per cent now which applies to both earned and unearned income. The basic rate of tax has fallen from 33 per cent to 25 per cent and husbands and wives are now taxed separately on all their income (not just earnings). There is also a new 20 per cent rate for the first £2,000 of taxable income and the Government proposes to increase the level of income which is subject to this lower rate of tax.

The method of calculating capital gains has changed dramatically due to rebasing rules. The tax is now aligned to the income tax rate whereas in the past capital gains were taxed at 30 per cent. The proposed annual exemption of £5,800 per person is very valuable and enables many individuals to avoid capital gains tax. Those with sufficient wealth to be concerned about capital gains may have been using offshore trusts as a means of deferring the tax, and there have been significant changes in the tax rules for such trusts.

Even the tax charge on death has not managed to avoid the Chancellor's red pen. Capital transfer tax was abolished in 1986 and replaced by inheritance tax which provides significant estate-planning opportunities.

Chart 1.1 illustrates the way in which the tax system can be used to

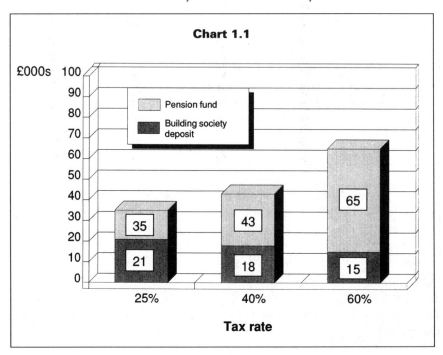

improve your wealth. It compares a net investment of £10,000 in a building society account with the same net investment in a pension scheme and assumes that each fund grows at ten per cent a year over ten years. It also compares the position if the taxpayer pays tax at the basic rate of 25 per cent, the higher rate of 40 per cent or if the top tax rate had increased to approximately 60 per cent under a Labour administration. This 60 per cent rate will not now apply.

The new 'TESSAs' (Tax Exempt Special Savings Accounts) also give the opportunity to improve the tax-efficiency of your available deposits. **Chart 1.2** assumes that maximum lump sum investments are made in a TESSA at

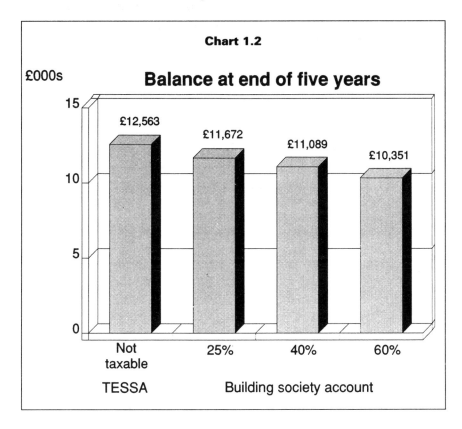

the beginning of each year and a similar amount invested in a taxable deposit account. Interest is credited at an average rate of ten per cent throughout the five-year period and higher-rate tax is withdrawn from the account during that period.

THE POLITICAL AND ECONOMIC CLIMATE

Before 9 April 1992 the possibility of a Labour government or a hung parliament was a serious one. To understand what this means, we need only cast our minds back to the very different tax world of early 1979 with income tax at rates of up to 98 per cent and capital transfer tax on lifetime gifts. While there was no question of a return to those rates, there remains a sharp difference between the Conservative and Labour Party proposals over tax matters.

On 16 March 1992, the Labour Party provided details of the Budget which they would have delivered in the Spring if they were to have formed the next government. At the lower end, they would have increased the personal allowance, abolished the two per cent national insurance charge on earnings up to £54 per week but also abolished the new 20 per cent income tax rate. At the higher level, they wanted to abolish the employee national insurance threshold and introduce a new 50 per cent income tax charge for taxable earnings over £36,375. **Chart 1.3** shows that the total charges would have risen steeply for middle managers and the higher paid.

The Liberal Democrats proposed total rates (tax and NI) starting at 35 per cent, increasing to 42 per cent at £33,000 and 50 per cent over £50,000.

While the tax-related illustrations in this book have been based upon the tax structure of the continuing Conservative administration, with a top tax rate of 40 per cent, some of the illustrations also show the effect had there been a change of government, with an effective top rate of tax and National Insurance of approximately 60 per cent. While those higher rates can be ruled out for the foreseeable future, they could return in five years or so.

As we struggle to pull out of the recession, the disciplines imposed by the UK's membership of the European Exchange Rate Mechanism and the closer integration of the Community's currencies and economic policies will limit the number of economic and tax weapons at any Chancellor's disposal. At

Chart 1.3 *Taxable earned income*

£	Conservative Tax %	NI %	Total %	Labour Tax %	NI %	Total %
0–2,000	20	2	22	25	–	25
2,001–2,808	25	2	27	25	–	25
2,809–21,060	25	9	34	25	9	34
21,061–23,700	25	–	25	25	9	34
23,701–36,375	40	–	40	40	9	49
Over 36,375	40	–	40	50	9	59
Personal allowance			3,445			3,625

the same time, these trends, particularly the gradual convergence of inflation and interest rates, also open up some opportunities for both borrower and investor.

Membership of the ERM, for example, provides a dilemma for those of us who have a mortgage. Interest rates are historically low, in that over the past 20 years various interest rates have often been at higher levels. Indeed, not long ago interest rates were around 15 per cent. However, it is not prudent for us merely to look at the way interest rates have changed in the past. Now that we are more closely linked to European currencies and interest rates (in particular the Deutsch mark), it is interesting to see how our rates compare with those in Europe. **Chart 1.4** gives food for thought, and this matter will be considered again in the chapter on mortgages. The rates were taken on 7 May 1991 and UK and certain European rates have fallen since then.

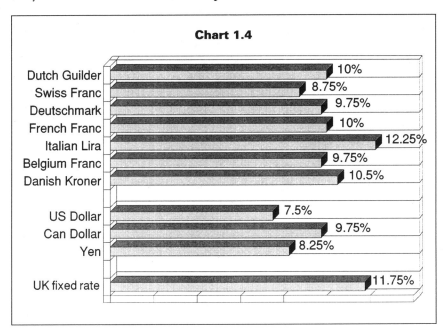

Chart 1.4

Dutch Guilder	10%
Swiss Franc	8.75%
Deutschmark	9.75%
French Franc	10%
Italian Lira	12.25%
Belgium Franc	9.75%
Danish Kroner	10.5%
US Dollar	7.5%
Can Dollar	9.75%
Yen	8.25%
UK fixed rate	11.75%

TAILORED ADVICE

There is no shortage of financial advice – from the golf club pundit to the glossy savings magazines – but the best financial planning consists of far more than just finding the right pension or insurance policy, or beating the taxman. It involves framing a comprehensive strategy based on a thorough knowledge of your personal and financial circumstances and objectives, and constructing the optimum financial portfolio at various stages of your life. This strategy must be flexible and capable of adaptation as your objectives change over time. Naturally, financial products play an important part in this strategy and we shall be reviewing a wide variety of these throughout the book and seeing how they can be slotted into your financial portfolio.

The recession of the early 1990s has had an enormous human cost. I have been asked by both public and private companies to provide financial advice for leavers on the financial effects of redundancy. Some companies have requested seminars illustrating the main points for consideration at this difficult time. The seminar may be a useful introduction, but it cannot replace the tailoring of advice to an individual's needs. The most valuable time is spent at a face-to-face meeting with the individual concerned.

Tailored advice is essential. Whatever your situation you must get specific recommendations and see how the proposals will affect your position. There is nothing worse than spending over an hour discussing your financial position only to obtain vague conclusions or no real recommendations at all. Your current financial position must be clearly illustrated to you and you must be able to see how the recommendations will benefit you, as well as understanding the risks involved and how your financial position will change.

FINDING THE TIME

Only a tiny percentage of the population has the knowledge and expertise needed to understand and evaluate the baffling variety of products now on offer from the financial services industry, let alone the income tax, capital gains tax and inheritance tax implications of financial decisions – implications that can have a serious impact not only on your own financial security but also on that of your spouse, children and grandchildren.

There is no mystique about this knowledge, but it can take a great deal of time to acquire. Pension regulations, tax laws, the workings of the financial markets and life assurance industry, and all the other disparate elements, can be baffling. Quite apart from all that, there is also an understandable reluctance when it comes to estate planning, to face up dispassionately to the implications of our own mortality.

WHERE TO SHOP

There is a need for specialist advice and there is no shortage of potential providers, but it is not always easy to know where to shop. 'One stop shopping' should be sought but adequate advice is difficult to find. Your advice should be from someone who has an in-depth knowledge of taxation, all available financial products and the financial houses who can provide those products. There is nothing worse than, for example, going to an accountant who can provide tax advice only and then being passed to an insurance broker for an insurance contract, and then on to a stock-broker and over to a solicitor. It is possible that certain of the financial products will need to come from different sources but it is essential that there is one person who can provide that initial overview and bring the advice together.

Not only should the advice be comprehensive in nature, it should also be independent and provided without an 'axe to grind': advice from a salesman who is only able to sell his or her company's products is unlikely to be the *best* advice. A company may, for example, be able to provide the cheapest life insurance product but may not be the best investment house. A salesman may be living off commission and will therefore need to sell you something to pay his way.

A fee-based system with all commission being rebated to you is the best approach. This will, however, require you to recognize the cost of obtaining good financial advice. Advice from commission-based salespeople may appear to be free but it can often turn out to be more expensive than the fee-based approach. Even your bank manager may not necessarily be independent, as some of the major high street banks and building societies have arrangements under which they tend to offer only one company's products. The same is true of some brokers and advisers.

This book cannot be a substitute for obtaining independent and comprehensive advice, since personal financial planning is precisely that – personal to each individual. What it does is examine all the constituent elements that go to make up a personal financial planning strategy and discuss which situations may be appropriate.

All law and practice alluded to in this book is as stated at 10 April 1992.

Barry Stillerman
Personal Financial Planning Partner
Stoy Hayward
10 April 1992

2

FROM CRADLE TO GRAVE

As you pass through life, your financial planning needs change and it is important that you recognize the changes in advance, plan for them and monitor your financial position. Part of the fascination of financial planning is that no two people are the same: their financial needs differ so it is not possible to produce a blueprint for all situations. However, most people pass through the established seven stages of life which are set out in **Chart 2.1**.

		Chart 2.1
Stage	*Approximate age*	*Description*
1	Up to mid-teens	Minority – not working – few responsibilities
2	Up to mid-20s	Pre-family – working or studying – few responsibilities
3	Up to early 30s	Building a career – family
4	Up to late 40s	Establishing a career – increasing expenditure on home and family
5	Up to mid-50s	Adult children – high earning level – reducing expenditure on home and family
6	Up to mid-60s	Working towards retirement
7	From mid-60s	Retired

STAGE 1

This is normally the most financially secure period of your life as your financial security is normally provided by your parents and comes out of their net spendable income. Many more parents are now less reliant upon the State to provide their children's education and school fees can become an ever-increasing burden. If children leave school at 16, parents may then feel less inclined to provide for them on an ongoing basis if their salary covers their cost of living, though there may still be a need to assist in the purchase of a house at some point in the future and this should be borne in mind by parents.

A child may be fortunate enough to have parents who could provide him or her with a capital sum. It is often not appreciated that children have a separate personal allowance for income tax purposes and this can be beneficial, as illustrated in **Chart 2.2**.

Of course, a child will need to be responsible enough to receive the money outright and use it wisely. Minor children will not be in a position to handle their own financial affairs, and this is where trusts may be appropriate.

If a parent settles money on a child who is under 18, any investment income received will be taxed to the parent; if a grandparent settles the money this problem does not arise. It is also currently possible to accumulate income in a bare trust for a minor child, where assets may be held by guardians or parents in trust for the child who has an absolute beneficial entitlement to the assets and income, without tax being payable (see p.200). This technique, however, may not last for much longer.

Children also have their own capital gains tax exemption, currently to be increased to £5,800. If parents are likely to be paying capital gains tax at the rate of 40 per cent, then this annual exemption could be worth £2,320 a year. Using the exemption may, however, be a little more difficult: again the child may not be responsible enough for the parent to transfer assets directly into his or her name. However, assuming that this is not the case, then the parents could plan for a future sale of assets, eg shares in a quoted or private company, by making gifts to their children.

The simplified illustration in **Chart 2.3** shows how the annual capital gains

---

Chart 2.2

	£
Deposit interest received by parents on, say,	
£30,000 at 10%	3,000
Tax at, say, 40%	(1,200)
Net receipt	1,800
Deposit interest received by child	3,000
Personal allowance 1991/2	(3,295)
Saving	(1,200)

exemption can be used by parents and children to reduce the tax burden. However, in this situation, the parents must recognize that the children will then each hold shares worth £10,500.

Chart 2.3

A husband and wife each have quoted shares worth £21,600 with a capital gains tax base cost of £10,000. They each transfer half their holdings to their two children and all the shares are sold in the next tax year at the same share price.

	£
Gain on gift to children	5,800
Annual capital gains tax exemption	(5,800)
Gain per person	5,800
Annual exemption	(5,800)
Tax saving (£2,320 × 2)	4,640

STAGE 2

This covers the stage of life when you are likely still to be single. (If you have left the family home, then the section on budgeting in Chapter 3 is very important to you.) You may now be taking on the expense of providing your own flat or home and if you have started work you need to ensure that your expenditure is more than covered by your income. One criticism of many financial institutions following the boom of the late 1980s is the way in which credit facilities were provided to the unsuspecting public. How often have you received a mailshot from a bank or building society offering you credit facilities? Too often credit has been taken without enough thought as to the way in which the loan is to be repaid, and if you do not balance your books on a regular basis you may be in line for a nasty shock.

The most important financial commitment you are likely to face at this stage is the mortgage payments. When taking out a mortgage you must carry out some form of budgeting exercise to ensure that you will be able to meet your mortgage payments. Often a mortgage is taken out without considering the economic and political climate: interest rates can fluctuate greatly. You need to be sure that you can meet the mortgage payments should interest rates increase by several percentage points. In addition, you need to consider the security of your income, in case your annual bonus decreases or you find yourself out of work.

	£	£
Chart 2.4		
Annual income after tax		20,000
Annual outgoings		19,500
Surplus		£500
Existing £50,000 mortgage		
Interest at, say, 11%	5,500	
Less basic-rate relief		
£30,000 × 11% × 25%	(825)	
		4,675
Cost of mortgage at 14%		
Interest	7,000	
Less basic-rate relief		
£30,000 × 14% × 25%	(1,050)	
		(5,950)
Additional cost		(1,275)
Original surplus		500
Revised deficit		£(775)

STAGE 3

This should be a very exciting stage of your life. It has been assumed that you have now started a family and have established your career path. You now have the responsibility of providing for your children. While you may be able to provide for their immediate needs, you may not have considered the future costs involved. As mentioned earlier in this chapter, you may be facing school fees in a few years and it is very difficult to produce an effective school fees plan unless it is started some years before the fees are due to be paid. Looking further ahead, you may wish to provide a down payment for a child's first flat. Indeed, it is difficult to see how any child can afford their first home without some form of parental financial assistance, unless they are very high earners. There may also be the future cost of a wedding to be considered.

It is again important at this stage to determine whether you have any surplus net spendable income. If so, you could contemplate a savings plan to provide for these needs. In most cases, there is little surplus income so you will need to plan to provide for these costs in some other way.

If both parents are working, there may be the added expense of a nanny for the children. If one parent stays at home full time to look after the children, the birth of the first child will lead to a loss of income for the family as only one spouse will now be working. Such a change in income flow must be planned and recognized in advance so that you can adequately plan for your outgoings. This reinforces the need to save wisely when you have net spendable income.

Obviously, the untimely death of a parent could cause serious financial hardship. If the remaining parent has given up work to look after the children, he or she may not easily be able to move back into a previous job, and capital or the income from it may be needed to cover the cost of looking after the children.

Life assurance cover can avoid such financial hardships relatively inexpensively. There may already be some death–in–service cover if the parent was in a company pension scheme. It is important to assess the total level of cover required as the pension fund may not provide significant financial resources. It may also be appropriate to take out a policy on the life of the remaining parent as well as other forms of insurance, such as private medical insurance.

It is surprising how many people do not have a will. The assets within the estate could now be significant, taking account of the value of the home and life policies. The mortgage would normally have been repaid from the mortgage protection policy but the rules of intestacy (as shown in **Chart 2.6**) can leave an estate in a tax-inefficient manner and against the wishes of the deceased person. (This matter will be considered further in the chapter covering estate-planning.)

Most people in their early years do not take pensions very seriously. Unfortunately, it is too often regarded as a matter of concern for much later in life and little thought is given as to how you will be able to live when you are retired. Where will the money come from to ensure that you can live as comfortably in retirement as you have throughout your working life? The personal pensions revolution has made more people aware of the choices available, and the opportunity to take the pension at age 50 has brought it into focus at an earlier age. It is often unwise to take the pension that early but the mere fact that a person aged 35 could take the benefits in 15 years' time makes the subject more meaningful.

Many people anticipate that their home will provide a 'pension' as they will be able to trade down and buy a smaller home in retirement, pocketing the difference in the values. Often this is a false hope as the retirement bungalow or flat is more expensive than originally anticipated, leaving less capital available.

You will see from **Chart 2.7** that you defer consideration of this subject at your peril.

Although the man in **Chart 2.7** has started his pension and initially pays £1,650 a year, the fund will only produce a pension of 11 per cent of his final income and this is unlikely to be anywhere near sufficient.

Chart 2.5

A 40-year-old man is married with two young children. He earns £30,000 a year and his wife does not work. His assets are a house worth £100,000 (on which there is a £30,000 endowment-linked mortgage) and investments of £10,000.

Net spendable income	Current position £000	£000	Position after death £000
Salary		30	
Gross income from investments, say		1	1
		31	
Mortgage and endowment policy payments	(4)		
Income tax	(6)		
		(10)	
		21	
Expenditure, say		(18)	(12)
Net surplus/(deficit)		3	(11)

Chart 2.6 *Intestacy rules under English law*

Beneficiaries – Spouse and children

Distribution of estate
First £75,000 and any personal possessions to spouse
Balance held on trust
  50% life interest for spouse
  50% for children

Chart 2.7

A 33-year-old man is earning £33,000. He pays 5 per cent a year into a pension plan. His salary increases at 5 per cent a year and he retires at 60. The fund grows at 8 per cent a year.

	£000	£000
Final salary		131
Pension fund at retirement	165	
Pension based on an annuity rate of, say,		
9%(single life, 5% escalation, no guarantee)		15
Pension as a % of final salary		11%

STAGE 4

At this stage it has been assumed that you are establishing your career. You may have taken on additional responsibilities at work. The demands of work and family may leave very little time for anything else. During this stage of your life your income should be increasing but so will the expenditure on your home and family. You may have moved house and have greater outgoings on the mortgage.

It is possible that you now have the resources to start to provide for the future. Even if your expenditure is increasing, increases in earnings may mean that you are still able to set a sum aside each month in some form of savings plan.

During this stage of your life, taxation may become more of an irritant than before. Your income may be much higher so the tax take will be much larger. While many of the tax-avoidance loopholes have been closed, there have always been opportunities to mitigate your tax bill. In recent years, the introduction of tax shelters and independent taxation planning has provided many opportunities.

It is difficult to divorce taxation from politics as tax changes are often politically-driven. For example, Nigel Lawson introduced the assured tenancy business expansion scheme to encourage mobility of labour. The Labour Party was planning to use the scheme to encourage investment in manufacturing companies rather than in property, and also to provide greater tax incentives for training and capital investment in industry. It may be possible to take advantage of these politically-driven tax incentives to reduce your tax bill and we will consider this in more detail later in the book.

STAGE 5

During this stage it has been assumed that your children are less of a financial burden. If you are in your late forties, your children may now have left school or university and be making their own way in life. This will have led to a significant reduction in your outgoings. At the same time, your income level may be increasing further as you may be in your peak earning years. You may now have accumulated cash deposits and should be looking for alternative forms of investment to fit into your risk profile. The pension scheme will become of even greater significance as you can now focus more readily upon the likely pension you will receive. You should by now have adequate insurance cover and a review of your insurance policies may lead to the conclusion that some are surplus to requirements.

In many households, both spouses will now be working and should be careful to maximize the benefits from independent taxation. While this may not be the time to make large capital gifts to children, it may be possible to start the process in a modest way. This may also be an appropriate time to begin an estate-planning exercise. Also the restructuring of your capital assets and the writing of a will can go a long way towards mitigating death duties without reducing your capital base. For example, the use of the nil rate band can save up to £60,000 of inheritance tax. (Other planning techniques will be covered by the chapter on estate planning.)

STAGE 6

Many people will be working towards retirement from 60 to 65. One of the changes which has taken place over the past decade has been the emergence of the 'third age'. There has clearly been a trend towards earlier retirement and the recent recession has caused companies to look carefully at the retirement policy of their workforce. Early retirement has often been taken voluntarily or compulsorily and there are now many people in their 50s looking for a new career. Others feel that this is the time of life when they should be able to reduce work pressures and enjoy more free time. Money and freedom are linked – if you have sufficient capital to produce enough income to meet your outgoings, you need not work so hard. It is sad to see people working long hours past the state retirement age if they do not really enjoy their work and are only doing so to pay the bills. One of the keys to any strategy is to plan: if your wish is to take life easy in your mid-50s, you must have a financial plan for how you will create sufficient financial resources to do so.

During this period of your life, you may be looking to significantly top up your pension but may be questioning whether additional cash resources should go into the pension scheme or whether they should be invested elsewhere. This is particularly relevant if you have only a couple of years to go before the pension benefits are to be taken. There are significant tax advantages in making additional voluntary contributions to a company pension scheme, but that money may only go towards providing an annuity (ie an income flow), so you may wish to invest your money in a less tax-efficient manner but in a way which enables you to receive the funds as cash. However, **Chart 2.8** shows the significance of the tax benefits.

If you are a shareholder in a private trading company, you may be looking for an exit route. It is essential that you structure your affairs in the most tax-efficient manner so that you can mitigate the ultimate tax charge as far as possible. The sale of a family business can give rise to the largest tax charge of a lifetime. While you may have been paying income tax during your working life, capital gains tax on the sale may be a very significant sum.

In the past, UK 'freezer' trusts and offshore trusts have been used to reduce significantly the capital gains tax charge. However, radical changes to the taxation of offshore trusts have now made this route less effective. The recent consultative document on the tax treatment of trusts must also be borne in mind. There are many other tax-planning opportunities, however, and indeed it may be more appropriate to have considered these at an earlier time. Investment structuring, inheritance tax planning, etc will also be relevant during this stage of your life.

STAGE 7

You may now be enjoying a well-earned rest in retirement and must live off the capital you have accumulated during your lifetime plus your state and private pensions. Just prior to retirement you will have had a number of choices to make. The pension scheme needs to be examined very carefully to determine the maximum tax-free cash sum that can be taken and the investment of that money. Usually, but not always, it will be advisable to take the maximum tax-free cash sum and the reduced pension. In a few cases it may be appropriate to look at reducing the tax-free cash sum and taking a larger pension.

It is often assumed that you must take your annuity from the existing pension provider, ie that if you have a personal pension with one company then this company will provide the annuity for you. You should take advantage of the open-market option. This enables you to establish the value of the pension fund and shop around to find the company which provides the best annuity rate. Often the best investment house will not provide the best annuity rate, so it may be better to transfer your fund to another company to obtain a greater income stream during your lifetime. As you will see from the chapter on annuities, there are a number of different forms of annuity and the most appropriate one must be selected to protect your family.

Chart 2.8

A 55-year-old higher-rate taxpayer is considering a net investment of £10,000 for a 5-year period.

Pension plan	£	£
Gross investment	16,667	
Tax relief at, say, 40%	(6,667)	
Net investment	10,000	
Tax-free growth at, say, 10% pa		
fund after 5 years	26,842	
fund used to buy a pension (75%)		20,132
plus tax-free cash (25%)		6,710
Investment bond		
Cost of bond	10,000	
Value of fund assuming 7.5% pa growth in a		
taxed fund	14,356	
Higher-rate tax on profit at, say, 15%	(653)	
		13,703

Note: this illustration ignores commissions and charges of both plans.

Chart 2.9

Man aged 60	
Sun Life annuity	£798.36
Equitable Life annuity	£855.48

Notes: (1) Annuity cost £10,000 escalating at 5% pa, guaranteed for 5 years
(2) Annuity payable monthly in advance

Source: Planned Savings masterfile, 5 November 1991

Investment planning is most critical during this stage of your life as you need to protect against the ravages of inflation and the possibility of having to provide for nursing fees in the future. You now have a finite capital sum with which to meet these requirements. Estate-planning will be even more relevant as you may wish to pass capital to members of your family to reduce the burden of death duties.

The following chapters will cover your requirements during the seven stages of life outlined here. Some may be more relevant to you at present and you may wish to turn to those chapters which most interest you, but nearly all the chapters will have some relevance to your financial position either now or at some time in the future.

You will have seen from this chapter that your financial requirements are unlikely to stay static. Changes in your financial circumstances may not be dramatic year on year, but after a few years you may look back and find yourself in a very different situation and this is why financial planning is not a 'one off' exercise. Many companies provide annual financial planning for their employees. Generally, it is not feasible for you to be fully conversant with all available products and opportunities, and it is important that you recognize the need for advice early enough, select the right financial advisor and follow through the recommendations which make sound financial and commercial sense to you.

3

BANK ACCOUNTS AND BUDGETING

Billions of pounds lie idle in old bank and building society accounts, ordinary shares, old national insurance issues and certain life policies where the returns are very small. With up to 1,000 different rates available from various financial institutions, all changing from week to week, it is little wonder that this wastage occurs. It is impossible to keep completely abreast of these changes, but there are certain golden rules which everyone should keep.

Firstly, keep your financial affairs relatively simple. Once you have established where your money should be, it is very important to review it every year or so. This chapter will concentrate on bank and building society accounts, and I will cover National Savings issues separately. However, you should dust off any British Savings bonds, national development bonds and defence bonds as these are likely to be earning comparatively little.

Keep your current building society passbook easily to hand, and retain all longer-term investment certificates, pension policies, insurance policies, your will etc in a deed box. The box should be kept in a safe place: a safe at home or a deed box at your bank. You should keep a separate record at home of all the documents which are in your deed box and let your next of kin know where the box and key are kept.

PLANNING YOUR ACCOUNTS

Consider how many accounts you should have and where they should be. Obviously you will need a current account so that you can write out cheques and find a home for your wages and certain other income, but the current account balance should not be large as the interest rate is either nil or very low. Some banks can arrange for an automatic transfer to take place once the account exceeds (or falls below) a certain figure, but are likely to charge for this service.

If you receive a salary at the end of the month, you must be sure to have sufficient money in the account at the beginning of the month to cover your likely expenses until the next salary cheque. You need to strike a balance between holding large sums in your current account which will provide a poor rate of interest – and too little in your account which will give rise to a periodical overdraft. You should certainly avoid running up an increasing overdraft as overdraft interest can be very expensive.

You need only have two or three accounts. If you have many more than this your financial affairs may become overly-complicated. You should have a current account for your normal expenditure and a deposit account. Shop around to find the best interest rate for your deposit account. You may find that the best rate is from a building society which doesn't have a branch near you, but as you may not need to use that account very often, the amount you allocate to it could be placed there for the longer term while you maintain a local deposit account with your bank or building society for easy access.

If you have large cash resources, you need to decide how much is to remain in bank and building society deposits and how much is to be invested elsewhere. We will be looking at this later.

POOR RETURNS

Some people have old building society accounts which were originally attractive but have since been superseded by much better-paying accounts. It is somewhat unfair for organizations to attract new investors with high-interest accounts without properly advising their existing investors, and the Government is just as guilty as some old National Savings issues give a very poor return.

Chart 3.1

	Current account % net of basic rate	7-Day deposit gross
	%	%
Barclays	2.06	1.00
Lloyds	1.12	1.50
Midland*	1.50	2.50
Nat West	1.50	1.51
(*Slightly higher rates for larger amounts)		
Building Societies – typical rates	*% gross*	
Ordinary Shares	3.70–3.90	
Deposit accounts	2.75–3.70	

Source: The Sunday Times, 20 October 1991

At the end of October 1991, the Halifax had a seven–day extra account which was paying 6.2 per cent gross and a 28-day extra account paying 6.5 per cent gross. By transferring the money into a new instant extra plus account the return could be increased to 8.75 per cent for £2,000 or 9.75 per cent for £10,000 plus. The Halifax ordinary share account was paying just under three per cent for sums of £50–250 and 3.9 per cent for investments above this figure. Its deposit account was only paying 2.75 per cent and 3.7 per cent respectively for the same capital sums. Most building societies suffer from the same problem of having a number of old accounts which are giving a relatively poor return.

DIFFERENCES TO WATCH

Consider carefully the kind of accounts you need. We will assume that you already have a current account and are looking for the best return from your cash deposits. You should also consider how much could be invested for the longer term. By spreading your money around different building societies, you are unlikely to be getting the best return because the institutions normally provide a better return for a larger sum invested, so it could be in your interest to consolidate your deposits. **Chart 3.2** illustrates the point.

Chart 3.2 *Building Society accounts*

Notice accounts gross %

Society	Days	£ 500	2500	5000	10000	25000	50000	No Loss if Balance
Bristol & West	30	9.10	9.10	9.45	10.05	10.6	10.9	(Instant on 90-day loss)
Halifax	90	8.65	8.65	9.05	9.85	10.35	11.0	£5,000
Lambeth	60	10.14	10.14	10.14	10.14	10.86	11.66	(60 days notice and loss)
Leeds & Holbeck	90	–	9.52	10.12	10.12	10.78	10.78	£10,000

Instant Access Gross %

Society	Note	1	£ 500	2500	5000	10000	25000	Interest paid
Bristol & West		3.40	8.40	9.10	9.10	9.70	10.00	Yearly
Halifax	(1)	3.00	8.60	8.75	8.95	9.75	10.00	Yearly
Lambeth		3.86	3.86	3.86	3.86	3.86	3.86	6 months
Leeds & Holbeck	(2)	8.60	8.60	8.60	9.42	9.90	10.50	Yearly

Notes: (1) £50 minimum
(2) £100 minimum

Source: Money Facts, November 1991

You need to be careful about the *type* of account you use. As you will see from **Chart 3.2**, some enable instant access but these do not normally provide the best rate of return. For example, the Lambeth instant access account was only providing 3.86 per cent while their 60-day account was providing between 10.14 per cent and 11.66 per cent depending upon the amount invested. Certain accounts require that the money is invested for, say, 90 days and exert penalties if you take the money out early unless you are able to give notice of the withdrawal 90 days in advance – though some do not impose a penalty so long as a certain amount of money is invested. If, for example, you have £40,000 in a 90-day account where the minimum investment against penalties is £5,000, you effectively have instant access to over £35,000 without penalty, and need to give notice only on the balance of £5,000. If you are unlikely to need more than £35,000 at any one time then this account may be appropriate.

Some of the best interest rates are from the smaller building societies, though the fact that some have only a few branches could be inconvenient if you wanted to make regular withdrawals. However, as previously mentioned you may wish to have some money deposited with a local building society or bank and the long-term deposits in the society which provides the best return.

Chart 3.2 also shows that by consolidating your deposits you can obtain a better return. If £6,000 was in the Lambeth account, the interest rate was 10.14 per cent. If you transferred £44,000 into the account from other sources the interest rate would increase to 11.66 per cent. **Chart 3.3** provides further examples.

Chart 3.3		
	Minimum investment £000	Net of basic rate tax return %
Coventry Building Society		
Money maker instant access account	5	7.88
10-day option account (if £5000 retained)	10	9.30
National Provincial Building Society		
Instant access account	10	9.66
Private Reserve 90-day return account		
(interest access over £10,000)	10	9.75
Source: Money Management, July 1991		

SECURITY

Following the collapse of BCCI, there has been a significant loss of confidence in institutions which were once regarded as 'gilt-edged'. You should ensure that any investment is covered by the Investor Protection Scheme. Since the war no ordinary investor in a building society which is a member of the Building Societies Association has lost any of their savings. On the few occasions when societies have run into financial difficulties, other societies have always stepped in to ensure that savings are fully protected.

The Building Societies Act 1986 ('BSA') provides a new legislative framework for building societies and includes provision for a statutory Investor Protection Scheme. This replaces the voluntary scheme set up by the BSA in April 1982 and covers all authorized building societies.

The statutory scheme is along similar lines to that which exists for the banks, with two important differences. Firstly, unlike the banks' scheme the building society Investor Protection Scheme does not have a permanent fund of money. The reason given for this by the Treasury minister concerned is that 'experience suggests that calls on the scheme are likely to be much less frequent than those on behalf of depositors with small licensed deposit-takers under the Banking Act Scheme.' Secondly, the maximum level of protection is 90 per cent of amounts up to £20,000, compared with 75 per cent for banks. In the case of joint accounts, the protection applies to £20,000 per individual.

Appendix 1 of this book contains a full extract from the Building Societies Association's Fact Sheet 6, dated 9 October 1991, on the subject of investor protection. Most of the smaller building societies are members of the association but you should check Appendix 2 before making your investment.

BANK MONEY-MARKET ACCOUNTS

For larger deposits (over £100,000) you can usually obtain a better return from a bank money-market account. All the main clearing banks operate a money-market or treasurer's account with special interest rates. Again, interest rates increase the more money is held in the account so shop around to get the best rate. Remember that if you receive a gross rate of, say, ten per cent from a building society then this should produce a greater fund than a 7.5 per cent net of basic-rate tax return (gross equivalent ten per cent) due to the tax deferral. Over a year, assuming that you are a basic-rate taxpayer, you would need to receive approximately 7.78 per cent net (gross equivalent 10.37 per cent) to produce the same return from a monthly income account which pays ten per cent gross with the tax payable upon assessment. **Chart**

3.4 provides an illustration of the increased return which could be obtained from a larger deposit on 4 December 1991.

Chart 3.4

	Gross return %
Barclays Bank Treasurer's Account	
Deposit	
£250,000	10.31
£500,000	10.50

CREDIT CARDS

Credit cards are dangerous. It is easy to get carried away when you are shopping and some people seem to regard a credit card expense as though it is a gift. Credit cards provide an easy way to pay for goods but it is essential that you keep track of your spending, perhaps by recording credit card expenditure in the same way that you would record a cheque. You may have a high credit limit of, say, £1,000. Credit card companies are happy to see you failing to pay off the full expenditure in any one month so long as they can recover the balance in due course. This is because they charge extremely high rates of interest – as illustrated by Appendix 3 which shows the credit and store card rates applicable in November 1991.

If you were offered a mortgage at the rate of 20 per cent I'm sure you would not take it, yet the interest payable on overdue credit card accounts is well over 20 per cent. If you use a credit card, make sure that the outstanding balance is settled each month within the required time limit.

BANK RECONCILIATION

You should reconcile your capital and your bank account on a regular basis. **Chart 3.5** provides a simplified illustration of a bank reconciliation statement.

Chart 3.5

Bank reconciliation statement as at 31 January 1992

Balance per cash book		1,170.30
Add Uncleared cheques		
Barclaycard	27.34	
J Small	10.00	
Marks & Spencer	32.15	69.49
		1,239.79
Less Receipt not yet cleared – T Lyons		25.00
Balance per bank statement		£1,214.79

You may wish to keep a cash book separately from your cheque book or at the back of your diary so that you can record cheques and receipts. In the illustration in **Chart 3.5** your cash book is showing £1170.30 while the bank statement shows £1214.79. This is on the basis that you record your credit card expenditure in your cash book which some people may not wish to do. You will see that the reason for the difference is that you wrote out a cheque to Mr Small for £10.00 and this has not yet been passed through your bank account and that certain credit card expenditure with Barclaycard and Marks & Spencer has been incurred but you have not yet settled these liabilities.

Also, Mr Lyons gave you a cheque for £25 which was paid in at the end of the month but has not yet gone through your bank account. Therefore you would be unwise to assume that your bank balance of £1214.79 is available as certain cheques have not been presented and your true available cash account balance is £1170.30. You may find that the difference between your cash book and the bank account could well be over £1,000 depending upon how many expenses are outstanding, so it is important that you do not fall into a false sense of security.

4

YOUR CURRENT POSITION

CAPITAL POSITION

Before embarking on a financial planning exercise, it is essential that both you and your advisor are fully aware of your current financial position. The ascertainment of financial data need not be a time-consuming exercise but it is likely to provoke a number of questions. In accordance with the Financial Services Act, all registered financial advisors must carry out a fact find. **Chart 4.1** provides an illustration of the start of this process.

	£000	£000
Chart 4.1 *Estimated capital position*		
Home	250	
Mortgage	(50)	
		200
Building society deposits	110	
Bank deposit account	10	
Bank current account	–	
		120
Value of shares		40
		360

In the example in **Chart 4.1** the home is valued at £250,000 and there is a £50,000 mortgage. This individual also has cash deposits and shares so that the total estate is worth £360,000. People are often surprised to see how much they are worth when all the assets of the estate are included. In **Chart 4.1**, I have assumed that the shares are easy to value. If you own shares in a private trading company their value may not be readily to hand: your accountant should be able to advise in this regard. In many cases the value of private company shares is the largest asset of the estate.

CURRENT INCOME POSITION

Having reviewed the capital position, it is now necessary to examine your current income and financial needs. The example in **Chart 4.2** shows:

- Your taxable income

- Your tax liability and top marginal rate

- Your net income after tax

- Your net income after tax and living expenses

In **Chart 4.2** the right hand column shows gross spendable income (therefore benefits in kind and personal allowances are ignored). The husband's gross income is £54,000 and the wife receives £15,000. The income includes the deposit interest assuming a gross rate of ten per cent and the gross dividend income. You will see that the husband pays nearly £18,000 of tax leaving £36,000 net before mortgage interest and approximately £31,000 after such interest net of MIRAS relief.

The wife's income of £15,000 suffers tax of approximately £3,000, and the total net spendable income for the couple if £43,000 after tax. The expenditure of £38,000 a year shows that the couple are able to save. The capital statement shows that they are relatively liquid so their investment needs should be carefully examined.

The 1992 Budget proposals introduced a new 20 per cent tax band for the first £2,000 of income. This could save £100 but has not been taken into account in **Chart 4.2** as the tax reduction is not significant.

ANNUAL EXPENDITURE

In **Chart 4.2** the couple spend £38,000 a year and have surplus income. Many people do not have an accurate assessment of their expenditure. A broad-brush approach is to consider the deposits held a year ago and the deposits held now: if there have been no other financial changes, and those deposits are approximately the same, then expenditure is roughly in line with income; if the deposits have increased or other assets have been acquired, then some saving is occurring; and if the deposits have fallen or there is an increasing overdraft, income must be insufficient. However, it is useful to carry out a budget of expenditure as illustrated in **Chart 4.3**.

You will see from the above that the £50,000 mortgage costs £5,875 pa including the cost of the endowment policy which has been structured so that it should pay off the mortgage and leave a surplus. You will see that £30,000 of the mortgage attracts basic-rate tax relief. Higher-rate relief is no longer

---

Chart 4.2 *Estimated net spendable income*

	Taxable income £000	Spendable income £000
Self		
Remuneration	40	40
Benefits in kind	4	
	44	
Deposit interest 120 @, say, 10% gross	12	12
Dividends 40 @, say, 5%	2	2
	58	54
Personal allowances	(5)	
Taxable income	53	
Tax £23,700 @ 25% £5,925		
29,300 @ 40% 11,720		
53,000 17,645		(18)
		36
Mortgage interest £50,000 @, say, 11% (5,500)		
Tax relief 30,000 × 11% × 25% 825		
(4,675)		(5)
		31
Partner		
Remuneration	15	15
Personal allowance	(3)	
Taxable income	12	
Tax @ 25%		(3)
		43
Expenditure		(38)
Net surplus income		5

---

available for mortgages.

Obviously, the figures for many items in this chart will vary dramatically from person to person. If you have access to a computer, convert this annual analysis on to a monthly spreadsheet showing the income and outgoings on a monthly basis so that you can plan the peaks and troughs of expenditure during the year.

	£	Annual expenditure £
Chart 4.3 *Estimated expenditure*		
Monthly payments		
Mortgage interest £50,000 @ 11%	5,500	
Less tax relief £30,000 @ 11% × 25%	(825)	
Net payments (£389.58 pm)		4,675
Endowment policy, say, £100 pm		1,200
		5,875
Household spending money £550 pm		6,600
Cash drawings £400 pm		4,800
Standing orders £100 pm		1,200
Credit card expenditure/clothes £550 pm		6,600
		25,075
School fees		6,000
Irregular payments		
Insurance: household	675	
buildings	450	
Car expenses	4,000	
TV licence, electricity, gas	2,000	
Poll tax, water rates	1,000	
Annual subscriptions	1,000	
Holidays	2,000	
Sundries	800	
		11,925
		43,000

ESTIMATED INHERITANCE POSITION

Having considered the capital and income position, it is necessary to examine the way in which the estate would be affected by a premature death. **Chart 4.4** sets out a further illustration based upon the above case study.

The net estate in the example in **Chart 4.4** was originally shown as £360,000, but this will be increased by at least £50,000 from the maturity of the endowment policy which contains life cover so that the mortgage should be repaid upon a premature death. Indeed, if the endowment policy has been running for some time, it is possible that a surplus will be received by the estate. The illustration assumes that there is death-in-service life cover of

---

Chart 4.4 *Estimated inheritance tax position*

	£000
Net estate	360
Add Repayment of mortgage on death	50
Death-in-service life cover	150
Taxable estate	560
Inheritance tax	
150 @ Nil (as per March 1992 Budget proposal)	
410 @ 40%	164
560	

£150,000 for the family through a company pension scheme. With no other life assurance policies the taxable estate would be £560,000. Assuming that all assets are left by one spouse to the other, then no tax is payable on the first death: the inheritance tax charge would arise on the death of the surviving spouse. The first £150,000 of the estate does not suffer any tax if the Budget proposal is enacted and the balance is taxed at a flat rate of 40 per cent. Therefore, in this illustration. inheritance tax of £164,000 would be payable.

FUTURE INCOME REQUIREMENT

So far only the current position has been shown, but if advice is to be provided on the required investment structure or any other matter, it will be necessary to bare in mind certain other factors, including future requirements. For example, this couple may be looking to move to a more expensive house, in which case the cash resources may be used for that purpose and a larger mortgage may be required, thereby reducing the net surplus income each year. The advisor will need to know the likely future level of school fees as they may be increasing for a period of time before they cease altogether.

For investment purposes, you need to analyse your liquidity position and risk profile. Some people prefer to have more money readily to hand than others. The investment term may be partly dependent upon age. If the couple in **Chart 4.4** are in their seventies, then they will not wish to tie money up long term. However, if the couple are in their thirties, part of the surplus income could be invested into a long–term plan together with part of the cash deposits. This matter will be considered in more detail in the chapter on investment.

This analysis of the capital, income, expenditure and inheritance tax positions highlights a number of questions and opportunities. With falling interest rates, it is likely that, so long as your cash deposits are not readily required, a better return can be obtained elsewhere. For tax purposes, it is unwise for a high-earning partner to hold the investment as he or she will suffer a tax charge at 40 per cent on the investment income whereas a 25 per cent taxpayer would only pay 25 per cent on most of the investment income. Merely transferring the assets in such cases results in a substantial saving.

The life cover may be inadequate for the needs of the couple in **Chart 4.4**. If the husband and wife were to die together, the children would be left with an inheritance tax liability of £164,000 and cash proceeds of £200,000 from the life policies and cash deposits. This is unlikely to be sufficient to meet their future needs and may necessitate a sale of the family home at this traumatic time. In addition, the life cover has not been written as effectively as possible – the death-in-service cover could have been written in trust so as to reduce the inheritance tax liability. This would enable the death-in-service proceeds to fall outside the estate thereby saving inheritance tax of £60,000. However, when reviewing the life cover, it may be necessary to write only part of the death-in-service cover in trust for the children so that part of the proceeds go to the wife. It may also be necessary to take out a separate life policy for the wife since the husband is the higher-paid member of the family. The husband and wife have not made maximum use of the nil rate band for inheritance tax: by using their nil rate band appropriately through a well-drafted will (or a new codicil to an existing will) inheritance tax of £60,000 could be saved. (This is covered in more detail in Chapter 15.)

5

INVESTMENTS

Basic investment strategy is the same whether you have £20,000 or £200,000 to invest. It depends upon the following factors:

- Risk profile
- Liquidity position
- Investment term
- Income needs
- Inflation
- Taxation
- The political scene

The couple in the case study of the last chapter had cash deposits of over £100,000 and net surplus income. Assuming that there are no pressing requirements, we can now examine the investment opportunities for this couple.

RISK

Your risk profile must be determined from the outset. Some people are not willing to risk a penny of their money while others are happy to accept a high level of risk in pursuit of capital growth. If you are adamant that your investment must not fall in value then a number of investments cannot be recommended to you, such as stocks and shares, properties etc. For example, a unit trust may cost £20,000 then fall to £18,000 after a year. However, if it is sold for £30,000 in three years, then the drop in value earlier on will be of little consequence. Indeed, a good average annual compound return of approximately 16 per cent will have been achieved between the dates of acquisition and sale.

If you are seeking to maximize capital growth, then it is often the case that the greater the risk, the greater the potential return. Historically, over the longer term, equities have outperformed building society share accounts handsomely, though obviously this depends upon the investment period chosen. **Chart 5.1** illustrates this point. If you take the most risk-free approach, then your return is likely to be little more than can be achieved from cash deposits.

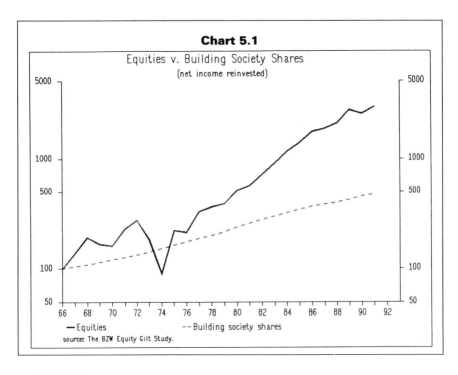

Chart 5.1

Equities v. Building Society Shares
(net income reinvested)

— Equities − − Building society shares
source: The BZW Equity Gilt Study.

LIQUIDITY

Capital growth is far more likely if you are able to invest long term. If you are seeking capital growth over only a one- or two-year period, then your requirement is difficult to satisfy as you may be forced to sell your investments at an inappropriate time. Any investment strategy should take account of the need for cash resources for identified needs, and also emergencies. In the case study of the previous chapter, there are cash deposits of £120,000 and, even if there are no other requirements for the money in the short term, it would be advisable for, say, £10,000 to be retained on deposit for emergencies. Of course, some people may wish to have greater liquidity and so retain more than £10,000.

INVESTMENT TERM

The term of an investment must be linked to liquidity. In this case, both lump sum and regular premium investments could be made. If part of the net surplus income is to be invested in a pension plan, then this may be considered to be a long-term investment if your normal retirement age is 20 years away. Therefore, you may be more willing to take a longer-term view on your investment and consequently accept greater risks for capital appreciation. For example, over a 20-year period, equities are more likely to outperform deposits or 'with-profit' plans, while it would be very difficult to recommend an equity investment if the term of that investment is to be, say, six months, unless it is felt that the stock market is very cheap. Very few investment houses anticipated the 1987 stock market crash. If you are looking six months to a year ahead, this may not leave enough time for any stocks to recover from market falls.

INCOME NEEDS

Income position is important. In the case study of the previous chapter, there is an excess of net spendable income of £5,000 after taking account of the deposit interest. Therefore, if part of the deposits are to be transferred into capital growth assets, the income is likely to fall. So long as the reduced income still covers expenditure and the liquidity position is protected, then there should be no problem. However, it is important that the income position is determined now, taking account of future requirements, and the future income position should be calculated after the proposed investments have been made. If your income needs are high, it is less likely that you will be able to structure all your portfolio for capital growth.

INFLATION

High taxes and inflation make cash deposits less attractive, as illustrated by **Chart 5.2**.

The combination of falling interest rates and an increase in tax rates could provide a real problem for those wishing to protect their capital against inflation, especially if most of the income is used to cover expenditure.

Chart 5.2

Gross deposit rate, say, 10%

	Tax rate applicable			
	0%	*25%*	*40%*	*60%*
Gross interest	10.0	10.0	10.0	10.0
Tax	(–)	(2.5)	(4.0)	(6.0)
Net return	10.0	7.5	6.0	4.0
Inflation, say	(5.0)	(5.0)	(5.0)	(5.0)
Net return if income is accumulated	5.0	2.5	1.0	(1.0)
Erosion of capital if net income requirement is 5% pa	–	(2.5)	(4.0)	(6.0)

TAXATION

The tax regime has changed dramatically since the late 1970s when some investment income suffered a top marginal tax rate of 98 per cent. Indeed in earlier years, it was possible for certain income which was subject to a special charge, to suffer tax of over 100 per cent! **Chart 5.3** shows the reduction in the basic and top marginal rates of income tax in recent years. While the

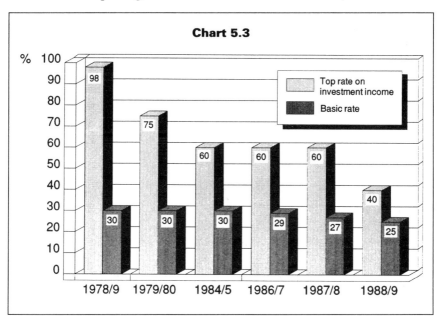

35

Labour Party wanted to reverse this trend, it is very unlikely that we would have returned to the crazy days of 98 per cent tax.

Taxation plays an important part in any investment strategy. There are a number of taxes to be borne in mind but the major ones are income, capital gains and inheritance.

The transfer of assets between a husband and wife can help to reduce the top marginal rate of income tax to 25 per cent (or even possibly 20 per cent) and it should be remembered that they may each have an annual capital gains tax exemption of £5,800. **Chart 5.4** is an illustration of how this exemption is often under-used.

Chart 5.4

£000

20,000 shares:	Cost	20
	Indexation allowance, say, 20%	4
		24
	Proceeds	28
		4
	Annual exemption	(5)
	Exemption not used	(1)

In this case, even though the shares cost £20,000 and are currently valued at £8,000 above cost, the indexation allowance and the annual exemption ensure that there would be no taxable gain if they were to be sold. As the exemption is lost if it is not used in a tax year, it may be advisable to 'bed and breakfast' the shares to use the exemption (as illustrated in **Chart 5.5**), but the costs and charges of the transaction should be borne in mind and professional advice sought.

As we have seen, inheritance tax can have a significant impact on the value of an estate and it is necessary to consider whether you are looking to provide greater capital growth for yourself or whether capital growth is to accrue to your children or other dependants. Therefore, the investment strategy can be combined with measures to save inheritance tax and, as mentioned above, income tax and capital gains tax.

THE POLITICAL SCENE

A change of government will not only affect tax. A different economic policy could have an effect on a number of important matters such as inflation and

---

Chart 5.5

Same facts as in **Chart 5.4** except the shareholding is 40,000 shares.

	£000	£000
Year 1 Sale and subsequent repurchase of 20,000 shares		
Gain covered by annual exemption as shown in **Chart 5.4** – tax due		<u>NIL</u>
Year 2 Sale of 40,000 shares: proceeds, say		56
Base cost: 20,000 shares, say	24	
20,000 shares repurchased in year 1	<u>28</u>	
		<u>(52)</u>
		4
Annual exemption		<u>(5)</u>
If all the holding is sold in year 2		
Proceeds	56	
Base cost and indexation allowance, say	<u>48</u>	
	<u>8</u>	
Annual exemption	5	
Taxable gain	<u>3</u>	

Notes: (1) The indexation allowance for year 2 has been ignored
(2) Dealing costs have been ignored
(3) It has been assumed that the share price has remained constant

---

interest rates. You will see from **Chart 5.6** that the capital would be eroded by almost 40 per cent over ten years if inflation was at only five per cent a year and by over 50 per cent if inflation was eight per cent.

The Conservative Party has used high interest rates as a means of controlling inflation but the recent recession has had a damaging affect upon profitability and company values. A change of economic policy could have a significant short-term impact upon the growth of the economy, interest rates, inflation etc.

Britain's entry into the European Rate Mechanism (ERM) has also had a significant effect. Our currency and interest rates are now linked more closely to the Deutschmark. Our economic fortune is now more dependent upon

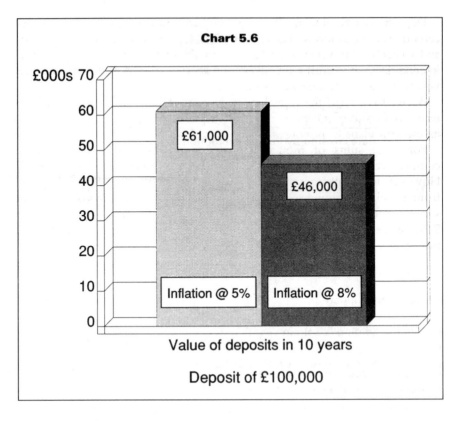

factors outside the control of the United Kingdom, and the cost to Germany of rebuilding the East German economy will clearly have a significant effect upon our own financial situation.

Most UK residents have all their investments in sterling as their income and expenditure are in that currency. However, many people are now looking to spread some of their investments into other currencies, even though this creates greater risks as there could be a fall in both the investment and the relevant currency. Sterling should be less volatile against other European currencies now that we are in the ERM, but if German interest rates rise while the UK economy is still struggling to move out of recession, this could conceivably lead to a realignment of sterling within the ERM.

DEPOSITS

Now that we have considered the investment criteria, let's look at the different investment vehicles, starting with deposits.

Deposits can be obtained from building societies, banks, post offices and certain other institutions. The advantage of deposits is that the money is safe and accessible. However, the rate of return depends entirely upon prevailing interest rates – if interest rates fall, so will your income; if the reverse happens you will enjoy an increasing yield.

As we have seen, the capital value of deposits will suffer erosion in real terms as a result of inflation. However, deposits are required as part of most investment plans to provide an emergency fund and income.

For large sums of money, the major clearing banks often give a competitive rate on their treasurer's accounts for sums in excess of £100,000. However, for small amounts, you may need to shop around for the best rate from a bank or building society, as illustrated in Chapter 3. Smaller building societies often provide the highest interest rates for depositors (see **Chart 5.7**), while certain larger building societies are more competitive on mortgages.

Chart 5.7	
Investment: £30,000 17 November 1991	
	Gross return %
Bristol & West 1-year account	12.25
Abbey National instant access account	8.85

The practical implications must be borne in mind as a smaller building society may only have one or two branches and this may not be convenient to you. It is normally advisable for you to retain a small sum of money in an account with the local branch of your bank or building society. Chapter 3 also shows how you can deposit larger sums elsewhere for a higher income yield if the money is not likely to be withdrawn on a regular basis.

The frequency of the interest payment may also be relevant. For example you may be offered an account which pays interest at the rate of 7.2 per cent a year with interest credited on a monthly basis. You would need to receive 7.3 per cent if the interest is credited twice a year or 7.4 per cent if interest is credited at the end of the year for the same overall return, due to the compound interest effect.

The tax system has now been changed so that if your money is deposited in an account which pays interest net of basic rate tax, basic rate tax may be recovered if you are due a repayment. (Previously, if you received building society interest, it was net of composite rate tax which could be reclaimed.) Many people who have money in a building society may be able to recover tax as shown by **Chart 5.8**.

This elderly couple and other non–taxpayers (such as children who inherit capital from their grandparents) should consider investing some of their money (approximately £6,000 in this case study) in a gross deposit account with a bank or building society, completing the appropriate form so that no tax is deducted at source and there is no need to make a repayment claim.

Chart 5.8

A married couple, both aged 70, each have £40,000 on deposit, earning 7.5 per cent net of basic rate tax (a gross equivalent interest rate of 10 per cent), and pension income of £2,000 in 1991/2

	Husband	Wife
Pension income, say	2,000	2,000
Building society interest (gross), say	4,000	4,000
	6,000	6,000
Personal allowance	(4,020)	(2,355)
Taxable income	1,980	3,645
Tax @ 25%	495	911
Tax paid	1,000	1,000
Tax repayable	(505)	(89)

TESSAs

This scheme has been running since 1 January 1991 and it makes sense for most taxpayers to transfer some of their bank or building society deposits into a tax-exemption special savings account (TESSA). These are tax-efficient and normally have no real downside.

The scheme is available to anyone over 18 years of age, and benefits accrue as long as the savings are left in the account for a period of five years, although the interest earned can be withdrawn. If you do not wish to withdraw any of the interest you can leave the capital and interest to roll up within the account for the five-year period. So long as no more than the net interest from the fund is withdrawn, there will be no tax to pay on the interest arising whether withdrawn or left to accumulate and the interest need not be declared on your tax returns.

Interest is provided net of basic-rate tax during the five-year period and if the capital remains in the account at the end of that period the basic-rate tax which has been deducted will be credited back to the account. If you withdraw more than the net interest during the five-year period, the exempt account will be terminated and all the tax advantages lost. The tax repayment will then be denied, and if you are in the higher-rate tax bracket you will be liable to higher-rate tax. However, you will be in no worse a position than if your money had remained in a normal taxable deposit account – unless your capital is withdrawn in a year in which your tax rate has increased.

You can make regular monthly payments up to the maximum limit of £150 per month into the account so that the capital invested is £9,000 spread evenly over five years. Alternatively you can invest the maximum permissible as early as possible by investing a lump sum at the start of each year, the maximum being as follows:

Year 1	£3,000
Year 2	£1,800
Year 3	£1,800
Year 4	£1,800
Year 5	£600
Total	£9,000

A husband and wife can invest a total of £18,000 over the five-year period. If you make the first investment of £3,000 on, say, 1 February, then the next investment of £1,800 cannot be made until the following 1 February.

Chart 5.9 compares the maximum annual investment in a TESSA with the same investment in a building society investment, assuming that interest rates are 7.5 per cent net of basic-rate tax throughout. All income is retained in the account which settles any tax due from interest received.

You should shop around for the best TESSA rate. A premium rate is often provided for a 'feeder' account as the full £9,000 is invested in a deposit account which feeds the maximum into the separate TESSA each year.

Many people are bemused by the choice of TESSA accounts so take no action due to lack of time and too great a choice. I suggest that, rather than doing nothing, you take advantage of the tax benefits, even if it means taking out a plan with your existing bank or building society which may not be giving the best rate, so long as it is comparable with the return from your other deposit accounts.

FIXED-INCOME ACCOUNTS

Part of your deposit income could come in the form of fixed income, particularly when interest rates are high. This provides the security of income which will not fall, but if interest rates rise during the investment term, you will lose out. Normally you will lose an element of liquidity as the

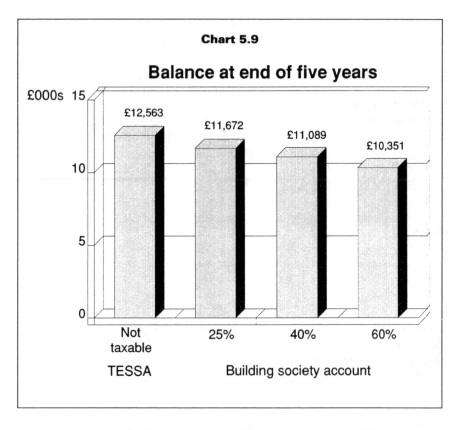

Chart 5.9

Balance at end of five years

arrangement normally has a fixed term. In some cases there will be a penalty for withdrawing the money early; under other arrangements the penalty will only arise if interest rates have risen during the period so that encashment prior to the end of the investment term could lead to a loss of part of your initial capital (by a fall in the unit price).

If you have surplus money in, say, December 1992, you could invest it for a fixed term of, say, 16 months so that it matures just after 5 April, and ask for all the interest to be credited at the maturity of the investment period. In this way, the tax on part of the income will be deferred for an entire fiscal year, as illustrated in **Chart 5.10**.

You can see from **Chart 5.10** that if all the interest for the period from 1 January 1993 to 30 April 1994 is credited on the latest date, all the higher-rate tax is deferred until 1 December 1995.

	Interest received net of basic-rate tax	Higher-rate tax payable
Chart 5.10		
Interest received quarterly	31 March 1993	1 December 1993
	Year to 31 March 1994	1 December 1994
	Interest to 30 April 1994	1 December 1995
Interest for 16 months credited on	30 April 1994	1 December 1995

Gilts

Another way in which you can invest for a fixed level of income is by acquiring a 'gilt', or government stock. Most of the available gilts are quoted in the *Financial Times* under the heading 'British Funds', or in certain other daily newspapers, and can be acquired by your stockbroker. There are a number of different gilts: some are short-dated and will mature within the next five years; some will run for between five and 15 years; and others will not mature for over 15 years or are open-ended.

The price quoted for the gilt will depend on the prevailing interest rate and the term to redemption. For example, if gross interest rates are running at around 11 per cent, then a gilt which provides more than 11 per cent of income will normally cost more than £100 for every £100 of nominal value stock. For example, on 15 November 1991, 13 per cent Treasury Stock 2000 cost £117.63p. This is because the interest rate was high, but the capital value is likely to fall over the next decade until redemption in the year 2000. If interest rates were to fall this year then the price could rise further as a premium income yield is being received. However, the price will need to fall eventually as it can only be redeemed at par (ie redemption at £100 for every £100 of nominal value).

Stocks which have little time to run until maturity are likely to move towards their redemption price of £100. Therefore if interest rates fall, the longer-dated stocks will rise while the shorter-dated stocks will normally move less dramatically as the premium yield will be received for a shorter period. Conversely if interest rates rise, the longer-dated and higher-interest stocks will normally fall more sharply than the shorter-dated stocks.

You can therefore select a stock which coincides with your investment period. The only downside of selling the stock within that period is that if interest rates have moved against you at that time you may take a lower return than was anticipated. For example, in November 1991 the average yield to redemption was approximately 9-10 per cent and the 9.75 per cent Treasury Stock 1998 cost £100.06p. If you are seeking a fixed income of around ten per cent this stock may be appropriate. However, if interest rates rise in, say, 1994 to 15 per cent you will still only be receiving around ten per cent a year and the sale price is likely to be less than £100.

In recent years gilts have not been quite so attractive because other fixed-interest arrangements have provided a slightly higher return. One of the attractions of gilts is that part of the return comes from income and part from a capital gain as stock can be purchased at a discount. Any capital gain is now completely tax-free (in the past the gilt had to be held for a year to obtain the tax-free gain).

Guaranteed income bonds

These are particularly attractive when interest rates are high. They are issued by insurance companies and the investment is normally covered by the Policyholders Protection Act 1975 so that up to 90 per cent of your original investment should be protected even if the insurance company runs into financial difficulties.

The guaranteed income bond is a fixed-interest investment which differs from a cash deposit or a building society account in that the interest to be earned is fixed at the outset and guaranteed over the term of the investment. The guaranteed income bond also has an income tax advantage over cash deposits in that the higher-rate income tax charge is levied on the net interest received rather than on the gross equivalent. Also, the higher rate charge could be avoided under independent taxation rules if the investment is made by a spouse whose income, including the gain from the bond, is likely to be within the basic rate band.

The return depends upon the term of the bond, which is usually between one and five years but can be longer. The rates fluctuate constantly and need to be reviewed before making any investment, but in November 1991 it was

Chart 5.11 *The best rates on guaranteed income bonds in November 1991 were as follows:*

		40% taxpayer		60% taxpayer	
	Year 1	Net of 25% tax %	Net return %	Gross equivalent Net return %	Gross equivalent %
General Portfolio	1	8.50	7.23	12.05 5.53	13.81
Property Life	3	8.75	7.44	12.40 5.69	14.22
Providence Capitol	5	9.30	7.91	13.18 6.05	15.13

possible to get 8.5 per cent net of basic-rate tax for a one-year bond and 9.3 per cent for a five-year bond – a greater yield than that obtainable from gilts at the time. The gross equivalent return would have been greater under a Labour administration as the top-rate tax charge is only levied on the net figure.

The problem with a five-year contract is that the money is locked way for five years and the bond, unlike a gilt, cannot be sold.

Zero coupon stocks

Zero coupon stocks have also become very popular in recent months. Certain stocks do not require any underlying capital growth and are taxable as income, while other zero coupon preference shares or split-level capital investment trusts may be taxed as capital gains. They are normally redeemable shares from a term of between four and ten years and have no income. While fixed-interest deposits from a bank, gilt and guaranteed income bond are not dependent upon any form of capital growth from the provider company, zero coupon stocks are, but in general, they are low-risk investments because the rate of return can be calculated at the outset and usually very little growth is required.

The redemption value is not guaranteed but usually the trust's assets need to grow by only a small percentage a year (say, one or two per cent) to ensure repayment at the projected value. Some zero coupon stocks protect the capital even if the company's underlying assets fall by up to 40 per cent but you will need to take specialist advice on this matter so that you are aware of the potential downside of the investment.

An article in the *Daily Telegraph* on 2 November 1991 quoted TR Technology's zero coupon stock as standing at 154.5 and projected to mature on 30 April 1998 at 313.2p – an average annual compound growth of 11.5 per cent. If we assume that inflation runs at five per cent a year, then only part of the gain will be taxable, as explained in **Chart 5.12**.

You can see from **Chart 5.12** that the net after-tax return is almost nine per cent and that the annual compound growth is fixed at 11.5 per cent gross over the period. Even if gross interest rates were to remain at 11.5 per cent, the net return to a 40 per cent taxpayer would be 6.9 per cent, a benefit of two per cent as the growth is taxed as capital. The returns can be higher than these but there are normally greater risks involved. Often, higher growth will depend upon the investment performance of the trust during its life so if you are looking for an alternative to the other fixed-interest arrangements, you may wish to consider zero coupon stocks which have a small element of risk, so long as you choose the trust which only needs to grow by around one to two per cent a year to provide the projected returns.

Zero coupon stocks are very popular as gifts to young children. Normally,

---

Chart 5.12

	%	%
Annual average growth	11.5	11.5
Inflation, say	(5.0)	
Taxable gain	6.5	
Capital gains tax @, say, 40% (Effective rate 23%)		(2.6)
		8.9

---

income received by a child who is under 18 in the form of capital passed across from the parent will be taxable upon the parent until the child reaches the age of 18. However, these settlement provisions do not apply to capital gains made by a child resulting from a *gift* from the parent. It might therefore be desirable to buy zero coupon stocks to use the annual capital gains tax exemption of the child so that no tax is payable at all. It is also possible to acquire the zero coupon stock through a personal equity plan, but this investment is not available for children under 18.

INFLATION PROOFING

We have already looked at some of the problems of inflation. You may remember that during the 1970s inflation reached over 20 per cent and while, at the time of writing this book, inflation was below five per cent, there is no certainty that this will continue. Twice during the 1980s, inflation got out of control and we have seen how measures to overcome the destructive effects of inflation have led to economic misery.

The case study in **Chart 5.13** refers to a married couple with cash deposits of £120,000 and a net surplus income of £5,000. It assumes that they are in the same position upon retirement. Net income is shown as £35,800 and I have assumed that it is represented by a flat rate after-tax pension and that the deposit interest is received at six per cent net of tax. I have assumed that expenditure increases at 7.5 per cent a year.

While there is surplus income in years one and two, as the pension income and deposit interest is not index-linked and as the expenditure is increasing in line with inflation (which is assumed to be 7.5 per cent a year here), then by year three there will be net surplus expenditure. You will see that this increases dramatically so that at the end of year ten the expenditure is approximately £35,000 more than the capital, which will be exhausted in year 11.

Clearly, in this situation the couple cannot continue to incur the same level of expenditure and will have to lower their costs. This shows the importance of building up a large enough capital base during your working life to have sufficient capital and index-linked income to offset the effects of inflation.

Index-linked gilts

In the past, index-linked gilts have not seemed to be a good investment although some fund managers do not expect the same level of growth from equities during the 1990s as was experienced during the previous decade so there may be a case for having some index-linked gilts in your portfolio to mitigate against high inflation in the future.

In November 1991, they were providing a real return of approximately 4.25 per cent of which approximately two per cent was income which would be subject to tax. Therefore, after tax, the net return is between three per cent and 3.5 per cent. Both the income and the capital value is index-linked and the above figures assume inflation at five per cent. While these stocks are tax-efficient, (as the index-linked gain is tax-free when sold) they produce little income and it is often necessary to have some assets which produce income to meet ongoing expenditure, some assets invested for capital growth and some index-linked stock to hedge against high inflation.

National Savings

As a hedge against inflation, the Fifth Index-Linked National Savings certificate is good value. A maximum of £10,000 in this issue may be held by any one person. Therefore a husband and wife can hold a total of £20,000 in index-linked certificates. It is also possible for one spouse to acquire the maximum of £10,000 in trust for a spouse. If both spouses acquire the maximum in their own name and the maximum in trust for their partner, a total of £40,000 could be acquired for this issue. This issue guarantees a fixed return over and above the rate of inflation. To obtain the best returns, this certificate should be held for the full five years to earn 4.5 per cent a year compound on top of inflation. If we assume that gross deposit interest rates remain at ten per cent and inflation is five per cent for the next five years, the benefit of this form of investment is as set out in **Chart 5.14**.

The gross equivalent return on this form of investment to a 40 per cent taxpayer would be 15.8 per cent to produce the same 9.5 per cent net return after tax. Obviously the benefit of this certificate depends upon future rates of inflation and taxation. If inflation were to fall to 3.5 per cent, then the net return of eight per cent would be equivalent to a gross deposit rate of 13.3 per cent to a 40 per cent taxpayer, which is still relatively high. However, if inflation increases to 7.5 per cent, then the supplement would provide a net of

Chart 5.13 *Net income*

Year	1	2	3	4	5	6	7	8	9	10
Pensions etc net of tax	35,800	35,800	35,800	35,800	35,800	35,800	35,800	35,800	35,800	35,800
Deposit interest @ 6% net of tax	7,200	7,500	7,647	7,619	7,392	6,938	6,229	5,232	3,912	2,228
Expenditure increasing @ 7.5%	(38,000)	(40,850)	(43,914)	(47,207)	(50,748)	(54,554)	(58,645)	(63,043)	(67,772)	(72,855)
	5,000	2,450	(467)	(3,788)	(7,556)	(11,816)	(16,616)	(22,011)	(28,060)	(34,827)

Deposit

Year	B/F	Surplus Deficit	C/F
1	120,000	5,000	125,000
2	125,000	2,450	127,450
3	127,450	(467)	126,983
4	126,983	(3,788)	123,195
5	123,195	(7,556)	115,639
6	115,639	(11,816)	103,823
7	103,823	(16,616)	87,207
8	87,207	(22,011)	65,196
9	65,196	(28,060)	37,136
10	37,136	(34,827)	2,309

tax return of 12 per cent which would require gross deposit interest of 20 per cent to produce the same net return to a 40 per cent taxpayer.

The other national savings issue which is very popular is the 36th issue. The maximum which can be invested is £10,000 per person (£20,000 for a husband and wife). Also, a further £10,000 can be invested in this issue from old maturing certificates. Like the index-linked certificate, no income is received but the certificates grow in value and should be held for the full five years. The 36th issue provides a fixed return of 8.5 per cent if held for the five-year period, which is equivalent to 14.17 per cent to a 40 per cent taxpayer. The above certificates can also be acquired for children and as they are free of tax and produce no income, they can be a worthwhile investment.

National Savings will introduce a new guaranteed growth bond in the summer. This will provide fixed rates of interest (yet to be announced) guaranteed for one year and paid after deduction of basic-rate tax. Up to £0.25m may be invested and there will be no maturity date; holders can cash them at any anniversary date without a penalty.

National Savings issues change from time to time so it is advisable to visit your local post office for details of the latest ones. Many people have old National Savings issues which have reached their five-year term but have not been cashed. Many of these old issues provide a lower return than you can get from later ones. National Savings issues from 7 to 31 are earning their general extension rate of 5.01 per cent and it is understood that there is still £2.85 billion in these issues yet, as we have seen, you get a much better rate from the 36th issue. Holders of the original index-linked certificates, issue numbers one and two (so-called 'granny bonds') are also advised to switch. Changing to the 5th issue, for example, means index-linking plus an extra 4.5 per cent while granny bonds offer only index-linking.

Chart 5.14	
	%
Deposit interest	10.0
Less tax, say	(4.0)
Net return	6.0
Index-linked certificate	
Inflation-linked growth, say	5.0
Add supplement	4.5
	9.5
Benefit	3.5

Offshore deposit funds

In the past, many people invested in offshore deposits, such as a Jersey-based bank deposit account, to get *gross income* instead of *interest*, which is subject to the composite rate of tax.

Many UK investors now consider currency deposits as a means of hedging against sterling: they perhaps have all their assets in sterling; their salary comes from a UK company; their expenditure is in sterling; and all their investments are in sterling.

A sound investment policy, however, is to avoid putting 'all your eggs in one basket'. For that reason, there is some merit in investing outside the UK so as to hedge against poor economic performance in the UK and a fall in sterling. However, it opens up the greater risk that you are now exposed to currency fluctuations. In the past, UK interest has been at a much higher rate than that of other currencies. However, now that interest rates have fallen comparatively and Britain is in the ERM, UK rates are closer to other currency deposit rates. Wide fluctuations between sterling and European currencies are now less likely.

Towards the end of 1991 many people were expressing concern at the likely future performance of sterling, especially if there is a change of government and a possible initial loss of confidence in sterling. Is it conceivable that a future chancellor may have to devalue sterling within the ERM? Could the yen or the dollar outperform sterling in the longer term? These questions are best answered by the specialists. A number of currency fund managers, such as N M Rothschild, have specialized in the management of currency deposits.

Offshore currency funds

Offshore currency funds are open-ended investment companies registered outside the UK in tax-shelter countries such as the Channel Islands and the Cayman Islands. There are two types of currency funds, namely 'roll-up' or 'accumulator' funds, and 'distributor' funds. These are classes of shares invested in various currencies, the gross income from which is accumulated and reflected in the share price. For the UK-resident there is, therefore, no income tax to pay until the shares are encashed, at which time the tax on the gain on the shares will be charged in full at the rate then prevailing.

A 'roll-up' fund is appropriate where you wish to defer income tax on sterling deposits as the gain is only taxed when the proceeds are received. Distributor funds, on the other hand, pay out all the income each year. The gain on the sale of the shares is taxed as a capital gain and this will be more appropriate if you wish to invest for capital growth in non–sterling deposits as a hedge against a fall in sterling.

The problem with the 'roll–up' fund for non–sterling deposits is that the Inland Revenue does not distinguish between income and capital when the shares are encashed. Therefore, if you make a currency gain in addition to the rolled–up income, it will all be taxed as income. For this reason, the distributor fund may be more appropriate for non–sterling currency deposits, especially if the future income tax rate exceeds the capital gains tax rate.

Companies such as Rothschilds charge a monthly management fee and administration charge which can amount in total to around one per cent a year. You should examine the prospectus before proceeding with the investment. Past performance of the specialist currency fund managers is reasonably good but careful selection should be made.

With-profit contracts

The with–profit concept is attractive to those seeking a return which has been traditionally better than deposits in the building society or bank but does not have the same risks as a stockmarket investment. A with–profit investment can be made in a number of ways but we start by looking at a simple lump–sum investment in a with–profit bond. The overall growth of the bond is determined by the declaration of bonuses to the policyholders in addition to the original capital invested.

Investment guarantees

If you invest in a with–profit bond with one of the large UK insurance companies the money is invested by the relevant fund managers in the equity markets and, to a lesser degree, in property and fixed–interest securities. The insurance company increases your original capital by providing a bonus at a minimum rate of between three and four per cent a year compound. However, the annual bonus is normally much higher than this and in November 1991 a number of companies were offering an annual bonus of 9.75 per cent net of basic rate tax. This rate is likely to fall to around 8.5 per cent during the summer of 1992.

Bonuses

Insurance companies declare bonuses to the with–profit fund which are a reflection of investment performance and the reserves held. Therefore, during years when they were able to achieve significant capital growth, they tended to top up their reserves so that they are able to draw money from these reserves during 'bear' markets. The effect of this was seen in October

1987 when the UK stock market fell by 20 per cent to 30 per cent whereas the bonuses declared on with-profit contracts shortly after the crash were at approximately the same level as those declared in the previous year.

Loyalty bonuses

If you hold a with-profit bond for some time, a special loyalty bonus is normally declared and attaches to the plan (some companies pay loyalty bonuses after one to three years; some may provide it from the commencement of the policy). This will apply regardless of whether the plan is being cashed or not but, should the plan be cashed prior to receipt of the loyalty bonus, say, after two and a half years, then this bonus may be received by way of a terminal or final bonus.

How bonuses operate

Some companies provide a large annual bonus while others favour a smaller annual bonus but greater loyalty and terminal bonuses. Some leading with-profit insurance companies are proposing to maintain their annual bonus rates in line with, or slightly ahead of, building society interest rates.

Single-premium with-profit bonds have only been in operation for the last few years but the structure is similar to the with-profit endowment policies which have been running for several decades. During the 1980s, the top performing with-profit offices produced average annual compound returns of up to 18 per cent, after basic rate tax. While these returns are unlikely to be repeated over the next decade, it is anticipated that the net of tax return rates should exceed those from banks or building society deposits, especially if held for the longer term. However, there are obviously no guarantees that this will happen, especially if interest rates rise sharply.

The 1980s saw tremendous growth in equity markets so the insurance companies were able to build up their reserves. Unless fund growth is matched at the same rate over the next decade, funds will probably need to be withdrawn from those reserves to such an extent that bonus rates will fall. This has already begun and it is anticipated that bonuses will be at lower levels over the next decade but may still produce a reasonable return.

You must get sound professional advice on choosing an insurance company. There are a number of actuarial surveys not widely known to the public but extracts are printed in financial magazines from time to time. It is important that your financial advisor has access to actuarial support as the with-profit office should be selected upon a number of factors, including the financial strength of the life office, current reserves, fund performance, size and charges.

As interest rates have fallen, with-profit contracts have been actively marketed. Some companies have taken a more conservative approach and have stated that no loyalty or terminal bonus will be provided for the first three years, but that thereafter the loyalty bonus will be provided on an increasing basis so that the longer the policy is held, the greater the return. Other companies say they may provide a loyalty bonus in the first couple of years while others have actively marketed their loyalty bonuses which commence immediately.

Ultimately, the return will depend upon the factors mentioned above. Whether or not a company gives a larger 'up-front' bonus is something of a marketing ploy because unless they can sustain that level of bonus, they are more likely to impose the market adjustment factor mentioned below. Do try to judge companies upon sound criteria rather than a good marketing approach.

Caveats

Full or partial encashment of the plan would, under normal circumstances, be at the full bid value of the units, together with any additional bonus that applies at the time. However, if asset values are *severely* depressed, a *market adjustment factor* may be applied to protect the interests of existing plan-holders. Use of the market adjustment factor by the insurance company would reduce the value of with-profit units cashed.

In practice, conditions would have to be very severe for insurance companies to introduce a market adjustment factor. The first move in a deteriorating investment environment would probably be to reduce or remove the terminal or loyalty bonus. Investment conditions would then have to deteriorate further before introduction of a market adjustment factor would be necessary. This factor would similarly apply if units are being switched out of the with-profit fund into other unit-linked or fixed-interest funds of the plan.

Companies are unlikely to impose the market adjustment factor on a regular basis. In fact, one leading company for this type of investment has indicated that it would only have operated this adjustment at one point in its history since World War II, and that was during 1974 when the stock market crashed from over 500 to under 200.

Tax treatment

Profits within the bond are subject to the life offices' rate of tax which is currently approximately in line with the basic rate of 25 per cent. Therefore, the higher rate of income tax is deferred. Five per cent a year can be withdrawn from the original investment each year for the first 20 years without an income tax charge. You may carry forward the five per cent allowance from previous years in which income was not taken or received fully up to the five per cent limit. A charge to higher-rate income tax would arise on the profit from the bond including the five per cent withdrawals only upon encashment of part or all of the bond. There is no charge to capital gains tax.

Any gain upon encashment of the bond is 'top-sliced', as illustrated in **Chart 5.15**.

If the top-sliced gain can be kept within the basic rate band, by, for example, switching the bond to a spouse with lower income, or by sheltering £4,300 of income, tax of £6,450 can be saved.

Chart 5.15

	£000
Bond held for 10 years	
Gain	80
Top-sliced gain (80 divided by 10)	8
Other taxable income in 1991/2, say	20
	28
Top-sliced gain:	
£3,700 – within basic-rate band – tax Nil	
4,300 – within higher-rate band – tax at 15%	(£645)
£8,000	
Top-sliced gain £645 × 10 (effective higher rate 8.06%)	6

Commission and charges

Although various companies have slightly different structures, the following is fairly standard. There is a charge of five per cent but an allocation rate of around 101.5 per cent by some companies on larger investments.

Most intermediaries will retain the commission as their income for advising on the matter, so your bond will initially fall in value by up to five per cent. However, you should view this plan in the longer-term – if bonuses exceed deposit interest rates you should benefit. Other advisors charge on a fee basis and rebate all the commission so that the initial value of the bond can be brought back to its purchase price.

Other advantages

Further advantages of an investment bond are as follows:

- Wide choice of funds and investment spread, coupled with easy and inexpensive fund-switching facilities so investment can be switched from with-profit fund to UK equity fund or cash deposit

- Professional management of funds by large institutions with considerable investment expertise

- No personal liability to capital gains tax (but a possible charge to higher-rate income tax) and corresponding reduction in amount of paperwork

- Ability to break down investment into a cluster of smaller policies to give maximum flexibility and tax advantages.

However, as the bond effectively suffers tax at approximately 25 per cent which is paid by life companies on their profits, it is likely to be less tax-efficient than an equity investment which suffers no tax on capital growth until the investment is sold, at which time it attracts the capital gains tax indexation allowance.

Chart 5.16 *Investment of £100,000*		£
Investment:	101.5% × £100,000 × 95%	96,425
Commission:	£100,000 × 4% × 130% uplift	5,200

With-profit endowment policy

A more traditional way of investing in a with-profit contract is to take out a with-profit endowment policy. You may have an endowment policy linked to your mortgage. The policy can be for a term of, say, 25 years so as to mature when the mortgage is to be repaid, or could be for a period of only ten years. The ten-year with-profit endowment policy is a very attractive medium-term investment: bonuses are provided on a slightly different basis from that of the bond but funds and reserves are maintained in approximately the same way.

If you were to pay, say, £1,000 a year into a ten-year endowment policy, the initial sum assured is guaranteed and bonuses will be credited to the policy each year. At the end of the term there may be a further bonus, depending on investment performance; in recent years this 'final bonus' has been substantial. The market adjustment factor can be applied to these policies, especially upon early encashment.

The with-profit concept smoothes out the fluctuations in equity markets and, as mentioned above, in the past the top performing with-profit companies have provided an after-tax return of up to 18 per cent. While this is not likely to be repeated over the next ten years, growth could still be reasonable. If you get a quote from an insurance company, you will note that the growth rate chosen can only be in accordance with LAUTRO (Life Assurance and Unit Trust Regulatory Organization) rules so that you are likely to see a quote based upon seven per cent or 10.5 per cent growth. Again, the need for expertise in the selection of a life office cannot be over-stressed, since the best results for with-profit policies are dramatically better than the worst, as shown by **Chart 5.17**.

While the with-profit contracts are designed to smooth out the fluctuations in equity markets, it is interesting to note how the with-profit offices invest their with-profit funds, as shown by **Chart 5.18**.

The with-profit endowment policy is very tax-efficient as the life companies' rate of tax is broadly in line with the basic rate of 25 per cent. If the plan is retained for 7.5 years, then there will be no higher-rate income tax charge upon encashment, so if the plan is held for the full ten-year term the proceeds are received tax-free. Commission of up to 40 per cent of the first year's premium is normally payable to intermediaries and this is why the surrender value is normally very low in the early years as the charges are 'front-end loaded'.

There is a very active market in second-hand with-profit endowment policies. Approximately 80 per cent of home-buyers take out an endowment policy and about the same proportion cash in their policy before the maturity date. Many are victims of salesmen who derive their income from commission but others encash their plans when they move house and take out a new mortgage. Many policies have been encashed due to financial difficulties because of the recession. For those who have available cash, this provides an opportunity to take advantage of these policies: due to the front-end loaded charges, the policy performs badly in early years (in terms of its surrender value). However if the policy is retained until maturity, a good return can be obtained, but you really must be sure to get best advice here.

If you can acquire the policy after the initial charges have been incurred, you are likely to get a better return from the investment than if you take out the policy at the start of the term.

There are a number of brokers willing to sell second-hand qualifying endowment policies and there is an active auction for these policies at Foster & Cranfield in London. If past bonuses can be maintained, it is possible to get a return of around 14 per cent from a second-hand policy and you may not need to wait as long as ten years – some policies may only have five or six years to run. However, as mentioned above, it is quite possible that future bonuses will not be as high as in previous years, but the returns could still be very favourable. If a second-hand qualifying policy is acquired without any change to the policy arrangement, then the gain on maturing is likely to be subject to capital gains tax.

Due to the indexation allowance and your annual exemption, this may be a very tax-efficient investment. Those who set up offshore trusts before the change in the tax system in 1991 may wish to consider this form of investment as the gain would then be tax-deferred until a capital payment is received from the trust.

The plans include life assurance in case the named party dies before the maturity date.

If you do not wish to invest in a second-hand endowment policy, the choice is between the single premium with-profit bond or the ten-year with-profit endowment policy. Many people prefer to invest a lump sum but also take advantage of the greater tax-efficiency of the ten-year endowment policy. One option is to take out a bond and withdraw five per cent a year, then use this money to fund a ten-year with-profit endowment plan.

Alternatively, you could use your cash deposits or fixed-interest deposits to fund the ten-year plan. In the past, gilts have been a popular means of providing annual premiums for the ten-year plan. Normally the first year's premium is paid and nine gilts are acquired with one maturing in each of the

---

Chart 5.17

Actual payouts in 1991 on policies taken out by a male aged 30 next birthday at outset; £30 per month gross premium, 25-year endowment policy, maturity value on 1 August 1991.

	£
Standard Life	67,872
Average (1)	54,411
NEL Britannia	31,113

Note: (1) Average of all the companies in the survey

Source: Money Management, October 1991

---

following nine years to pay the future premiums. The gilts provide tax-free growth and you can construct the plan so that part of the proceeds from the maturing gilt can be used as income with the balance being paid into the ten-

---

Chart 5.18   *Investment spread of with-profit funds, 1990*

	Proportion of with-profit assets invested in			
	Gov & other fund interest	*Equity*	*Property*	*Cash etc*
	%	%	%	%
Equitable Life	17	57	15	11
Norwich Union	0	60	34	6
Provident Mutual	25	46	19	10
Scottish Widows	19	63	12	6
Standard Life	1	75	24	0
Sun Life of Canada	14	38	29	19

Source: Money Management, November 1991

---

year plan. You can also write some of the plans in trust for children or grandchildren for estate-planning purposes. Other forms of fixed–interest investments, such as guaranteed income bonds or zero coupon stock could also be used for this purpose. I consider use of a temporary annuity to fund the plan in Chapter 7.

Equities

For those seeking long–term capital growth, an equity portfolio may be suitable for part of the available cash sums. **Chart 5.19** sets out the past performance of UK equities compared with Treasury bills.

The tax treatment of equities is normally more beneficial as only real gains are now taxed (ie the gains are reduced by an indexation allowance). While historically equities have been a good investment, there is no certainty that the next decade will be as good as the last. The UK stock market is supposed to be looking six to 18 months ahead so you would expect it to have discounted some recovery from the recession, but if profits of UK companies increase substantially over the next few years, then the share price may also move ahead. Sometimes the share price moves down following publication of a good set of accounts, but only if the market is expecting a higher profit figure.

One problem with an equity investment is that it is long–term. It is also subject to the vagaries of the stock market. While the investment houses have significant research facilities, very few anticipated the stock market crash of 1987 when clients saw their share values reduced by up to 30 per cent in the space of a few days. This is worrying to the wealthy – for those with a smaller capital base, it can produce sleepless nights.

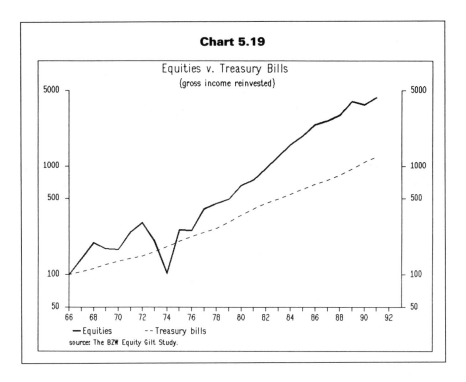

Chart 5.19

Equities v. Treasury Bills
(gross income reinvested)

Equities — · — Treasury bills

source: The BZW Equity Gilt Study.

The problem is that many people are not well-advised and tend to have short memories. At some point during the 1980s, an equity investment seemed too good to be true: you could subscribe for a new share issue and be almost assured of a premium, so many people 'stagged' a new issue to make a quick short-term gain. This encouraged many others to invest in the stock market on the assumption that it was a way of making money very quickly. Alas, reality returned and many people were brought back to earth with a thud. Even in the current recession, some shares have performed very well and **Chart 5.20** shows the performance of Wellcome over the last few years.

You will see how the share price fluctuated over that period and the graph also show the effects of the October 1987 crash. The problem is one of timing. Some people are very reluctant to invest one penny in the stock market, especially if they have already had their fingers burnt. It is very uncomfortable to see the value of your money fall, but while it may be more reassuring to place your money in bank deposit accounts, or even in with-profit plans, the long-term return from equities may be greater.

For those with a faint heart, equity investments should either be made in moderation or not at all. There are sound reasons for investing in equities but only if you are willing to accept the roller-coaster effect of the markets. If we take the Wellcome shares as an illustration, you will see that during 1987, the

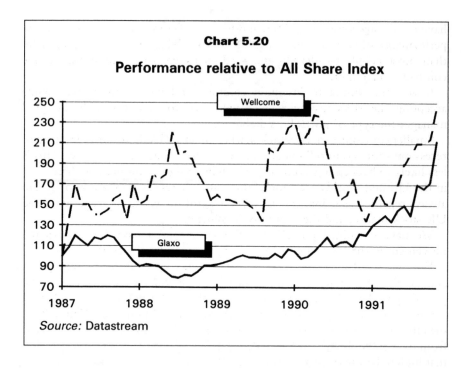

Chart 5.20

Performance relative to All Share Index

Source: Datastream

share price was in the region of 120p. Within five years, the share price had increased to over 240p showing an average annual compound return of over 15 per cent. However if you had bought the stock in 1988 at £2.10 and had seen it fall to below £1.40 in 1989, you may have been very depressed about the position. If you decided to 'cut your losses' and sell this would have been bad timing because the share price leapt back to over the 1988 peak. Although it fell again in 1990, it then climbed back to an all time high for the period under review.

Had you held the shares throughout that period you would have experienced the roller-coaster effect. However, over the longer term it has been a good performer. If you invest in equities you really need to take a somewhat detached view, leave the investment performance to the specialists and review the matter every three months or so, but be prepared to wait for five to ten years to see the longer-term growth. This takes great discipline and this is why I am always anxious to establish whether clients are willing to approach their investments in this way.

You need to consider whether you wish to have a 'hands on' or a more dispassionate approach to investments. Some people like to select their own stocks and shares as it provides greater interest: I would guard against this approach unless you are a specialist in this field. Specialist fund managers have enormous research facilities and have a full-time manager to check the performance of various companies and sectors. That manager is more likely than most people to identify the need to move from one sector or one company to another.

If you are willing to invest in equities for longer-term growth while accepting the risks involved, you will need to establish with the fund manager the type of portfolio suitable for you.

Smaller companies on the stock market are more likely to suffer in times of recession: some go into liquidation so their shares become worthless. This is less likely to happen to a company which has a significant market-share both in the UK and worldwide. Such 'blue chip' shares, as they are known, are always regarded as being less risky but are still subject to the vagaries of the UK stock market and the economy in general.

We have examined the effects of inflation and **Chart 5.21** shows the movement in the FT Industrial Ordinary Index since the 1950s.

You will see that the index has moved steadily upwards through its peaks and troughs. The graph which is adjusted for inflation shows that during the period up to the 1970s, real returns were achieved. During the 1970s inflation was exceptionally high and the fund performance was not good. You will see the effect of the stock market crash in the mid 1970s, when the index moved from over 500 to below 200. It took a number of years to recover and during that high inflationary period there was a loss in real terms. However, during the 1980s, the index recovered.

Professional fund management

If you are willing to seek professional fund management, you must decide on the type of management to be chosen. For a portfolio of £100,000 or more a stockbroker may be appropriate. Some investment houses use a stockbroker for investments of less than £100,000 while others (and especially for those seeking international funds) tend to use unit trusts and investment trusts for investments of over £100,000.

It is important to establish a good rapport with your broker, but it is normally advisable to allow discretionary fund management so that action can be taken at short notice where necessary. There is nothing worse for a broker than having to report back to a client and finding that the client is not available just when he or she needs to take action in a volatile market. Your accountant should be able to assist in finding an appropriate fund manager. You should determine at the outset whether you want your money in UK equities or international funds.

Many UK investment houses are very good at managing money in the UK market but have less expertise in foreign markets. If you want a truly international portfolio, you will need to go to one of the specialist houses

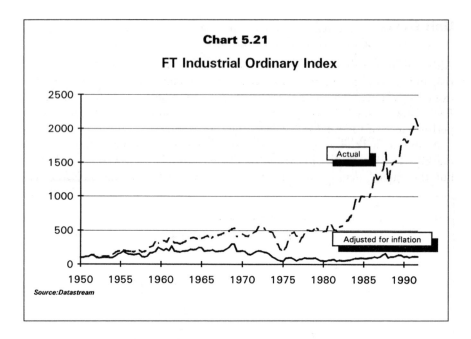

Chart 5.21

FT Industrial Ordinary Index

Source:Datastream

which have a good reputation for international fund management, with specialist managers who are resident in, and have inside knowledge of, the international markets. Managed funds are popular but you can see from **Charts 5.22** and **5.22a** that in many cases a large part of managed funds are invested in the UK market. If you are really seeking an international fund, you must go to the specialist managers.

It is interesting to note how the UK market has performed against other markets around the world. The Japanese market has performed badly during 1991 and 1992 but at some times during the 1980s, it showed remarkable growth. **Chart 5.23** sets out a comparison for your consideration.

It is important that you obtain a good spread of investment. If you have your money in one or two shares, then you will be greatly affected by those companies. Have your money invested in a basket of 30 or 40 companies, then if one performs badly it will not have such a great impact upon your portfolio. Some people have a significant part of their wealth in one company for historical or family reasons – perhaps a parent was the driving force behind a private company which subsequently went to the market. That company may have made the family millionaires – but there may be no good reason now to retain such a large holding in that company.

For those who have less than £100,000 to invest, unit trusts or investment trusts may form part of the portfolio or be the only means of obtaining a good spread of investments without high charges.

Unit trusts

Although primarily equity investments, unit trusts offer a greater spread of risk and each fund will normally hold within it some 30 to 40 shares. If, for example, you had ten unit trusts, you could be investing in some 400 shares. Each fund is unitized: you purchase a number of units with the subsequent performance of the fund reflected in the unit price.

A unit trust fund adopts a managed approach to various sectors of the market. The income arising from a unit trust fund is subject to income tax, but the capital gain within the fund is only taxable on the investor on

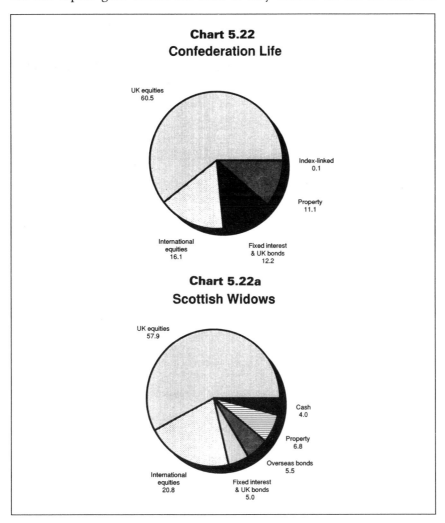

Chart 5.22
Confederation Life

UK equities
60.5

Index-linked
0.1

Property
11.1

International
equities
16.1

Fixed interest
& UK bonds
12.2

Chart 5.22a
Scottish Widows

UK equities
57.9

Cash
4.0

Property
6.8

Overseas bonds
5.5

International
equities
20.8

Fixed interest
& UK bonds
5.0

Chart 5.23 *Pension fund performance over last five years*

£1,000 invested offer to bid, net income reinvested

	Average of funds		Best performance	
	£			£
UK equity	1,650		CML Rainbow	3,768
Managed	1,493		CML Rainbow	2,243
Far Eastern	1,341		NM Far Eastern	2,583
North American	1,301		Premium Life	2,458
International	1,214		General Portfolio	1,591
European	1,156		Clerical/Fidelity	1,506

Source: Money Management, December 1991

encashment. Therefore, provided you remain within your capital gains exemption (proposed to be £5,800 a year) on encashment, there is no tax to be paid on your capital gain within the fund.

As a husband and wife now have separate capital gains tax exemptions it may be worthwhile investing part of the proceeds in the spouse's name so that you both realize your investments tax-free up to the annual capital gains tax exemption. If the gain exceeds any available capital gains tax exemption, then tax at up to 40 per cent may be payable.

A number of products have been introduced to enable you to invest money in equities without the risk that your capital may fall in value in total terms (however, in real terms, if your capital remains the same, then there will be a loss). The plans are split so that a small part of the money is invested in unit trusts or equities with the balance invested in a guaranteed income bond, zero coupon stock or some other form of investment which is projected to return the initial capital value. An alternative course of action is to make the allocation yourself in respect of your capital.

Investment trusts

Investment trusts are similar to unit trusts. You acquire shares in the investment trust – its share price can normally be found in the financial newspapers. The investment trust company invests in other companies and their value is reflected in its share price. The share capital is fixed and can only be increased with the approval of the shareholders. Its share price is subject to the law of supply and demand so market forces, as well as equity performance of the underlying investments, will be reflected by it.

As mentioned above, one of the benefits of unit and investment trusts is that they are structured to provide capital growth which is subject to capital gains tax. After taking account of the indexation allowance and the annual exemption, there may be no tax to pay. You can select some investment trusts or unit trusts which are geared towards income, but if you are seeking capital growth then normally the income return will be relatively low.

Personal Equity Plans

For tax purposes you may also wish to consider investing part of your equity funds in a personal equity plan (PEP). A UK resident may subscribe a maximum of £6,000 to a personal equity plan (PEP) in any calendar year. Investing in a PEP involves payment to plan managers who will buy and hold shares for you. Investments which may be held under the plan are:

1. Ordinary shares in UK companies quoted on a recognized stock exchange or dealt in on the Unlisted Securities Market (USM).

2. Investment trusts and authorized unit trusts.

As long as dividends and proceeds produced from the sale of shares within the plan are reinvested, no capital gains tax is payable on any gains made (nor will any loss produce tax relief), and any dividends received within the plan are free from income tax (no higher-rate tax charge is payable and the fund managers will reclaim the tax credit).

A PEP is suitable for all investors but particularly those paying 40 per cent tax on income and gains. Other features of PEPs include:

*   Husband and wife can each have a PEP

*   Sale proceeds may be reinvested without affecting the £6,000 annual allowance

*   PEP holders must be UK-tax-resident and ordinarily resident

*   It is possible to sell shares and keep the proceeds in the PEP for more than four weeks prior to reinvestment

*   It is difficult to spread your investment, though a spread can be obtained by varying the investment plan from year to year.

For the first time from January 1992, corporate PEPs are permitted: a company can issue its own personal equity plan so that if you wish to invest in, say, the Marks & Spencer plc plan - as an employee or as an outside investor – you can do so if the company has a plan. As certain PEP providers enable you to have discretion over the selection of equities, it is possible to invest £9,000 per person in an ordinary or corporate PEP (£18,000 for a married couple) and have all the money invested in one company.

The main tax benefits of investing in a PEP are that income is received tax-free and there is no capital gains tax to pay. However if you do not pay capital gains tax then the benefit of receiving the dividends tax-free needs to be set against the additional charges of operating a PEP.

Chart 5.24 compares a unit trust and a PEP.

If capital gains tax is payable, then the PEP has an advantage over the Unit trust. If you pay no capital gains tax, then the benefit of the PEP is reduced.

There are a number of other more risky vehicles such as futures, warrants, options and commodities which are not detailed here. Advice on these can be obtained from specialist brokers. Such vehicles carry far greater risks but also greater potential for capital growth.

Chart 5.24

Unit trust (see Note 1) value in year 5	8,649	
Capital gains tax, say	(396)	
		8,253
PEP (see note 2) value in year 5		9,323

Notes: (1) Assumes initial investment of £6,000, 6% initial charge, 1.5% pa annual charge, income 2.4% net of 40% tax, inflation 5% pa, annual capital growth 8%.

(2) Assumes initial investment of £6,000, 6% initial charge, 1.5% annual charge, gross income 4%, capital growth 8% pa.

PROPERTY

For many people, the family home is the most valuable asset in the estate. Over the past few decades, property has proved a good investment, but the last two years have shown that nothing can be taken for granted and property values have fallen in many parts of the country.

For those with available capital, buying a property as an investment rather than simply a place to live in may be worth considering. You could acquire a residential property and get a tenant: short-term property lets have proved popular but there tends to be a lot of administration involved and a general concern about the ability to re-let the property after the tenant has left. In addition, you will need to consider carefully who would be responsible for repairs, insurance, etc.

Many investors seek a commercial property such as a shop or office building. If a property can be found with an existing tenant on a tenant's repairing lease, there may be fewer problems involved, but there are still a number of factors which must be carefully borne in mind, including the following:

- Whether the purchase price represents good value today
- Recent movements and likely future movements in property values
- Location of property
- Security of tenant
- Rental yield

Unless you are a property specialist, you should seek professional advice before proceeding with any property investment. Unfortunately, most property advisers have an 'axe to grind' as they tend to be remunerated on a percentage of the purchase price so it is therefore in their interest to ensure that you acquire a property. However, there are a number of reputable property advisers who should be able to provide sound advice.

If a tenant is secure and if rental values are likely to increase over the period of the lease, you should obtain an increasing income yield from the property together with capital growth. However, as we have seen in recent years, rental values don't always grow. In addition, the current recession has thrown up many problems associated with tenants taking on the obligation of a long-term lease and then experiencing difficulty in meeting the long-term rental obligations, and it may be more common in future for there to be a 'break clause' in a lease.

So long as the property is let commercially 26 weeks a year, you can borrow to buy the property and have the interest set against the rent for income tax purposes. This is one of the few fully deductible loans and **Chart 5.25** shows the benefit of using loan finance for a property investment.

Other property investments could include farms or woodlands. However, since the income tax relief has been withdrawn from woodlands, their values have significantly fallen, but they do provide inheritance tax relief and gains from the sale of timber can be received tax-free. Pension funds have traditionally invested in forestry, but since the income tax reliefs have been withdrawn private investors have been few and far between.

The acquisition of a farm has also been popular in the past but it is often difficult to get a reasonable return from a working farm. The 1992 Budget proposal to increase inheritance tax relief for working farms up to 100 per

	£000	£000
Chart 5.25		
Investment of cash	250	
Rent @ 8% pa		20
Tax payable at, say, 40%		8
Net income after tax		12
Investment of cash	100	
Loan	150	
Total investment as above	250	
Rent @ 8%		20
Loan interest at, say, 12%		18
Net income		2
tax at 40%		(1)
Net income after tax		1

cent could make them more attractive. If you borrow to acquire a farm, the interest paid, together with any farming losses, can be allowable for income tax purposes. However, it is very questionable as to whether the farm will prove to be a good long-term investment and, again, specialist advice should be sought.

The Business Expansion Scheme

The property-based expansion scheme has been very popular in recent years. Introduced by Nigel Lawson as a means of improving job mobility and creating a UK rental sector on an assured-tenancy basis, the scheme was designed to encourage individuals to invest in unquoted companies by providing income tax relief on the amount subscribed for ordinary shares. You can get tax relief at the top marginal income tax rate of 40 per cent for an investment of up to £40,000 a year in any tax year so that an investment of, say, £1,000 would only cost £600 after tax relief of £400. Shares can be sold after five years free from any income tax or capital gains tax. Moreoever, a BES company can start off trading in a qualifying way (eg letting out properties on insured tenancies), but once the qualifying period has passed, it can carry out non-qualifying activities (eg letting out non-qualifying properties) and the growth in the company's shares will be tax-free. To qualify for tax relief, the following conditions must be met:

- You must not own more than 30 per cent of the equity share capital of the company ie you must be a minority shareholder

- You must subscribe for, rather than acquire, the shares
- The shares must be held for five years otherwise the income tax relief is claimed back
- The company must carry on a trade of letting properties under an assured tenancy or must be a trading company or a member of a trading group
- You cannot receive remuneration from the company, although you can receive dividends or, if you are an unpaid director, a reimbursement of expenses incurred in connection with the company's trade.

The rule restricting you to 30 per cent of the equity share capital includes shares held by a spouse and/or children, but does not include brothers, sisters or certain other relatives. It does, however, include trading partners.

The tax relief can be carried back to an earlier year but the maximum relief which can be carried back if an investment is made before 5 October is 50 per cent of the investment up to a maximum of £5,000, with the balance of the relief allowed in the year in which BES investment is made.

BES companies can invest in properties in Greater London costing not more than £125,000 each and not more than £85,000 in the rest of the UK.

It is possible for four individuals to form their own BES company. **Chart 5.26** shows how a husband and wife can each acquire a 12.5 per cent equity stake in the company so that over a two-year period, a considerable sum of money can be invested.

Most people are not looking to make such a significant investment in a BES company and choose the available issues which are promoted heavily before the end of the tax year. Many of these involve the BES company entering into a contract with a housing association which rents the properties from the BES company for the first five years. At the end of the five-year period the BES company can exercise its option to sell those properties to the housing association for around 35 per cent above the original purchase cost.

Examine these issues carefully. In some cases, the housing association may not have entered into the option agreement before you invest your money. In addition, there is no guarantee that the association will be financially secure at the end of the five-year term when the option can be exercised (there is no guarantee that the option *will* be exercised). However, if, for example, a 35 per cent uplift is provided and you also get 40 per cent tax relief on the investment, then it is possible to get an attractive return. If you also feel that residential property values have been depressed, this may be a reasonable time to invest. The 1992 Budget proposes to end the BES in December 1993 so there is likely to be a great interest in these arrangements 'while stocks

	Chart 5.26		
		£000	*£000*
Investment year 1		40	
Investment year 2		40	
12.5% equity investment for self		80	
12.5% investment for wife		80	
		160	
Total investment by four families			640
Company borrowings			640
			1,280
Rent @, say, 8%		102	
Interest @, say, 12%		(77)	
Gross income before tax available			
for distribution			25

last'.

While a BES issue is very tax–efficient, it is clearly a risk investment so the tax benefits should not override the commercial aspects of it. At the end of five years, you would own a minority interest in a company which, if successful, may be able to sell the assets and distribute the net proceeds. Alternatively, the company may acquire your shares. If the company has not been successful, you could be locked into a private company with little prospect of a reasonable return.

Lloyds

Membership of Lloyds used to be very popular but losses have been incurred in recent years and this has made many people wary of involvement in a Lloyds syndicate. Also, the tax treatment was more favourable in the past so many passive investors became Lloyds Names.

The principle is that you use your assets to become an underwriter so that you share in the profits or losses of the syndicate. There is no significant capital injection as the assets are deposited with Lloyds but you still enjoy the income therefrom. However, there is unlimited risk and even if you take out a 'stop loss' policy and reduce the level of risk, you still need to be very wary in view of the losses which can be caused by disasters.

You (or your spouse) must demonstrate wealth of £250,000 in readily realizable assets, and pay the initial non–returnable entrance fee, normally £3,000. You will need to deposit assets with Lloyds equivalent in value to 30 per cent of the business you propose to write. By showing wealth of

£250,000 you can write up to £3m of business. Although the assets will be deposited with Lloyds trustees, their title will remain vested in you. As an alternative the deposit can be covered by a bank guarantee. An underwriter will not only participate in the fortunes of a syndicate but will also share in the interest, dividends and capital appreciation arising from the investment of premiums pending the receipt of claims.

The means test

At least 60 per cent of the wealth you wish to show should consist of stock exchange securities, cash at bank, building society deposits, the surrender value of life policies, a bank guarantee or letter of credit secured on your assets including your home, an absolute interest transferred from a trust or gold at 70 per cent of its market value. Up to 40 per cent may include the value of private houses (excluding your principal private residence) and commercial property less any secured indebtedness, farmland and buildings (again excluding your principal private residence).

The risks involved

As with any business offering a high return, there is a very real element of risk as your liability is unlimited. However, this risk can be mitigated by taking out a stop loss policy. Normally the policy will have a *de minimus* limit so that, for example, the first £25,000 of loss (which is tax deductible) may be borne by you but the policy will cover the loss from that *de minimus* limit to an upper limit of, say, £200,000. Normally, the upper limit will be sufficient to cover any losses. An underwriter's return is clearly dependent on the performance of his or her syndicate, so careful selection of a syndicate is extremely important and advice should be taken on this from an underwriting agent.

Taxation treatment

The underwriting profit, including the investment income, is assessed in the fiscal year in which the underwriting year of account ends, eg the underwriting year ending on 31 December 1992 will be assessed in the fiscal year 1992/3. The underwriting profit and investment income will be taxed as the top slice of your income and any underwriting losses will give rise to income tax relief, again at the top marginal rate.

An underwriting account runs for a calendar year but is not closed for a further two years so that claims can be accepted against the risks written on that account. As a result of this three-year accounting procedure, there is a delay in determining the results and paying tax on any profits and investment income.

Tax benefits

The following benefits will be of interest to a higher-rate taxpayer:

- A large proportion of the premium income tends to be invested in gilts and the capital gains on the realization of these investments are entirely tax-free

- Up to 50 per cent of the underwriting profits (including investment income) can be set aside in a special reserve fund, subject to an overriding maximum of £7,000. This fund is invested on your behalf and may be used to meet future losses. The profits transferred into this fund escape tax at the higher rates when transferred, but will be taxable in the year in which they are withdrawn from the fund. It is therefore possible to transfer profits to the fund during a 'high income' year and be liable to tax thereon upon resignation from Lloyds during a subsequent 'low income' year, or any year in which tax rates are reduced. If tax rates increase, the converse is true

- On death, the 'underwriting interest' of your estate is deemed to be a business asset so 50 per cent of its value is exempt from inheritance tax. The Budget proposals could increase the relief to 100 per cent. The 'underwriting interest' consists of the Lloyds deposit, special reserve fund and profits, less losses on open underwriting accounts at the time of death. In addition, some of the profits transferred into the special reserve fund escape income tax altogether

- The underwriter may receive annual lump-sum payments from the underwriting accounts in respect of the profits of a particular financial year before paying income tax on such payments

- When computing the underwriting profit or loss, personal accountancy fees based on a fixed scale, annual subscriptions, annual expenses (not the setting-up costs) of letters of credit and bank guarantees, stop loss policy premiums and the cost of an estate protection plan are all allowable for income tax purposes.

Election of new Names

As a new Name, you will need to be sponsored by an existing Name who has been personally known to you for at least a year. The sponsor's letter and your application form must be submitted to Lloyds before 30 June if you wish to become an underwriter on the following 1 January.

The Lloyds market is somewhat cyclical and it is possible that underwriters will enjoy a better return in future years. Due to the unlimited liability aspect of this business, it should not be undertaken lightly and professional advice must be sought both from an underwriting agent and from an accountant or solicitor.

REVISED CAPITAL POSITION

Although it has covered a number of investment possibilities, this chapter is by no means exhaustive. To return to our case study, you may recall that there were deposits of £120,000 which could be reinvested as the couple had surplus net spendable income of £5,000. **Chart 5.27** illustrates some investment proposals.

Chart 5.27 shows that in our case study, the mortgage is to be reduced by £20,000 to get basic-rate relief from the remaining loan. There is no risk in this but it reduces the available liquidity.

The single premium with-profit bond should provide a better return than the deposit account and the risk is low/medium. It is semi-liquid as it can be encashed at any time but, to obtain the best returns, it should be held for five to ten years. It is tax-efficient as the investment is to be made by the wife and any profit should be covered by her basic rate band so that no higher-rate tax is payable on any profit.

The unit trust and PEPs are risk investments as they are volatile and their price movements could change dramatically, but they are invested for long-term capital growth. They are liquid in that they can be encashed at any time.

Chart 5.27

Investment proposal	£000	Risk	Liquid	Tax-efficient
Reduction of mortgage	20	Low	No	Yes
Single premium with-profit bond	30	Low/Medium	Semi	Yes
Unit trusts	20	High	Yes	Yes
PEPs	4	High	Yes	Yes
TESSA	6	Low	Semi	Yes
National Savings	10	Low	Semi	Yes
BES	10	High	No	Yes
Deposits	20	Low	Yes	No
	120			

The unit trusts are reasonably tax-efficient as they are geared for capital growth and any gain should be covered by the annual capital gains tax exemption. Unit trusts can be structured so as to produce relatively low taxable income. The PEPs should provide a tax-free dividend and any gains will be exempt from capital gains tax. The maximum amount is not invested in PEPs so that the equity exposure is not too great in accordance with the client's risk profile.

The TESSA is a deposit-based investment which is low-risk and semi-liquid (in that it can be encashed within the first five years although encashment during that period would mean losing the tax benefits). If held for the full five years it would be tax-efficient as all interest would have been paid after deducting the basic-rate tax which would be repaid at the end of the five-year period.

Similarly, National Savings Certificates are tax-efficient and semi-liquid as they can be encashed but should be held for the five-year term. They are low-risk investments.

The BES investment is high-risk and tax-efficient. It is the least liquid investment as there is no control over the way in which the capital will be repaid. This leaves £20,000 on deposit for emergencies. The revised capital and income positions are set out in **Charts 5.28** and **5.29**.

Chart 5.29 takes no account of the income from the TESSA, the tax relief and income from the BES issue or any capital appreciation. You will see that the income would have fallen by a few thousand pounds as the portfolio is now structured for capital growth. However, there should still be surplus net

Chart 5.28 *Revised capital position*

	£000	£000
Home	250	
Mortgage	(30)	
		220
Single premium with-profit bond	30	
Unit trusts	20	
PEPs	4	
TESSAs	6	
National Savings	10	
BES investment	10	
Deposits retained	20	
		100
Remaining shares		40
		360

spendable income of approximately £3,000. Investments have been switched into the wife's name to take advantage of the benefits from independent taxation.

Chart 5.29 *Revised net spendable income*

			Taxable income £000	Spendable income £000
Self				
Remuneration			40	40
Benefits in kind			4	
			44	
Personal allowance			(5)	
Taxable income			39	
Tax	£23,700 @ 25%	£5,925		
	£15,300 @ 40%	6,120		
	£39,000	12,045		
				(12)
				28
Mortgage interest £30,000 ×, say, 11% =		3,300		
Basic rate relief @ 25%		825		
		2,475		
				(2)
Wife				
Remuneration			15	
Deposit interest £20,000 @ 10%			2	
Income from units trusts £20,000 @, say, 4%			1	
			18	18
Personal allowance			(3)	
Taxable income			15	
Tax @ 25%				(4)
				40
Income from bond £30,000 @, say, 5%				1
				41
Annual expenditure				(38)
Surplus net spendable income				3

Be sure to get specific advice on the way your investments should be restructured.

6

PENSIONS

Pensions are one of the most tax-efficient long-term investments available – and probably the most misunderstood. Complex issues surround pension benefits and there have been significant changes to pensions legislation over the past few years (see Appendix 4). Following the Maxwell scandal more changes are due to protect members' funds. You may wish to ask yourself the following questions:

1. Why do I need a pension scheme?

2. Do I understand what my pension benefits will be?

3. Should I invest in a pension or another investment?

4. Is my pension fund performing well?

5. How secure is my pension benefit?

6. Am I happy with the advice I have been given?

It is important that you appreciate the basics of pensions and take an active interest in your own pension arrangement. In some cases, the fund created to buy your pension at retirement will be the biggest asset of your estate, even larger than your home.

TAX BENEFITS

Pension schemes have enjoyed special tax benefits since the 1920s. These special privileges have been under attack and in 1989 the Government surprised the nation by introducing restrictions on the level of income on which these benefits could be obtained.

Since March 1989, higher-paid employees who join a new occupational pension scheme can only obtain pension benefits in respect of earnings up to £71,400. This is the rate applicable for 1991/2 (£75,000 for 1992/3) and it is to be index-linked thereafter. In addition, employees and the self-employed who only have personal pension arrangements rather than the old-style retirement annuity policies (which were in existence up to 1 July 1988) are similarly restricted on pension benefits in respect of their earnings. Some schemes have higher-paid employees who can obtain full benefits while others are 'capped' and must find some other way of providing for their income in retirement if the capped pension will be insufficient.

There are a number of alternative methods of providing for benefits in excess of the 'cap'. These include Funded Unapproved Retirement Benefit Schemes (FURBS) where the payment into the FURBS creates a tax charge but no national insurance is paid. The fund grows tax-free and can be extracted in cash. Specialist advice is required on different methods of funding 'capped' benefits.

It was understood that the Labour Party wanted to remove the higher rate of income tax relief from pension contributions and allow only basic-rate relief. Any such further restriction would be unfortunate: there should be greater encouragement for people to invest in a pension scheme and build a sufficient fund with which to enjoy their later years in moderate comfort.

Any payment into a pension scheme attracts full tax relief. This applies not only to your payment but, if you are part of an occupational scheme, to payments made by your employer. The pension fund does not suffer tax so any income and gains accrue tax-free. The exception to this rule is if a pension fund is trading rather than investing, though this is unusual in practice. Part of the pension fund can be taken as tax-free cash at retirement.

These benefits apply to occupational schemes so long as the pension is not over-funded and the benefits are within accepted Superannuation Funds Office guidelines. Directors who set up their own pension schemes before 1987 can take all their pension benefits as tax-free cash depending on the value of the fund and final remuneration. This is obviously very attractive as it gives the director greater flexibility over the way in which the money is reinvested.

For most of us, however, the pension fund will provide some tax-free cash and the balance of the money must be used to buy an annuity (a taxable pension). The part of the fund which can be used to provide tax-free cash will depend upon the type of scheme. In the case of personal pensions, 25 per cent of the fund can be used to provide for cash and the balance will provide the pension. In most cases, it is advisable to take the tax-free cash at retirement, although professional advice should be sought at that time.

The combination of tax relief on contributions to the pension scheme and tax-free growth is very powerful. Basic-rate tax is 25 per cent and the higher rate 40 per cent. For the purpose of illustration, we assumed that the top tax rate would have increased to 60 per cent had the Labour Party won the election. **Chart 6.1** shows the power of tax relief and compares the benefits to a basic-rate and higher-rate taxpayer under the continuing Conservative administration and based on a Labour Government.

The basic-rate taxpayer will only get 7.5 per cent net of tax in the building society account and the 40 per cent taxpayer six per cent net. As the pension fund does not pay tax, its return will remain at ten per cent throughout the 20-year period. In addition, the basic-rate taxpayer is able to invest £13,333 to produce a net return of £10,000, the 40 per cent taxpayer can invest £16,667. A 60 per cent taxpayer can invest £25,000 as the tax relief will be £15,000, producing a net cost of £10,000. A Labour Government would probably restrict tax relief on pension contributions to the basic rate so that the fund is likely to be approximately £89,697 (as only £13,333 could be invested to produce £10,000 net) while the likely deposit balance could be £21,911.

You will see that the basic-rate taxpayer could accumulate a pension fund of more than twice the value of the building society deposit whereas the 40 per cent taxpayer will produce a fund 3.5 times as large due to the twin effect of tax relief on the contribution and the tax-free roll-up. These dramatic figures show the tax-efficiency of pension schemes and why to much time has been devoted to them by the major political parties.

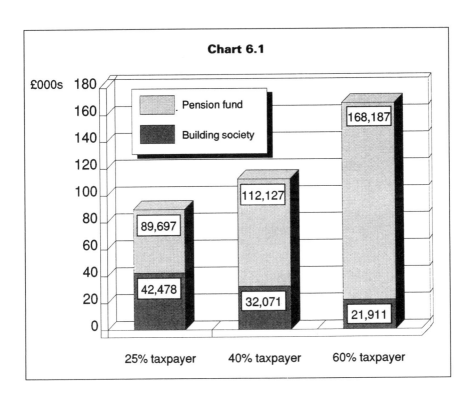

STATE BENEFIT

A very unfortunate misapprehension surrounds state pension benefits: they were never intended to *replace* your income at retirement but merely to *supplement* that income.

The state pension is provided in two forms. The basic pension is payable to everyone. A man can take the state pension at 65 and a woman at 60.

For the majority of taxpayers, the basic retirement pension will be totally inadequate to cover their annual expenditure, as will be the state earnings-related pension scheme (SERPS). SERPS was introduced in 1978 as a means of 'topping up' the basic state pension and is funded by the additional national insurance contributions which contracted-in employees pay on earnings between the lower and upper limits, currently £2,808 and £21,060. Under the existing scheme, the pension accrues at a rate of 1.25 per cent a year up to a maximum level of 25 per cent. You will see from **Chart 6.2** that in 1991/2 this could provide a SERPS pension of £4,394. If the man is entitled to the basic and SERPS pensions but the wife to only the basic pension, they will receive a maximum of £8,723 before tax. Indeed, if the man's earnings did not reach the upper limit, the pension will be less than this.

While the SERPS pension will be index-linked, it will probably be cut in future years by a Conservative administration. The Labour Party, on the other hand, wanted to improve basic state pensions.

The number of people expecting to receive SERPS is growing rapidly, while the number of contributors is falling. For this reason SERPS will be modified by the following changes:

Chart 6.2 *Maximum state pensions 1991/2*

		£	£
Basic state pension:	male/widow	2,704	
	wife	1,625	
			4,329
SERPS			
Upper NIC level £390 × 52		20,280	
Lower NIC level £52 × 52		2,704	
		17,576	
25% thereof			4,394
			£8,723

- From 2009 people retiring will receive a SERPS pension based on 20 per cent of lifetime earnings rather than 25 per cent of the best 20 of these years

- For people retiring before 2009, the pension will be on a combination of the old basis up to 6 April 1988 and the new basis thereafter

- Provision will be made to protect the SERPS pension of people unable to work because they are looking after a child or a disabled person or are themselves disabled

- Widows and widowers over 65 will inherit half their spouse's SERPS pension rather than all of it. This change will not affect people widowed before the year 2000.

If the changes proposed by the Conservative Government continue, then a SERPS pension for someone aged 40 will be reduced from around 25 per cent of relevant earnings to approximately 21 per cent. The long-term effect will be a 50 per cent saving for the State in providing the SERPS pension.

CONTRACTING OUT

The alternative to claiming the SERPS pension is to contract out of the state scheme so that only the basic retirement pension is received. This reduces national insurance contributions paid by employee and employer and the difference in contributions can be transferred into a personal pension. In addition to reduced national insurance contributions, there is an incentive payment (otherwise known as 'the bribe') of two per cent of band earnings and this will be paid into the personal pension scheme until 1993.

You should consider the likely fund produced by the personal pension as against the likely SERPS pension. If the projected personal pension is greater, it will be advantageous to contract out of SERPS in order to fund the personal pension. The cut-off point is approximately 20 years before the state benefits are taken so people in their 30s would normally be advised to contract out. If you are in your 50s, then it is advisable to remain in the state scheme. A man in his early 40s or a woman in her late 30s would normally be in a marginal situation. **Chart 6.3** compares the two options.

It is possible for one person to contract both in and out of SERPS. For example, a man could contract out during his 30s and then contract back in

---

Chart 6.3 *Extract from payroll*

Sex	Age	Salary	State pension	Projected alternative pension	Should the member contract out?
		£	£	£	
Male	51	20,752	273	264	No
Male	31	34,344	374	1,469	Yes
Female	55	10,789	122	50	No
Male	34	38,169	353	1,150	Yes

Growth rate assumptions: Salary 6.5%, Fund 8.5%, Inflation 5%
Annuity: Male 9.5%, Female 7.5%

---

when he is, say, 48.

Some employers may wish to contract in their *scheme* but then contract out the relevant *employees* on an individual basis. This means that the employer does not have to provide the guaranteed minimum pension ('GMP'). Other companies may be providing very good pension benefits and will be happy to contract out of the scheme to take advantage of reduced national insurance contributions, providing the GMP as part of the benefits of their plan.

While the SERPS pension will be index-linked, you will be depending upon the government to increase the basic pension. For the vast majority of people, it will be necessary to have an alternative means of securing income for when you retire. I have seen many tragic cases where people have relied

---

Chart 6.4

A company has ten employees earning £9,620 ('lower paid') and 20 employees earning over £21,000 ('higher paid').

Reduced annual NI payable	Saving per employee £	Total saving £
Employee's NI		
Lower paid	138.32	1,383.20
Higher paid	351.52	7,030.40
Employer's NI		
Lower paid	210.08	2,100.80
Higher paid	666.64	13,332.80
		£15,433.60

---

upon the state pension and possibly a very small private arrangement, and have found that they could not afford to retire. Financial pressure during your twilight years is most definitely to be avoided.

SERPS is complex so professional advice should always be sought.

FUNDING RATES

It is critical that you have an idea of the appropriate level at which you should be funding your pension scheme. Unfortunately, there are a number of unknowns in this calculation, including your future salary, the fund growth of the scheme and the future rate of inflation.

The illustration in **Charts 6.5a** and **6.5b** assume that a 40-year-old man earns £35,000 a year and does not start his money-purchase pension scheme until that time. Thereafter five per cent of earnings is paid into the non-contributory pension scheme until age 60 and he makes no individual contributions. It has been assumed that the funds grows at nine per cent a year, that his salary increases at seven per cent a year and that the average RPI increases six per cent. While these assumptions may seem very low we may be entering an era of low inflation and equity growth. In any case, it is the interaction *between* these assumptions that is important. For example, we have assumed a real growth of two per cent in the fund over and above his salary increase. It may be that the fund growth and salary increases are higher but it is this differential which is important to the computations.

You will see from **Chart 6.5a** that the projected fund is £165,000 at age 60. If we assume that at that time, the annuity rate is seven per cent for a pension which increases at five per cent each year and provides a widow's benefit, then the projected pension will be £12,000 a year.

Too often, pension illustrations are shown only in the manner of **Chart 6.5a** by pension salespeople. If this is the only advice received, you may be heading for a rude shock. While the projected pension fund and pension may seem attractive, it will only produce a pension of around £3,000 in today's terms. Indeed the final salary is projected to be £126,000 so that the pension will be nine per cent of final salary.

It is much better to see benefits as a percentage of final salary so that you can relate them to your earnings today. You will see from **Chart 6.5b** that the current salary is £35,000 and that a funding rate of 35 per cent will be needed in the company scheme to produce a total projected pension of 64 per cent of final salary. In this illustration, the state benefits have not been included and would increase the total benefits further. However, as mentioned above, the SERPS pension is likely to be cut so it is unwise to rely too heavily upon these benefits throughout your working life.

The person in this illustration should be aiming for around 70 per cent of

Chart 6.5a

	5% Funding rate			35% Funding rate		
	%	£000	£000	%	£000	£000
Current salary			35			35
Projected pension fund		165			1,158	
Projected pension			12			81

Chart 6.5b

Final salary	126		126
Pension as % of final salary	(9)		(64)
Projected income in today's terms	3		22

This illustration assumes that the required funding rate excludes the state and SERPS pension.

final salary, including state benefits, so that if his salary is just about providing enough money for the family to live at a reasonable standard, then it should be possible to cut expenditure by around 30 per cent in retirement – there may be no need to provide for children and people tend to spend less in their later years.

The conclusion in this case is that the five per cent funding rate is insufficient. If this man is in a company pension scheme and his employer is paying five per cent then he should pay the maximum additional voluntary contributions if he wishes to increase the funding rate to 20 per cent. He will need to convince his employer to increase the funding rate further (normally an unlikely scenario) if he wishes to receive benefits which are more appropriate. Indeed, the position becomes more dramatic if he delays making the pension increases. For example, if he pays five per cent together with a company's contribution of the same rate, then ten per cent will be paid into the scheme initially. At age 50 he would need to arrange for the company scheme to be funded significantly in excess of 35 per cent. This may not be possible as the maximum personal contribution is 15 per cent and the company is unlikely to be willing to increase the funding rate as that company would normally apply a standard funding rate throughout.

This dramatic picture arises from the delay in topping up pension benefits. If money is paid in at an earlier time, the fund will grow for a longer period and produce a better return.

A similar position arises if early retirement is taken. Many people now wish to take their pension benefits at 50 or 55 rather than 60. Indeed, personal pension benefits can be taken at 50. In **Chart 6.6** it is assumed that the employee is earning £35,000 at age 40 and only starts to make pension contributions from that time; if the pension is funded at 12 per cent throughout until his 50th birthday, then he will retire on a final salary of approximately £64,000. While the projected fund will be approximately £91,000, the projected pension (using an annuity rate of 5.5 per cent) would be a little over £6,000. As this would represent only nine per cent of his income at age 50 it would normally be inadequate.

Again, the reason for the shortfall is that the pension contributions have been paid at too low a rate for too short a period. In addition, an annuity rate at age 50 is lower than that at age 60 as the life expectancy is ten years longer. Therefore, while it may be attractive to take benefits early, you must consider whether you can afford to do so. If you wish to plan towards early retirement, you should take steps to increase the pension benefits as early as possible so that you will be in a financial position to do so. If you are in a company scheme, then additional voluntary contributions ('AVCs') may be an answer. However, these are restricted to 15 per cent of current remuneration and you must deduct from this maximum limit any contributory pension payment you make. For example, if the pension scheme requires you to pay five per cent then you will only be able to pay ten per cent as an AVC. If your AVC arrangement has been taken out after 7 April 1987, then the pension benefits will only be able to fund additional pension entitlement rather than tax-free cash.

The above illustrations have been based upon a person in a *money purchase*

Chart 6.6

Facts as in **Chart 6.5** except the man funds the pension at 12% throughout and takes the benefits at age 50.

	%	£000	£000
Current salary			35
Fund at 50		91	
Projected pension			6
Final salary			64
Pension as % of final salary	(9%)		

---

arrangement. In a *final salary scheme*, the situation will be different. The company will have promised you a percentage of your final salary when you retire. If you stay with the company for that period then you are guaranteed a certain level of pension benefit.

The illustration in **Chart 6.7** shows that John has been promised a pension of one 60th of his final salary for each year he is in the scheme and if he stays with the company until retirement at 60, he will have completed 20 years service. Therefore his projected company pension benefits will be approximately 33 per cent of his final salary. If he pays the maximum AVC of 15 per cent (assuming that it is a non-contributory scheme), then the AVC fund will be just under £500,000. This AVC fund will provide a pension of approximately £34,000 a year based on a seven per cent annuity rate. Together with the underlying company pension, he should get a pension benefit of 60 per cent of his final salary. This will, however, require maximum funding throughout the next 20 years. In addition, part of the benefits may not be inflation-linked, depending on the terms of the company's scheme and, as shown earlier, inflation is a very important subject. For example, it could cost an additional 50 per cent to buy a pension which is index-linked, rather than a flat pension which will erode in real terms. Therefore it is important that you provide projections based upon an increasing pension in respect of your own contributions, and if you are in a company scheme you should find out what inflation-linking is promised by that scheme.

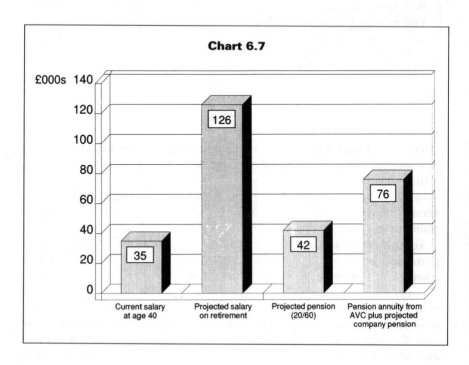

THE DIFFERENT PENSION ARRANGEMENTS

If you are self-employed or are not in an occupational pension scheme, you can pay into a personal pension scheme. These replaced retirement annuity contracts on 1 July 1988. You are limited by the amount which can be paid into the scheme but not on the benefits you receive. If you have old-style retirement annuity policies, then it may be worth keeping them going if your earnings are near the pensions cap. **Chart 6.8** shows the benefit of retirement annuity plans (RAPs).

Chart 6.8

John is 52. He is self-employed and wishes to make the maximum premium payment in 1991/2.

	Earnings	
	£000	*£000*
	80	120
PPS £71,400 × 30%	21	21
RAP earnings at 20%	16	24
PPS excess/(deficit)	5	(3)

You will see from **Chart 6.8** that if earnings are £80,000, then a higher percentage of income can be paid into a personal pension scheme (see Appendix 5) so that more money can be paid into personal pensions than retirement annuities. However, if the earnings are £120,000, then more money can be paid into the retirement annuity scheme because even though the contribution rate is 20 per cent rather than 30 per cent, the earnings are not 'capped'. It is not possible to 'mix and match' personal pension and retirement annuity payments in the year so it may be necessary for you to stop paying into the personal pension and only increase your retirement annuity plans. It may be worth searching through your records as the old plans may be of significant value to you in the future.

There are two main types of occupational pension arrangement, the money purchase scheme and the final salary arrangement. Under a money purchase scheme, the principal involved is 'the more you put in, the more you get out'. As I have already said, the funding level is crucial to the projected benefits you will receive and the investment performance is very important. For example, if your salary is £35,000 a year and the company pays ten per cent into the scheme and you pay five per cent, then a total of £5,250 will be invested and the money will be invested for capital growth.

On retirement, your account will be identified and the fund will be used to buy a pension for you. Each member can identify his or her own 'account' and less input is needed from an actuary to determine benefits. Therefore the pension receivable by the member will depend upon the amount paid into the scheme and the returns (after expenses) which have been achieved from the investment of the money. While the money purchase scheme is easy for the employer and employee to understand, it suffers from a lack of guarantee as the pension benefits will decrease if the investment performance of the fund is poor. Also the benefit is very much dependent upon the annuity rates upon retirement. The company is not liable to supplement the pension if it is less than was originally projected so the risk is borne by the employee rather than the employer.

The alternative is the final salary scheme. In this arrangement, you are promised a certain percentage of your final salary at retirement. For example, if it is a 60th scheme you will be provided with one 60th of your final salary for each year's service. Therefore, to obtain the maximum Inland Revenue entitlement of two thirds of final salary, you will need to have worked for 40 years with the company (unless you are in an enhanced executive arrangement). Indeed the Inland Revenue limits also allow an index-linked pension to be taken so there may well be scope to top up a final salary scheme even if you may serve 40 years with the company, if the scheme does not provide for the maximum index-linking.

By setting up a final salary scheme, the employer is committed to a contribution level which will produce a fund to meet the promises made. This complex funding arrangement will require a guiding hand from an actuary. It is important for the employer to estimate the costs of providing the promised benefits. Unlike the money purchase scheme, the employee does not have a readily identifiable 'account'. Also, the costs to the employer are unknown and the funding rate will be determined upon a number of factors including the following:

- Company's payroll

- Age and sex of members

- Increase of salaries in future years

- Level of growth and inflation in future years

- Level of benefits under the scheme

- Number of employees leaving the scheme before retirement

- Eligibility conditions of the scheme

- Expenses of the scheme

In recent years, the funding rates of final salary schemes have been adversely affected by a number of changes. In particular, the proposal for future pensions to be increased by the RPI or five per cent, whichever is the lower, could significantly increase the funding rate and some schemes may find that their pension fund costs increase by up to 50 per cent. In the current recession many employers are reconsidering whether they wish to have an 'open cheque book' scheme which is likely to cost more each year. Many have moved across to a money purchase scheme where costs are controlled.

Under the final salary scheme, there are no investment risks for the employee as he or she has been promised a certain level of pension. All the investment risks are taken by the company.

If you are in a final salary scheme, your pension benefits can be provided on both final salary and money purchase bases. The underlying promises of the scheme will be on a final-salary basis. However if you take out an AVC to top-up these benefits, then these will be on a money-purchase basis. As you will see, investment forms an integral part of the pension benefit. All employees and the self-employed need to consider carefully the investment performance of their fund while a company needs to consider carefully the investment performance of final salary schemes as this will affect the funding rate.

All that has been explained here is the main structure of pension schemes. There are a number of other variations, for example, controlling directors may wish to set up a small self-administered pension scheme so that they can control the investment of the money rather than pass all the cash across to an insurance house to be managed. In addition, there are often special executive 'top-hat' schemes to augment the pension benefits paid to other members of the company.

INVESTMENT PERFORMANCE

The combination of tax relief and good investment management should make the pension fund a very attractive benefit. Investment performance is a key factor because of the long-term nature of the pension fund, but it is often overlooked or monitored in a haphazard way. Too often, the plan is sold to people who take little interest in the investment performance until they near retirement. This is far too late to be examining the fund's performance.

As your pension is a long-term investment, you should consider carefully the structure from the outset and then monitor it from time to time. If you are in an occupational scheme, you may not have a choice and the trustees may be taking the investment decision for you. However, it may be possible to arrange for your 'account' to be managed separately from the rest of the fund. In addition, you are able to take out a free-standing AVC so that it can be invested with the pension provider of your choice, rather than with your employer's pension company. Obviously the charges will need to be considered but if you would prefer to manage your AVC personally, then you can now do so.

We have considered investment separately in this book and there is no reason why the same investment criteria cannot be applied to your pension scheme. Traditionally, pension funds tend to be invested in the following areas:

- Equities, both UK and international
- Cash deposits/deposit administration
- With-profit contracts
- Gilts
- Property

Often the funds will be invested in an insurance company's managed fund so that it obtains exposure to most of the above investment areas. If your pension benefits will not be received for, say, 20 years, then you can take a long-term approach to the fund. For example, you may wish to invest 70 per cent in a managed fund or a unit-linked contract for long-term capital growth, and the balance in gilts and with-profit funds. Alternatively, if you are within ten years of retirement, I suggest that you gradually secure the pension benefits.

Timing is of the essence but as you move towards retirement, you should look towards moving the money across into with-profit, cash or gilt funds rather than leaving all the funds in equities. For example, a man who retired in November 1987 would have been very disappointed to learn that his unit-linked fund has dropped by around 20 per cent due to the October crash. Conversely, it would be unwise to transfer money away from property or a unit-linked contract if it is felt that the relevant funds have been severely depressed and should increase over the next couple of years.

However, if you are 50, you should gradually look towards moving the money into safer funds so that you can secure the benefits which have accrued to date. Otherwise you will be gambling upon short-term investment performance the nearer you get to retirement.

The investment performance of different funds and different companies can be quite dramatic, as shown by **Chart 6.9.**

You should choose a reasonable-sized fund which has performed consistently well in the past and which has been in existence for a long time. It is easier for new funds to go to the top of the ratings list as they are able to take more risks early on. As the pension fund is a long-term investment, then a good long-term performance should be chosen, although it must be accepted that the past is no guide to the future.

Before choosing the relevant insurance company, it is worth considering the investment sector for your fund.

Britain's entry into the European Monetary System could lead to lower interest rates and currency stability within the European Community. This may make index-linked gilts more attractive but it is hoped that as Britain moves out of recession, the performance of British companies will improve and give rise to a greater equity performance in the future. **Chart 6.10** shows the performance of funds in the past, but you will need to consider carefully the future strategy.

Many individuals invest in either the managed or with-profit sector, leaving the investment choice to the fund managers. The investment could be spread among various sectors, as shown in **Chart 6.11**, for example.

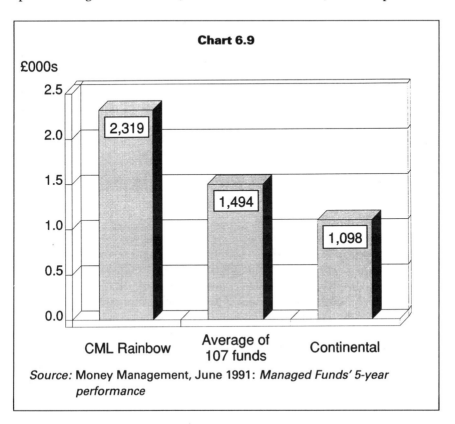

Chart 6.9

£000s

Source: Money Management, June 1991: *Managed Funds' 5-year performance*

The investment mix will vary from company to company and you may feel that you would prefer the relative security of a with-profit fund (covered separately in this book). You will see from **Chart 6.12** that if the investment performance of the fund is 15 per cent rather than nine per cent as shown in **Chart 6.5b** the projected fund would almost double and the pension will be 17 per cent rather than nine per cent of final salary. Fund performance should not be taken lightly.

LIFE COVER

The need for life cover, permanent health insurance and other forms of cover is explained separately in this book. However, cheap life assurance can be obtained through the pension scheme. It is possible for a pension fund to insure a member for up to four times remuneration so that if you are earning £35,000, you could get £140,000 of life cover through the pension scheme. In addition, it is possible to write the benefits under a discretionary trust so that they fall outside your estate for inheritance tax purposes. This could save £60,000 of inheritance tax at current rates based on the 1992 Budget proposals.

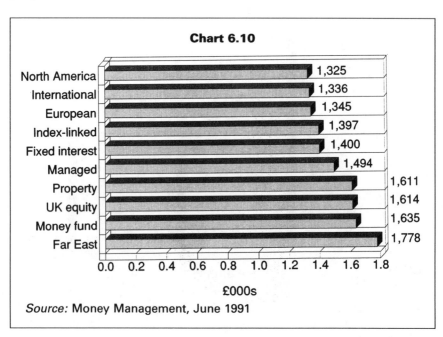

Chart 6.10

	£000s
North America	1,325
International	1,336
European	1,345
Index-linked	1,397
Fixed interest	1,400
Managed	1,494
Property	1,611
UK equity	1,614
Money fund	1,635
Far East	1,778

Source: Money Management, June 1991

Death-in-service cover is normally taken out as term assurance until age 60 so it will disappear when you take your pension benefits or leave the scheme. Loss of life cover is often overlooked when leaving a pension scheme.

LEAVING THE SCHEME

You should immediately enquire about your life cover when you leave a company pension scheme. Your new scheme may not have the same life cover or there may be a qualifying period. If you are setting up on your own, you will need to take out temporary assurance so that your family is covered.

The deferred pension is often overlooked when people leave a scheme. Funding calculations in this chapter have been made assuming that there are no deferred benefits. Indeed, if there are deferred benefits, then they should be taken into account when estimating your future pension entitlement.

You have a number of options regarding the pension benefit from your previous employer, including the following:

- Leave the pension as a deferred benefit

- Take a transfer value into a section 32 policy

- Take a transfer value into a personal pension

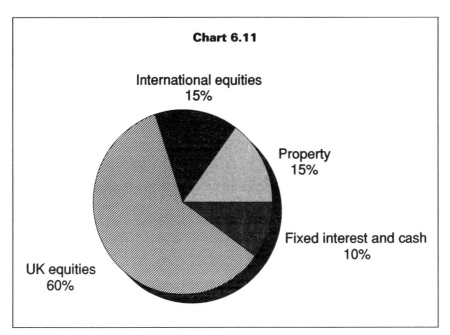

Chart 6.11

International equities 15%

Property 15%

Fixed interest and cash 10%

UK equities 60%

Chart 6.12

Facts as in **Chart 6.5**

	Pension fund	Pension as % of final salary
	£000	%
Fund growth at 9%	165	(9)
Fund growth at 15%	314	(17)

You could leave the funds where they are and get your pension benefits at the normal retirement age of your past employer's scheme. If this is a final salary arrangement, then this will be a percentage of your income; under a money purchase scheme it will be the value of the fund at retirement.

It is often beneficial to take the transfer value making sure that you take advantage of any recent improvement in the proposed transfer value. In addition, if you are likely to benefit from a surplus in a final salary scheme or from the projected five per cent escalation of pension payments, then this should also be taken into account.

You should seek professional advice at this time as you may well need an actuarial computation as a background for your choices. Clearly the calculation of the transfer value to which you would be entitled on leaving a company that operates a final salary scheme is very complicated. The first step is to calculate the member's deferred pension. If the scheme is contracted out, then the GMP must be protected. If you have been in a final salary scheme the benefit will be based upon your salary when leaving the scheme. Some schemes allow for some form of index-linking of the salary. The illustration in **Chart 6.13** is taken from my book *The Daily Telegraph Pension Guide* and shows the effective penalty of leaving the final salary scheme.

The computation of transfer values has changed since the illustration in **Chart 6.13** was published but there still remains the effective loss from moving between final salary schemes. Although many leavers have been disappointed with the deferred benefits and transfer value, it is often advisable to take the transfer value and invest it separately. Once the deferred benefits have been identified and the transfer value established, you need to consider the growth rate required to ensure that you meet those deferred benefits. You will see from **Chart 6.14** that in this case the fund would need to grow by 12.2 per cent a year to achieve the same benefits.

The case in **Chart 6.14** is a marginal one as over 12 per cent is required. However, often the computation requires a growth rate of less than nine per cent so that the transfer should be made.

Chart 6.13

A 45-year-old man leaves his job on a salary of £12,000. He has 20 years of service and will retire at 65 on £31,840. His salary grows at 5 per cent a year in line with inflation during the period. His new employer operates a similar scheme which provides for a pension based on one 60th for each year served.

	No escalation from first employer £ pa	Full escalation from employer £ pa
Pension from existing scheme £12,000 × 20/60	4,000	10,614
Pension from new employer £31,840 × 20/60	10,614	10,614
Pension at retirement	14,614	21,228
Pension if he remains with one employer throughout £31,840 × 40/60	21,228	21,228
Loss of pension by moving	6,614	Nil

Too often, pension benefits are left where they are. By doing this, you effectively lose out by not taking advantage of the likely future greater capital growth produced by the transfer value. Clearly, if the calculation shows that you require a growth rate of, say, 16 per cent, you would be advised to leave the funds as they are because it may be difficult to achieve 16 per cent a year throughout the remaining period.

Chart 6.14

A 45-year-old man is offered a transfer value of	£10,000
Projected pension at retirement (age 65) from existing scheme	10,613
Fund at 65 required to produce above pension	89,373
Growth rate required from transfer value to produce the same fund	12.21%

Note: assumes pension annuity rate 11.88%, inflation 5%, GMP roll up 7.5%, GMP annuity rate post-1988 8.5%, pre-1988 9.5%

The section 32 buy-out policy enables the fund to be transferred into a separate policy, the benefits of which can be taken at the same time as those which would be applicable to the normal scheme. However, if you transfer the benefits into a personal pension, they can be taken at age 50 but you will need to consider whether there would be any transfer benefits restrictions on them.

7

ANNUITIES

In retirement, you will need to live off the income produced from your capital and any pension benefits.

The illustration in **Chart 7.1** assumes that a man retires at 65 when his wife is 60 years of age. They have index-linked state pensions and a small income which covers some of their expenditure, leaving £13,000 of expenditure to be covered by the income from their cash deposits. The husband lives for a further ten years, when the expenditure falls by a third, and his wife lives until age 80. We have assumed that deposit interest rates are ten per cent gross throughout (7.5 per cent net of basic rate tax) and that inflation runs at five per cent throughout the period. (For a summary of general annuity rates, see Appendix 6.) Appendices 7.1 and 7.2 calculate the annual income and expenditure surplus and deficit which is shown in **Charts 7.1a** and **7.1b**.

You can see that the deposit balance of £175,000 is reduced dramatically over the couple's lifetime. While there is a very small surplus of income in the first year, inflation erodes the capital so that by the time the wife dies, there is only £36,000 left in the deposit account and the excess expenditure is almost £18,000 a year. If the wife were to live for a further five years, her capital would probably be fully eroded. She would then be in a very difficult financial position and would need to dramatically reduce her expenditure over her last few years.

As an alternative, **Chart 7.1b** assumes that £75,000 remains on deposit but that the couple take out a joint life annuity with £100,000 of capital. We have assumed that the annuity provides net income of seven per cent. Part of the annuity will be treated as capital and is therefore not taxable; the balance is subject to basic-rate income tax. The couple have taken out an annuity which increases at five per cent a year and provides the same income during their joint lives. In other words, the income does not fall when the husband dies. This illustration assumes that there is no income guarantee so if the husband and wife were to die a year after taking out the annuity, the insurance company would greatly benefit.

It is assumed that the couple are more interested in providing for their own security than that of their children, so they will want the annuity which best protects them. You can see that by the time the widow is 80, there is still a small surplus of income each year and there is also over £57,000 left in the deposit account. I would recommend an annuity as a last resort as there is no return of capital, but it can help to provide a plan which reduces the chance of money running out during a lifetime.

DIFFERENT TYPES OF ANNUITY

Compulsory purchase annuity rates are slightly different from pension annuities. The principle is the same in that the annuity provides income for

---

Chart 7.1a

Man 65, wife 60 with index-linked state pensions which cover certain expenditure, cash deposits of £175,000 (held by wife), expenditure £13,000. Husband dies at 75, expenditure then falls by a third

Deposit

Year	B/f	Surplus/ (deficit)	C/f
1	175,000	125	175,125
2	175,125	(516)	174,609
3	174,609	(1,237)	173,372
4	173,372	(2,046)	171,326
5	171,326	(2,952)	168,374
6	168,374	(3,963)	164,411
7	164,411	(5,091)	159,320
8	159,320	(6,343)	152,977
9	152,977	(7,734)	145,243
10	145,243	(9,274)	135,969
11	135,969	(3,919)	132,050
12	132,050	(4,919)	127,131
13	127,131	(6,029)	121,102
14	121,102	(7,260)	113,842
15	113,842	(8,621)	105,221
16	105,221	(10,126)	95,095
17	95,095	(11,786)	83,309
18	83,309	(13,617)	69,692
19	69,692	(15,630)	54,062
20	54,062	(17,846)	36,216

		Chart 7.1b	

Deposit

Year	B/f	Surplus/ (deficit)	C/f
1	75,000	(375)	74,625
2	74,625	(703)	73,922
3	73,922	(1,071)	72,851
4	72,851	(1,482)	71,369
5	71,369	(1,940)	69,429
6	69,429	(2,451)	66,978
7	66,978	(3,017)	63,961
8	63,961	(3,646)	60,315
9	60,315	(4,341)	55,974
10	55,974	(5,109)	50,865
11	50,865	1,100	51,965
12	51,965	1,046	53,011
13	53,011	983	53,994
14	53,994	907	54,901
15	54,901	818	55,719
16	55,719	714	56,433
17	56,433	594	57,027
18	57,027	457	57,484
19	57,484	300	57,784
20	57,784	122	57,906

you during your lifetime, but the tax treatment is slightly different. The pension annuity will be fully taxable; under the purchased life annuity you have exchanged a cash sum for an income stream, part of which is deemed to be a repayment of capital and will therefore not be taxable. The older you are, the greater the capital element.

Once you have purchased the annuity, the money cannot be reclaimed and you will be left with an income stream but no cash to fall back on. For this reason, it is necessary to have a mixture of cash and annuity income but only if the annuity is likely to provide a better return than an alternative form of investment. I have always been somewhat sceptical about the benefit of annuities. Do make sure that the annuity is appropriate in your case.

Appendix 6 shows a number of different forms of annuity. The first annuity is for a single person. For example, for a cost of £10,000, the annual annuity for a man aged 60 will be £1,184 and the annuity for a woman aged 60, £1,087. This is because the life expectancy of women is greater than of

---

Chart 7.2 £100,000 purchased life annuity payable monthly in arrears

		Male aged 65 £		Male aged 70 £
Annuity pa increasing at 5% pa		9,800		11,660
Capital content (44%/52%)	4,287		6,065	
Taxable content	5,513		5,595	
Income taxed at 25%		(1,378)		(1,399)
Annuity net of basic rate tax		8,422		10,261

Source: Standard Life, December 1991

---

men therefore the money would normally be paid over a longer period. However this form of annuity ends when a person dies: it will not provide for the surviving spouse.

The problem with a flat-rate annuity is that inflation will inevitably increase your expenditure while the annuity income stays static. An escalating annuity is better.

It is not possible to receive a company pension which provides the same level of income received when working: the maximum pension is two-thirds of the final salary, though this can be index-linked. It is possible to provide a widow's pension of up to two thirds of the member's pension but no more, under Inland Revenue limits. However, under a compulsory purchase annuity it would be possible to provide an annuity which continues at the same rate after the death of the first person. For example, if a man is aged 65 and the wife 60, £10,000 will secure an income of £1,034 throughout their joint lives or £671 escalating at five per cent a year.

However, it may not be necessary to provide the same level of income after the death of the first spouse as the expenditure is likely to be reduced following that event. For that reason, they may prefer an annuity which halves after the death of the first spouse, in which case the flat rate annuity is £1,147 and the index-linked annuity is £781.

An annuity is very good value if at least one partner of a marriage enjoys a long life. However, if they both die shortly after taking out the annuity, there will be no capital sum returned to the estate unless they take out a *guaranteed* annuity. It is normal for guarantees to be provided for periods of up to five or ten years. Much depends upon the person or persons to be protected. Is it to be the surviving spouse or the beneficiaries of the estate (eg children)?

PENSION ANNUITIES

At normal retirement age, part of a fund may be taken as tax-free cash and the balance as an annuity. It is normally advisable to take the maximum cash so as to provide additional funds at retirement, striking a balance between cash on deposit and annuity income – though your particular circumstances should be considered carefully.

Annuity rates depend on a number of factors, including interest rates, so timing is important. If interest rates are high, it may be advisable to buy the annuity rather than wait until a later date. Of course the later you leave it the higher the annuity as the income will be paid over a shorter period.

The tax payable by companies providing compulsory life annuities has recently increased. This is likely to reduce annuity rates.

What is often overlooked is that at normal retirement age, you have the option of purchasing your annuity. For example, if you have a personal pension with Standard Life, you do not necessarily need to take your annuity with that company. **Chart 7.3** gives sample annuity rates of some companies at the time of writing.

It is often the case that the best annuity can be bought from a different company from the one which holds your pension fund. For example, in this case, if your pension fund was with Norwich Union it would have been advisable to take the open-market option and take a pension from the Prudential to increase your pension income by over seven per cent.

DEFERRED ANNUITIES

You may want to avoid taking income now in order to secure a greater income at some time in the future. In this case, the deferred annuity may be appropriate, but at the time of writing few companies were providing this form of annuity.

TEMPORARY ANNUITIES

It may not be necessary for the annuity to be paid for the long term. Some investment plans are set up over a short period: you may wish to invest in a ten-year with-profit maximum investment plan. The premiums only need to be funded over the next ten years and thereafter the capital sum will be returned. You could finance the annual premium out of income or capital but may wish to buy an annuity for that purpose, the temporary annuity being a fully self-funding exercise. For a cost of, say, £100,000, the temporary annuity would fund the ten-year with-profit endowment plan. You would

Chart 7.3   *What the companies offer*

Figures are for 65-year-old male with 62-year-old wife. Annuity purchase price £100,000. Payout continues for five years even if man dies, and widow gets 50% thereafter.

	Level payments	Yearly payouts Increasing benefit options		RPI-Linked
		3%	5%	
Prudential	£12,140	£9,900	£8,500	£7,290
Confederation Life	£12,010	£9,820	£8,460	n/a
Providence Capitol	£11,900	£9,640	£8,230	n/a
Scottish Widows	£11,840	£9,590	£8,180	£6,960
Standard Life	£11,750	£9,540	£8,170	£7,470
Scottish Equitable	£11,600	£9,420	£8,050	n/a
Sun Life	£11,480	£9,170	£7,720	n/a
Eagle Star	£11,450	£9,080	£7,600	£7,350
Norwich Union	£11,280	£9,190	£7,900	n/a
Hill Samuel	£11,090	£8,730	£7,250	n/a

Source: Annuity Bureau, *Money Mail*, 13 November 1991

lose the flexibility of being able to withdraw the capital and fund the premiums in some other way but this may be more convenient for you. **Chart 7.4** illustrates a temporary annuity funding plan.

The fund produced in **Chart 7.4** from a temporary annuity is almost the same as the net fund produced from a gilt ladder.* In this case a gilt ladder provides the flexibility of being able to encash the gilts during the ten–year period and funding the savings plan premiums in some other way. You must consider carefully the various methods of funding the savings plan so that it fits your tax and liquidity profile and takes advantage of the most appropriate investment plans available.

* The gilt ladder is a series of government stocks which are structured so that each year one government stock will mature and the proceeds will fund the payment of the ten–year saving plan.

HOME ANNUITIES

These should really be a last resort but, like other annuities, they can be useful in providing an income flow for the rest of your life to ensure that money does not run out if you live to an old age. Many people do not have large cash sums to invest in annuities and if you are looking to find other ways of increasing your lifetime income, then you could consider a home annuity.

There are two main types of home annuity. You could effectively sell your home to an insurance company in return for an income stream. The difficulty with this is that if you wish to move at some time in the future you will not have the cash funds to buy a new home. However, if you are likely to remain in your existing home for the rest of your life, or possibly until you may need to move into a nursing home, you could consider this form of annuity. Instead of passing your home to your children after any inheritance tax has been paid, the home will no longer form part of your estate. Part of the

Chart 7.4		
Male aged 55, female aged 50	£	£
Total		100,000
First year's premium paid by cash		(13,282)
Balance used to buy temporary 10-year annuity		86,718
Gross annual payment commencing after 12 months		
Capital element	9,651	
Income	4,842	
		14,493
Income tax at, say, 25%		(1,211)
		13,282
Maturity of saving plan after 10 years assuming 10.5% growth pa	209,000	
Net annual annuity if tax rate 40%		
Net annuity as above		13,282
Less Higher rate tax at say 15%		
£4,842 at 15%		(726)
		£12,556
Annual income produced by a gilt ladder (6 December 1991) to fund savings plan		£12,530
Source: Norwich Union, 5 December 1991		

Chart 7.5

70-year-old man. Cost of annuity £30,000. Annuity and loan interest payable throughout life.

	£	£
Gross annuity		4,444
Capital element	2,671	
Income element	1,773	
Tax on income at, say, 25%		(443)
Net annuity		4,001
Interest at, say, 8.625% net of basic-rate tax		(2,587)
Increase in net spendable income		1,414

Source: Royal Life, 4 December 1991

---

annuity is a return of capital and is not therefore taxable. As it involves losing the ownership of your home, this is rather a drastic course of action.

If you have no mortgage, an alternative course of action is to retain ownership of your home but take out a loan against the value of the home and use the money to acquire an annuity. On your death the debt will need to be repaid from your estate, possibly from the sale of your house. One of the benefits of this is that a married couple over 65 years of age get tax relief at the top marginal rate on the loan interest. **Chart 7.5** illustrates this.

You should analyse your situation and think very carefully before proceeding with an annuity because once the money has been paid to the insurance company, it is not normally retrievable.

8

INSURANCE

PROTECTING THE FAMILY

If you die tomorrow, will your family be able to maintain your current standard of living? If the answer is no and, in particular, if the family income will be dramatically reduced, then you need life assurance protection.

Chart 8.1

40-year-old man, married, two young children. He is an employee earning £30,000 pa., wife does not work. His assets are a house worth £100,000 (on £30,000 endowment-linked mortgage) and investments of £10,000.

Net spendable income	Current position		Position after death
	£000	£000	£000
Salary		30	
Gross income from investments,			
say		1	1
		31	1
Mortgage and endowment policy payments	(3)		
Income tax	(7)		
		(10)	—
		21	1
Expenditure, say		(18)	(12)
Net surplus/(deficit)		3	(11)

The situation in **Chart 8.1** will be vastly improved if a life assurance policy is taken out; this would provide funds for the family in the event of death. The benefits from a policy can be inflation-proofed by index–linking the premium. The two main forms of life assurance are:

- *Whole life assurance:* explained in Appendix 8

- *Term assurance:* suitable if you want to take out life assurance for a limited period of time

You may believe that in ten years you will have accumulated sufficient wealth so that your family will not need to rely on life assurance and term assurance is all that is required. There is no surrender value to these policies but they are normally cheaper because at the end of a ten-year plan you will have paid money for no return, and they can be written to include a right to convert into a whole life policy.

Clearly, the ability to take out whole life assurance will depend upon the available net spendable income and capital. All the illustrations in the book assume that the assured is a non-smoker.

Chart 8.2

Facts as in Chart 8.1. The man uses his net spendable income of £3,000 and takes out a low-cost whole life policy on his life. Annual premium £1,650, minimum life cover £200,000.
Net spendable income position on death

	£
Proceeds from policy	200,000
Other investments	10,000
	210,000
Income thereon @ , say, 10% gross	21,000
Less tax, say	(4,430)
	16,570
Expenditure	12,000
Surplus	£4,570

THE NON-WORKING SPOUSE

If a woman looking after children full-time were to die, there would be significant financial needs. Actuarially, a woman is likely to live longer than a man so the cost of life assurance for a wife is normally cheaper. In addition, this life insurance may only be required for a relatively short period of time. For example if the children are, say, aged eight and five, there may only be the need to take out term assurance for the next 12 years or so, by which time they may be in higher education or working.

Chart 8.3 shows the cost of ten-year term assurance in respect of a woman aged 33, to provide a cash sum of £100,000 to produce income of approximately £10,000 a year plus an initial capital sum to fall back on.

DEATH-IN-SERVICE BENEFITS

Pension schemes, as we saw earlier, are designed to provide a pension for life, together with the option to take part of the fund as a tax-free cash sum on retirement. Death-in-service benefits are normally included in the schemes and this is where inheritance tax may be mitigated.

The pension scheme will normally permit benefits which arise from death while still a director or employee of the company. On death-in-service, the benefit will pass to the trustees who will exercise their discretion as to who should receive the payment. The director will normally provide a letter of wishes indicating who should benefit. This is not a legally-binding document but if the trustees of the scheme are, for example, the deceased's co-directors it would be unusual for them not to follow these wishes. Similar arrangements apply for personal pension plans, where life cover can be obtained and benefits paid directly to, or in trust for, the beneficiaries without an inheritance tax charge.

The death-in-service benefits of a company scheme can be substantial and are normally an amount equal to four times final remuneration plus the pension benefits which the company has purchased for the beneficiaries. The maximum benefits will, of course, only become payable if the pension scheme has sufficient funds to pay them out. It may be advisable for the scheme to 'top up' its funds by term assurance to ensure that the maximum benefits can be paid.

If death-in-service benefits are paid to the spouse they will form part of his or her estate and so aggravate the inheritance tax position. However, there is the opportunity to pay the benefits into, say, a trust for the children or grandchildren, and they will then pass directly for their benefit without an

---

Chart 8.3

Woman aged 33
Cover £100,000
10-year term assurance – annual cost
(monthly premium £7) £84

Source: Scottish Equitable, 4 December 1991

---

inheritance tax charge.

Chart 8.4

A man's final remuneration is £55,000. He dies in service and the pension fund has £220,000 which can be paid to his wife (whose wealth will exceed £150,000 on her death) or his two children equally.

	£
Payment to spouse	220,000
Potential inheritance tax at 40%	(88,000)
Estate net of tax	132,000
Payment to children	220,000
Potential inheritance tax on wife's death	–
	220,000
Tax saved	88,000

PERMANENT HEALTH INSURANCE COVER

Many people cover the position should they die, yet ignore the problems which can arise if they become disabled so that they can no longer work. This may be even more serious from a financial point of view, as not only will earnings fall or cease altogether, but there may be the need for financial assistance to provide for medical fees, etc. This potential difficulty can be met by a permanent health insurance policy which will pay out regular income in the event of the assured person becoming disabled.

The policy could be taken out personally to provide for the family or by a company in respect of an employee. It will normally end when the insured reaches the age of 60 or 65. The income from a policy taken out by an individual will become subject to income tax after one to two years depending on when the benefit commences. **Chart 8.5** gives an example of the cost involved for a policy to provide annual income of £20,000 a year to age 65.

The benefit in **Chart 8.5** is tax-free in the first year of the claim and will be taxed as income thereafter (it is possible to receive tax-free income for up to 23 months). Permanent health insurance can be set up in the following different ways:

- Level benefit. The benefit and the premium remain the same throughout the term of the cover

- Growth benefit. The benefit remains level until there is a claim then increases by five per cent a year compound until the end of the claim period, at which time it returns to the original level

- Optional increasing benefit. This gives the policyholder the option to increase the benefit by up to 25 per cent every three years without further medical evidence

- Index-linked benefit. The cover is automatically increased in line with the RPI throughout the term. The premiums applicable also increase and equate with the level of premiums applicable to the policyholder's age at the time the increments are added.

Chart 8.5

Age of insured next birthday	Income cover £20,000 pa – annual premium £	Income cover £20,000 pa index-linked – annual premium £
30	250	356
40	380	458
50	640	900

(The benefit commences 13 weeks after disablement.)

PRIVATE MEDICAL INSURANCE

The current National Health Service debate has focused many people's minds on whether they are happy to rely only upon the NHS or whether they wish to have some additional private medical care available. It is surprising how many people are covered for death but not for a serious illness. Many companies now offer permanent health insurance as a perk, and it is normally possible to obtain better rates through a group discount.

If you want private medical care, shop around. Major schemes like BUPA and PPP may not be the cheapest but their range of hospitals may be wider than some of the smaller companies. A broker should advise you. **Chart 8.7** shows the cost of medical cover. Annual costs are reduced if you are in a group company plan.

Chart 8.6 *Permanent health insurance benefit*

Monthly costs based on £20,000 pa benefit

	Benefit deferred	
	13 weeks £	26 weeks £
Level benefit	21.23	16.62
Index-linked benefit	29.58	26.16
Optional increasing benefit	23.20	13.27
Growth benefit	23.20	13.27

Chart 8.7

Basic

Age	Single £	Married £	Family £
18-24	697.20	1,278.12	1,597.68
25-29	699.72	1,340.28	1,675.56
30-34	722.16	1,384.68	1,730.64
35-39	754.20	1,445.76	1,806.84
40-44	779.52	1,493.52	1,866.48
45-49	827.52	1,585.08	1,981.08
50-54	931.68	1,787.04	2,234.04
55-59	1,081.44	2,072.52	2,590.80
60-64	1,221.00	2,338.56	2,923.44
65-69	1,528.08	3,056.04	3,520.32
70-74	1,816.80	3,633.12	4,159.44
75 +	2,234.52	4,468.68	5,094.96

Source: BUPA, December 1991 – Scale A

CRITICAL ILLNESS (DREAD DISEASE INSURANCE)

Dread disease cover (otherwise known as 'critical illness insurance') is now quite commonplace. It pays a lump sum in the event that you are diagnosed as having a life-threatening disease. The range of diseases covered is normally limited to cancers, heart attacks and certain other illnesses and you should check the policy very carefully before proceeding.

LONG-TERM CARE INSURANCE

This is relatively new. It insures against a person having to go into residential care towards the end of their life. This is likely to be an increasing problem for elderly people seeking residential care as the cost may well be beyond a family's means in critical cases.

In the example in **Chart 8.8** the return from unit trusts is not guaranteed and depends upon the investment performance over the five-year term: this may not be attractive enough for you in view of the risk involved.

An alternative course of action is to pay an annual premium to cover disability. Commercial Union has a plan which costs £3,818 pa (at 6 December 1991) for a managed fund to provide £25,000 pa for severe disability or £12,500 for moderate disability. The cover includes an inability to get into or out of a chair or bed, dressing, washing, continence etc.

Chart 8.8

Man aged 75. Investment £100,000.

	£	£
Capital-protected annuity		33,324
Unit trusts (income reinvested)		66,676
		100,000
Annual income from annuity		
Capital element		7,812
Income element		564
		8,376
Tax at, say, 25%		(141)
		8,235
Value at end of 5 years from unit trusts		
(assuming 10.5% growth pa)		100,000

Source: Clerical Medical, 6 December 1991

PERSONAL ACCIDENT COVER

This policy would cover you if you were to have a serious accident. **Chart 8.9** shows the amounts you would be likely to receive for certain injuries, and **Chart 8.10** the cost of cover.

Chart 8.9

Benefit A — death and permanent injury	*One unit*
	£
Accidental injury which results in:	
Death	25,000
Total loss of sight in one or both eyes	25,000
Total loss or loss of use of one or both hands	25,000
Total loss or loss of use of one or both feet	25,000
Total loss or loss of use of:	
Thumb	5,000
Index finger	3,000
Any other finger	1,000
Big toe	1,000
Any other toe	500
which occurs within 2 years of the injury from which the claim arises	
Permanent total disablement from any profession or occupation	25,000
Total loss of hearing in both ears	10,000
Total loss of hearing in one year	2,500

Benefit B — temporary injury	*One unit*
Accidental injury which results in temporary total disablement	£25 per week for up to 104 weeks

Benefit C — temporary sickness (only available with Benefit B)	*One unit*
Sickness which results in temporary total disablement	£25 per week for up to 104 weeks

Source: Norwich Union, 6 December 1991

KEYMAN COVER

If an individual is the driving force behind the family company or business, the value of that company or business is likely to be materially depleted on death. Even if another director is brought in to run the company it may take some time before confidence and profitability is restored.

In these circumstances, a keyman insurance policy is advisable to produce a capital sum for the company which would help alleviate these problems.

Chart 8.10 *Annual cost per unit of benefit*

| Benefit | Proposer's Occupation Group | | | | Spouse | Children |
	1	2	3	4		
	£	£	£	£	£	
A Death and permanent injury	20.00	30.00	40.00	55.00	16.00	£7.75 per child (£6.20 per child if a parent is insured by the policy)
B Temporary injury	5.00	10.00	20.00	25.00	4.00	–
C Temporary sickness	25.00	25.00	30.00	30.00	20.00	–

Notes: (1) The cost per unit of benefit for your spouse applies only if he/she is insured by the Family Plus policy in addition to yourself, and his/her occupation falls within Occupation Group 1 or 2.

(2) Policy minimum premium £25.

Instalments

If required, premiums over £50 can be paid by monthly instalments. A small additional charge of 6% (APR 31.7%) is made for this facility.

Examples of cost

1. Computer programmer selection 3 units of Benefit A £60.00
    Spouse (housewife) selecting 2 units of Benefit A £32.00
    Annual Premium £92.00
    Monthly Premium £8.13
2. Clerical worker selection 2 units of Benefit A and
    1 Unit of Benefit B £40.00
    1 Unit of Benefit B £5.00
    Spouse (hairdresser) selecting 1 unit of Benefit A £16.00
    Child with 1 unit of Benefit A selected £6.20
    Annual premium £67.20
    Monthly premium £5.94

Plus the free legal expenses cover for the family and the free £10,000 permanent total disablement cover for the child.

Source: Norwich Union, 6 December 1991

Similar insurance cover may be required by a partnership. The cost can be comparatively modest depending upon the age of the insured. **Chart 8.11** is an example of the costs of a level-term assurance plan to age 65.

Man aged	Sum assured £100,000 – annual premium £
	Chart 8.11
30	362
40	530
50	866
60	1,095

Type of protection

To protect itself from the loss of a key person, a company could effect either a term-assurance policy or a whole of life policy. The advantage of a whole of life policy is that it will exist throughout the service of the key person and produce a surrender value which can be taken at a later stage or assigned to the key employee in recognition of his or her services on retirement. This is unlike a term assurance policy, which would only produce a sum on death within the term of the contract and has no surrender value.

For the term assurance policy, premiums paid by the company would normally be tax-deductible against corporation tax and the proceeds will be treated as a trading receipt and charged to corporation tax accordingly. In order to have the premiums of a term assurance policy treated as tax deductible, the life assurance policy must be for the purposes of the trade and should be for a short period, such as five years. However, with a whole of life policy the premiums are not generally tax deductible but the proceeds may not be subject to any tax liability on payment in event of death.

SHAREHOLDER PROTECTION

In the event of the death of a shareholder/director, the cost to the company in buying the shares of the deceased director can be onerous. The purpose of share protection is to provide capital for the incumbent shareholder/director to purchase the deceased's shareholding from the estate.

By arranging a share purchase scheme of this kind, the directors avoid the shares falling into the hands of an uninterested party. It also ensures that the directors' beneficaries receive an adequate value for the shareholding.

A share purchase scheme consists of a life assurance policy which will provide funds for the purchase of the deceased director's shareholding. There are basically two ways in which this form of assurance can be set up, namely as shareholder share purchase or company share purchase.

Shareholder share purchase

Under the shareholder share purchase arrangement, shareholders enter into a mutual double option agreement which would be exercised upon the death of a director/shareholder. The options provide that the continuing shareholders could require the executors of the deceased to sell the deceased's shares to them and the executors could require that the continuing shareholders buy the shares from them.

Normally, a form of flexible or discretionary trust is used to ensure that the proceeds of the life assurance policy would be paid to the remaining shareholders in agreed proportions.

There is no tax relief on the premiums if paid by individuals. However, if the premiums are paid by the company and treated as a benefit in kind to the employee, the company avoids national insurance costs.

Company share purchase

Companies are allowed to purchase their own shares which are then treated as cancelled (under the Companies Act 1985). Therefore, the shares of a deceased's estate may be purchased by the company from their executors who would receive cash for the shares to pass on to the director's beneficiaries. There are a number of formal procedural steps to be followed before the shares can be purchased, for example, checking the articles of association, passing a formal resolution, and so forth. In addition, the company must normally have distributable profits to enable a distribution so that purchase of the shares can be made. Alternatively, the purchase could be made out of a fresh issue of shares for that purpose.

To enable the company to fund the purchase of shares, life policies on the lives of the directors/shareholders concerned will need to be effected. Policies should be set up on the life of another basis with the company actually effecting the policy as grantee.

There will generally be no tax relief on the premiums but the company may suffer corporation tax on the receipt. The money is then distributed to the personal representatives of the deceased. It is recommended that permission is sought from the Inland Revenue to have the distribution treated as a capital distribution, otherwise (if the relevant conditions are met) the payment could be treated as an income distribution. The conditions of such treatment include the need for the purchase to benefit the trade (to meet an inheritance tax liability would not be acceptable). The shareholder must be a UK resident for tax purposes and have held the shares for five years.

The share purchase scheme will involve arranging a term or whole life assurance policy on the life of each of the directors written into trust for the benefit of the other directors.

Certain insurance companies have term assurance policies for which the life office can review the premium and increase it accordingly if mortality experience moves against them. In other words, the premium is not guaranteed to stay the same throughout the term of the policy.

PROVIDING FOR DEATH DUTIES

A serious problem can arise if a large part of an estate comprises non–liquid assets, for example, shares in the family property business. The potential tax liability (or part of that liability) can be met by taking out life assurance, with the policy written (possibly under trust) for the benefit of family members. This is not necessary for one's spouse, as no tax charge will arise if assets pass to the spouse on death.

It may be advisable to take out extra cover in any event, as you may need to provide for both death duties and a capital sum so that your family have sufficient income.

The premium paid each year will be treated as a gift as the benefit of the policy will accrue to the beneficiaries. Premiums paid more than seven years before death will normally be exempt and only those paid within that seven-

---

Chart 8.12

Annual premium of a with-profit minimum-cost whole life policy written on a joint-life surviving-spouse basis. Sum assured £100,000.

Age of husband next birthday	Age of wife next birthday	Annual premium £
30	26	145
40	36	275
50	46	566
60	56	1,182

(The above quotes assume that the assured are non-smokers.)

year period will be chargeable. However, any chargeable premiums may be covered by the various exemptions (particularly that for gifts out of income) or by the nil rate band explained in Chapter 15.

For a husband and wife the policy can be written on a joint-lives, first-death or surviving-spouse basis. If the bulk of the estate is to be left to the spouse, the major tax charge will arise on the death of the surviving spouse. If a joint-life, surviving-spouse policy is taken out, the premiums become the liability of the surviving spouse after the first death, and the policy will not mature until the second death. The premiums are normally cheaper than those for a single-life policy.

The advantages of a life assurance policy written under trust to fund the inheritance tax liability are:

- Funds are made available at the right time outside the estate and so without liability to inheritance tax

- Funds are under trust and so free of inheritance tax liability

- The premiums for the life assurance policy normally come under the normal expenditure exemptions and are free of inheritance tax liability

- A substantial fund is available from the payment of the first premium.

So a life assurance policy is a means of gradually passing funds to the next generation in a tax-efficient manner to build up a fund to settle the inheritance tax on death. There are two types of cover:

1. *Standard cover*. Standard cover means that if a conservative growth rate is experienced by the life assurance fund and mortality charges do not change, then the same level of life cover will be maintained throughout the life of the policy without any need to increase the premiums. In other words, a level premium will provide cover until the second death.

2. *Maximum cover*. Maximum cover is the lowest premium required to meet the specified sum assured. The premium will remain the same for the first ten years then a review will normally take place and the premium will probably increase to maintain the same level of life cover, the level of that increase depending on the investment performance of the life assurance fund.

COVER IN RESPECT OF GIFTS MADE

The problem with a potentially exempt lifetime gift is that it is not known at that time whether the gift will escape inheritance tax, as gifts made within seven years of death are caught.

PERSONAL FINANCIAL PLANNING

Chart 8.13

A man with an estate of £450,000 wishes to make a £150,000 gift and protect against the additional tax if he dies within seven years.

No. of years between gift and death	Additional tax charge £
0–3	60,000
3–4	59,200
4–5	58,400
5–6	57,600
6–7	56,800
7–8	Nil

Cost of inter vivos assurance premium for seven years to cover the above tax

Man aged	Annual premium £
30	130
40	180
50	360
60	835

The Cost of an inter vivos plan which covers £60,000 for the first three years but falls by 20 per cent per annum is as follows:

Man aged	Annual premium £
30	82
40	110
50	249
60	543

A special term assurance policy called an *inter vivos* assurance policy can provide for the additional tax charge. The policy could be taken out by the donor with the proceeds of the policy passing to the beneficiaries. In this case the premiums will be chargeable transfers if death occurs within seven years. If the donor survives seven years the policy will lapse and no further premiums will be required. In some cases the cover will fall by 20 per cent a year after year three but in other cases the cover may need to be higher than this in the later years.

9

MORTGAGES

Buying your home is likely to be the largest financial commitment of your life and should be given serious consideration. Moving is traumatic. Often so much time is taken up in finding the right home, or trying to co-ordinate the sale of one house and the purchase of another that the mortgage is left to the last minute. This can be very dangerous as it can take several weeks to arrange a mortgage. Before committing yourself to exchanging on a property, you should leave yourself with enough time to arrange the mortgage properly.

Financing the mortgage should be planned well in advance, normally some months before you are likely to finalize the contract. This will require you to carefully budget your revised expenditure to ensure that you can meet the cost of the mortgage in the future. The case study we have been using has assumed that the couple's original home was worth £250,000 and they had a £50,000 mortgage and cash deposits of £120,000. The case study also assumes surplus income of £5,000. **Chart 9.1** shows the likely additional cost if the new house is valued at £380,000.

You can see from **Chart 9.1** that the couple should receive £200,000 net of the first mortgage from the sale of their home and are using £100,000 of their deposits so that £20,000 remains free for emergencies. If we assume that the new property costs £380,000 and that they increase their mortgage to £100,000, there will be £20,000 remaining. However, they will have to pay legal fees, stamp duty, survey fees, and the agent's commission on the sale of the house. There is also likely to be additional expenditure when moving into your new home – extra fittings, building works, etc – so the £20,000 surplus could reduce very quickly.

If we assume that mortgage interest rates are at 12 per cent, then there will be an additional £6,000 a year to pay and they may have to top up their investment plans to provide funds for future mortgage repayment, so additional expenditure could be around £7,000 a year. As the case study shows surplus income was £5,000, they will now need to cut their expenditure by £2,000. There might be extra difficulties if interest rates were to increase – a return to 15 per cent would mean an extra £3,000 a year. A

Chart 9.1

	£000	£000
Sale of home	250	
Redemption of mortgage	(50)	
		200
Cash deposits, say		100
		300
New property	380	
Mortgage	(100)	
		280
		20
Costs and emergency fund		(20)
Additional mortgage costs		
Interest £50,000, say, 12%		(6)
Endowment plan, say		(1)
		(7)
Surplus income to date		5
Need to cut expenditure by		(2)

property worth nearer £350,000 and a lower mortgage might have been more appropriate.

You should consider carefully the costs of moving. **Chart 9.2** shows the

Chart 9.2

Costs	Selling £	Buying £	Total £
Lender's valuation fee and your surveyor's fee		400	
Solicitor's conveyancing fee	575	583	
Stamp duty		2,000	
Land registry fee		220	
Search fees		35	
Estate agent's commission on selling the home, say	5,106		
Removal fees		407	
Total	5,681	3,645	9,326

likely costs of buying and selling a house worth £200,000.

If you are taking out a new mortgage there may also be an arrangement fee. If your mortgage is high (say, over 80 per cent of the value of the home) the lender may require a mortgage guarantee policy, so you should check the likely cost of this beforehand. (The cost of a mortgage guarantee policy can vary depending on the age of the individual.)

LENDING CRITERIA

If at all possible, you should avoid excessive borrowings on a home. Interest rates can fluctuate and many people who bought their homes in the late 1980s have found the value of their home fall. If they borrowed heavily, it is possible that the property is now worth less than their loan. The recession has led to many redundancies and this has given rise to an increasing number of home repossessions as homeowners could no longer afford to pay the mortgage. You should be very wary about the commitment you are making and need to consider 'doomsday scenarios' such as sharp interest rate rises, or the possibility of a cut in earnings.

Before buying a new home, you should first enquire into the likely value of your existing home. As estate agents may be competing for the instruction to sell your home, they may flatter you by overvaluing it. This can lead to disappointment later on when you find that you cannot in fact get the price you expected and therefore cannot afford the property you wanted to buy. You should get two or three different valuations and use the most cautious valuation as your benchmark.

The amount you can borrow depends largely upon your income. Building societies and banks will normally lend up to a maximum of 2.5 or three times your income plus one or 1.5 times a second income. Some will include regular overtime or spare-time earnings while others will not.

Proof of your income will be required. If you are employed, a copy of your last form P60 showing your salary in the last tax year will do as proof, or a letter from your employer. If you are self-employed you are likely to be asked to produce accounts.

Although you will be buying a house at a certain price, lenders may take a different view on its value, since they are more concerned with the price they will be able to get for it if you default on the mortgage. In such circumstances they would be looking to sell it off quickly. Therefore, although in the current market you may be buying a property for, say, £150,000, they may only value it at, say, 80 per cent of that price so that they know they could sell it for £120,000 fairly easily. When money is plentiful you may be offered a mortgage of up to 100 per cent of the lender's valuation; during recessionary times, lenders may be more cautious and lend up to only 80 or 90 per cent of the valuation.

You will normally be asked to take out some form of indemnity insurance or mortgage guarantee policy to cover the borrowings if they exceed around 70 to 80 per cent of the lender's valuation. Premiums can be around three per cent or more of the loan over the normal limit so you should be wary of this additional cost which will arise if you are heavily geared.

If your existing mortgage is too small, you can get additional cash by taking out a mortgage from another insurance company but the interest on this second loan is likely to be at a higher rate.

The traditional term of a mortgage is 25 years although some lenders will allow 30 years. It is advisable to take out the loan so that the end of repayment coincides with your retirement as you would normally wish the mortgage to be paid off by that time. However, if you wish to take out a mortgage at age 45 and have it redeemed at 60, there will only be 15 years to run, including the investment plan which is designed to pay off the mortgage, and this will cost more if there is only 15 rather than 25 years to run, as shown by **Chart 9.3**.

If you are in the happy position of being able to redeem your mortgage early, you should examine the lender's policy as some make a special charge if you end the mortgage early, such as three months extra interest. Consider this matter carefully before taking out the mortgage.

Chart 9.3

Mortgage £30,000	Investment term in years		
	10	15	25
	£	£	£
Annual premium	3446	1851	728
Likely maturity proceeds after repayment of mortgage (assuming 10.5% growth)	23,900	26,700	35,700

PROVIDERS OF FINANCE

There is no shortage of mortgage providers. Traditionally, building societies were the first port of call but the banks have now moved very heavily into the mortgage market. There are around 100 building societies in Britain and most of them are members of the Building Societies Association (BSA). The largest include the Halifax, Nationwide Anglia and Woolwich; Abbey National was a building society but has now become a bank. The societies normally give preferential treatment to people who have saved with them. If you are looking to take out a mortgage with one of the large building societies it makes sense to start a savings plan with them earlier on.

The main clearing banks, and many smaller banks, offer home loans. In addition, international banks, finance houses and several insurance companies now lend, often on the back of their investment policies. It is normally advisable to seek independent guidance at this time. Some very useful magazines such as *What Mortgage* can be bought for around £1.40 per month.

Specialist brokers can be helpful but you should bear in mind that many brokers earn their money from the investment plan which is taken out (see Chapter 17 for the levels of commission they often receive for this).

There are many different schemes around to attract new borrowers. The different forms of discount offered are almost endless and it can be very difficult to pick your way through the maze of offers to determine the best mortgage for you.

INTEREST RATES

Chart 9.4 shows the movement of interest rates over the last ten years.

During the late 1980s, interest rates exceeded 15 per cent; at the end of 1991 they were around 11 per cent and certain societies were providing mortgages below this level. Your mortgage interest rate is at the mercy of factors outside your control. For example, if inflation takes off again or if the economy is growing at too fast a rate, the government may increase interest rates. Now that we are in the ERM, economic changes outside the UK can have a serious impact on our interest rates. The cost of reunification in Germany could mean higher interest rates throughout Europe. During 1991, UK mortgage rates moved closer to those of other European countries (see **Chart 1.3** on page 4).

Now that interest rates have come down, many people are taking fixed-interest loans. The difficulty is deciding whether the interest rate being offered will seem reasonable in, say, five years time. Will interest rates fall further now that we are in the ERM? The benefit of a fixed-interest mortgage is certainty: even though interest rates may fall, you can plan your finances more accurately as you know what will be payable over the fixed-rate term. In November 1991 it was possible to get a fixed-rate loan at around 10.5 per cent for three to five years. A few institutions were lending for a longer term at a fixed rate.

'Cap and Collar' mortgages have also become quite popular. These are variable interest-rate mortgages but the interest can only fluctuate between given levels. For example, the arrangement could be structured so that the rate does not exceed, say, 11.9 per cent but will not fall below 9.9 per cent. This is an alternative to the fixed-rate mortgage and also provides some

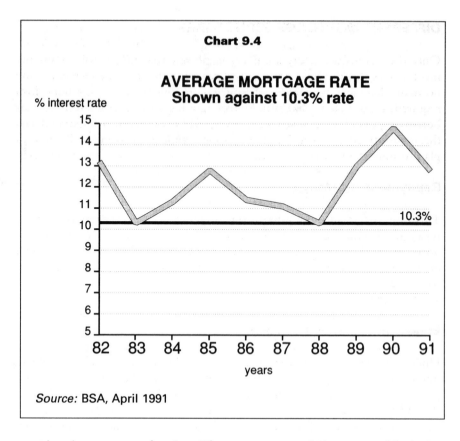

Chart 9.4

AVERAGE MORTGAGE RATE
Shown against 10.3% rate

% interest rate

Source: BSA, April 1991

certainty in mortgage planning. There are many variations upon this theme. Some societies will arrange for the interest to be paid at the same level even though the mortgage is a variable-rate mortgage. If interest rates increase, the additional interest is added to the loan. While this may appear attractive, you are taking on an increasing burden and it is normally better to clear your mortgage interest payments each month rather than have a loan which is likely to escalate.

Some start-up loans provide a preferential fixed rate for the first year or two. There are low-start deferred arrangements so that the initial mortgage rate is low but the reduction in the interest payments rolls up within the mortgage plan. Some mortgage interest rates are relatively competitive but only if you take out certain investment policies. You need to be careful here. In the past, non-profit endowment policies have been used by insurance companies to attract borrowers based upon a competitive interest rate, but the investment plans were poor value in the long term.

DIFFERENT MORTGAGE STRUCTURES

Only the seriously wealthy are likely to be able to arrange an interest–only mortgage as this provides no means of repaying the loan. Lenders will only normally lend in this manner if you have deposits in excess of the loan required. If so, you are likely to be paying a higher rate of interest on your borrowing than the interest you receive (which will normally be taxable) so this is a relatively unusual situation. For most people, the lender will require a plan to fund the repayment of the loan.

Repayment mortgage

This requires you to pay interest on the mortgage and, at the same time, repay the capital. The term is often for 25 years and the payments are normally made at a set monthly level over that period. The payments will increase or decrease only if interest rates change. In the early years most of the payment covers the interest rather than the capital so that the loan is repaid at a quicker rate towards the end of the term.

Endowment-linked mortgage

Under this arrangement the mortgage remains constant. You only pay interest and do not reduce the loan. You also need to take out an endowment policy, which is really a savings plan, and this should grow in value so that at the end of the mortgage term it matures to pay off the mortgage. A low–cost endowment policy will normally pay off the mortgage and provide a small surplus whereas a high–cost endowment policy will be more expensive but will produce a greater surplus.

Pension-linked mortgage

With a pension-linked mortgage you pay only interest on the loan and pay money into your pension scheme which is used as your long–term savings plan. On retirement, your tax-free cash sum from the pension scheme is used to pay off the mortgage. This will require a regular commitment to the pension plan and a projection of the likely future tax-free cash will normally be computed on the basis of an annual (rather than a single) premium.

PEP-linked mortgage

This is similar to an endowment mortgage except that you are then committed to pay money into a personal equity plan rather than an endowment policy. At the end of the term, the PEP can be cashed to eliminate the mortgage, or it can be cashed from time to time during the term of the loan. (The difference between a PEP and an endowment policy is covered in Chapter 5.)

You will note that the capital and interest repayment mortgage requires a mortgage-protection policy. This is because life assurance is required so that a policy matures on death prior to the redemption of the mortgage. There will normally be some form of insurance under the endowment or pension-linked mortgages. While the endowment mortgage appears a little more expensive, it is likely to produce a capital sum at the end of the term and many have proven to be good value. Under a repayment mortgage, at the end of the term the mortgage is fully repaid without any additional sum coming back to you.

Some people who took out mortgages 25 years ago were surprised at the large surplus from endowment plans. This obviously depends upon the investment performance. Under a unit-linked endowment, the profits from the plan are organized more like a stock market investment which could go down as well as up and many people have preferred the with-profit plan for its greater security. PEP mortgages are also linked to stock market performance and are therefore volatile in nature.

Chart 9.5 gives the approximate cost of the different types of mortgage. We have taken the example of a young couple where the man is aged 30 and the woman 28, taking out a £50,000 mortgage over a term of 25 years. The calculations are based upon an interest rate of 10.5 per cent.

As a savings vehicle, the pension plan is the most tax-efficient as the pension fund grows tax-free while tax is levied upon the gains made by the life company so that the endowment policy will effectively incur this charge. Also the premiums paid into a pension plan will attract income tax relief at your top marginal rate while those paid to an endowment policy attract no tax relief at all unless the policy was taken out before 1984. However, the endowment fund can be used to repay the mortgage while only part of the pension fund can be used in this way. These tax breaks provide a significant benefit, as illustrated by **Chart 9.6**, taken from my book *The Daily Telegraph Pensions Guide*, published in 1987. At that time you could get full tax relief of 60 per cent on the pension contribution.

The pension mortgage is likely to produce a greater return at the end of the term. This is because of the tax benefits and also because only 25 per cent of a personal pension plan can be used as the means of repaying the loan so 75 per cent of the fund will be used for pension purposes. However, if you take out a pension mortgage you must appreciate that the tax-free cash will be reducing the ultimate pension fund which will go to buy your retirement benefits. Therefore, when planning for the appropriate level of pension upon retirement, you will need to take account of the fund which is to be used to repay the loan.

In the past, pension-linked mortgages have not generally been available to employees in occupational schemes. This is because although the employee would be entitled to tax-free cash upon retirement, it comes from a scheme which was not under his or her control. New AVC schemes are no longer able to fund tax-free cash. However, if you are in an AVC scheme which was set up some years ago this may be possible. Finance houses have been happier to arrange a pension-linked mortgage for controlling directors and employees with individual pension arrangements, ie executive pension plans.

Chart 9.5

Monthly cost	£	£
Capital-and-interest repayment mortgage		
Monthly level-term mortgage payment	413.80	
Monthly mortgage-protection premium	11.15	
Total		424.95
Low-cost with-profit endowment mortgage		
Monthly mortgage payment of interest only	371.90	
Monthly endowment premium (joint lives)	59.50	
Total		431.40
Unit-linked endowment mortgage		
Monthly mortgage payment of interest only	371.90	
Monthly unit-linked plan payment	66.00	
Total		437.90
Pension-linked mortgage		
Monthly mortgage payment of interest only	371.90	
Monthly contribution to personal pension plan	97.54	
Total		469.44
PEP-linked mortgage		
Monthly mortgage payment of interest only	371.90	
Monthly PEP contribution	57.96	
Term assurance	17.62	
Total		447.48
Fixed-rate mortgage		
Monthly mortgage payment of interest only at, say, 9.95%		£363.10

Source: Bradford & Bingley Building Society

Chart 9.6

A 35-year-old man who is a 60% taxpayer takes out a £30,000 mortgage for a 25-year-term. The interest rate is 11% pa.

Monthly payments	Repayment mortgage Net £	Endowment-linked mortgage Net £	Pension-linked mortgage Net £
To lender	166.87	110.00	110.00
Endowment/pension premium	n/a	41.37	30.76
Life assurance premium (net)	3.52	n/a	3.72
Total payments	170.39	151.37	144.48
Proceeds after repayment of mortgage at the end of the term	Nil	16,863	Cash of £7,504 plus pension of £11,481 pa

TAXATION

In the past, mortgage interest relief on loans up to £30,000 attracted the highest rate of income tax relief. Therefore, if you were a 40 per cent taxpayer the interest was costing you only 60 per cent of the amount paid after tax relief had been taken into account. Following the Finance Act 1991, the higher-rate relief has been withdrawn so that you only get basic-rate relief on the part of the loan up to £30,000. If you are employed then you are likely to be in the MIRAS scheme. This means that the tax relief is deducted at source so that the interest you pay will be net of tax relief, as shown by **Chart 9.7**.

PAYING OFF THE MORTGAGE

If you find you have available funds, you may wish to consider whether the mortgage should be repaid. If we assume that your current mortgage interest rate is, say, 12 per cent, then the net cost to you after basic-rate tax relief is nine per cent. You will need to compare the cost of the mortgage with alternative uses of your money, such as having ready cash funds in case a good investment opportunity arises.

If you are always likely to have an excess of £30,000 on deposit, then there is a strong argument for paying off the mortgage, as shown by **Chart 9.8**.

Chart 9.7

Mortgage, say, £50,000. Interest rate, say, 12%

	£
Interest £50,000 × 12%	6,000
Tax relief £30,000 × 12% × 25%	(900)
Annual net interest	5,100
Monthly net interest	425

If you wish to pay off a mortgage which is linked to an endowment plan, it may be advisable to repay the mortgage but retain the endowment plan as a savings vehicle.

Chart 9.8

	£
Mortgage interest £30,000 at, say, 12%	3,600
Tax relief at 25%	(900)
Net cost	2,700
Interest receivable £30,000 at, say, 11%	3,300
Tax thereon at, say, 40%	(1,320)
Net income	1,980
Difference	720

10

SCHOOL FEES

In many ways, school fees planning is similar to pension planning although the requirement is normally over a shorter period. If you wish to have your children educated privately you should plan in advance. You can either fund the school fees out of your net spendable income or provide for them in advance. You should consider whether you will be able to meet the costs of school fees without cutting your standard of living if possible.

Chart 10.1 is a case study of a couple with two daughters. We have assumed that the eldest daughter is aged 11 and that in 1991 the school fees are £1,300 per term or £4,200 a year. It has been assumed that the fees increase at ten per cent a year and that there is the need to provide for these fees until she is aged 17. Of course there may be the need to provide for the cost of further education, but for the purposes of this illustration, we have assumed that fees are to be provided for both daughters until age 17.

If the couple in this case study have surplus net spendable income of £5,000 a year they should be able to provide for the eldest daughter's school fees out of income. However, in 1996, it is hoped that the youngest daughter will join her older sister at the school so the fees payable will double at that time. For the next two years, the fees increase to over £14,000 a year with inflation and then fall to just over £8,000 a year when the eldest daughter leaves the school. The total fees amount to over £100,000.

There are a number of different ways of providing for school fees but it depends upon how well you can plan. If the fees are to be payable in the next year or so, then there will be very little chance of building up sufficient capital through various investment plans to meet these needs.

Too often there is a certain mystique connected with school fees planning which really only requires an investment strategy. However, before considering the various investment plans, most of which have already been discussed in Chapter 5, and which ones could be applied to school fees planning, we should examine the various school fees education trusts.

Chart 10.1

Year commencing September	Eldest daughter Age	Fees £	Youngest daughter Age	Fees £	Total fees £
1991	11	4,200			4,200
1992	12	4,620			4,620
1993	13	5,082			5,082
1994	14	5,590			5,590
1995	15	6,149			6,149
1996	16	6,764	11	6,764	13,528
1997	17	7,441	12	7,441	14,882
1998			13	8,185	8,185
1999			14	9,003	9,003
2000			15	9,903	9,903
2001			16	10,894	10,894
2002			17	11,983	11,983
Totals		39,846		64,173	104,019

EDUCATION TRUSTS

Education trusts have become quite popular and can be a convenient way of providing for school fees. Normally a lump sum needs to be paid to the trust which then uses the money to buy an annuity (written on the life of the child) from a major British life office. At the commencement of the plan, the parents can select one of two options:

Option 1. The right to surrender the plan before the first fee payment.

Option 2. The right to surrender the plan in the event of death of the child or the child not going to a fee-paying school.

Normally, payment would be made by the parents but otherwise, the donor may wish to retain the right to nominate the school to which the child will go.

Some months before the first benefits are due under the plan, the trust will write to the parent or appointed person to establish which school the child will attend. The plan benefits are then paid in the form of a cheque to the school or the cheque is sent to the parents or appointed person to coincide with the payment of the term fees.

The plans can accommodate changes which need to be made in the level or pattern of the term payments. If, for example, the child obtains a scholarship then the benefits could be deferred to a later stage.

The education trust plan is normally exempt from capital gains tax and the payments made do not form part of the parents' income. However, if the plan is cancelled, then the monies are returned to the donor who may be taxed at that time. There may also be inheritance tax implications depending upon whether the payments are made before or after the school fees costs are incurred.

To return to our case study, if we assume that the first year's school fees of £4,200 are paid by the parents in November 1991 and the balance of approximately £35,646 for the older child is needed from 1992 onwards, the education trust would require a payment of just over £28,000 to meet those school fees. This provides an approximate yield of 6.4 per cent after tax. Therefore, a higher-rate taxpayer, paying 40 per cent tax would require a gross equivalent return of 10.67 per cent while a 25 per cent taxpayer would require 8.53 per cent.

Chart 10.2 _Eldest daughter_					
Year commencing September	Age	Balance B/F	Growth 6.4%	Fees	Balance C/F
		£		£	£
1991 (1)	11	4,200		(4,200)	
1991 (1)	11	28,150	1,802		29,952
1992 (2)	12	29,952	1,769	(4,620)	27,101
1993 (3)	13	27,101	1,571	(5,082)	23,590
1994 (4)	14	23,590	1,331	(5,590)	19,331
1995 (5)	15	19,331	1,040	(6,149)	14,222
1996 (6)	16	14,222	694	(6,764)	8,152
1997 (7)	17	8,152	284	(7,441)	995
1998 (8)					
1999 (9)					
2000 (10)					
2001 (11)					
2002 (12)					
Totals				(39,846)	

A payment of just over £33,600 was required to cover the school fees of approximately £64,000 commencing in 1996. The net yield was approximately eight per cent for a non-taxpayer, 10.67 per cent for a 25 per cent taxpayer, 13.33 per cent for a 40 per cent taxpayer.

Chart 10.3 Youngest daughter					
Year commencing September	Age	Balance B/F £	Growth 8%	Fees £	Balance C/F £
1991 (1)		33,631	2,690		36,321
1992 (2)		36,321	2,906		39,227
1993 (3)		39,227	3,138		42,365
1994 (4)		42,365	3,390		45,755
1995 (5)		45,755	3,660		49,415
1996 (6)	11	49,415	3,682	(6,764)	46,333
1997 (7)	12	46,333	3,410	(7,441)	42,302
1998 (8)	13	42,302	3,057	(8,185)	37,174
1999 (9)	14	37,174	2,614	(9,003)	30,785
2000 (10)	15	30,785	2,066	(9,903)	22,948
2001 (11)	16	22,948	1,401	(10,894)	13,455
2002 (12)	17	13,455	596	(11,983)	2,068
Totals				(64,173)	

When considering the benefit of this plan, it is important to consider whether a greater yield can be obtained than 6.4 per cent in respect of the older child and eight per cent in respect of the youngest child. The education trust is convenient when a lump sum is required and the income payments are then guaranteed. However, many people do not have the necessary cash sums available and will wish to consider other means of meeting school fees.

OTHER INVESTMENT PLANS

Tax exempt special savings accounts (TESSAs)

This plan and the following potential investments have been covered in detail in Chapter 5 so they are only covered here in terms of their benefits in school fees planning. As £9,000 can be paid into a TESSA by a husband and a similar sum by a wife, a married couple could invest £18,000 over a five-year period. If the capital can be retained in the plan for the five-year period, on the basis that the school fees are not required during that period, then this may prove to be a better investment than the education trust. If the tax-free income is likely to exceed the above yields of 6.4 per cent or eight per cent, then the TESSA will be more appropriate, although it is not possible to pay £18,000 into the plan initially as the investment must be made over five years.

However, a TESSA could be a good way of setting sums aside to meet future school fees.

Equities

You could invest a lump sum in equities in the hope that the capital growth over the period will exceed the yield from the education trust. If you can use your annual capital gains tax exemption together with the indexation allowance, then there may be little capital gains tax payable. However, stock markets are volatile and you may find that your investments perform badly just when you need the money for school fees. If you are able to invest over a longer period of time, you can seek to cash your equities at the appropriate time before the school fees are due.

Many people are unable to plan, say, ten years ahead and would not normally start to think about school fees planning until the child is born and the fees may then become payable after five years or so.

In view of the costs involved, it may be more appropriate for investment to be made through a unit trust or personal equity plan.

Single premium bonds

If school fees are not likely to be payable for at least five years, you may wish to consider a lump sum investment into a single premium bond. The investment can either be made in a unit-linked or a with-profit fund. It may be more appropriate to make a unit-linked investment through a unit trust, investment trust or personal equity plan, but the with-profit single-premium bond has been popular in recent years (as explained in Chapter 5). The investment could be made and the bond cashed after six or seven years to fund the future school fees. The bond has effectively suffered the basic rate of tax which a life company pays and any profit would be subject to higher-rate tax. (The way in which the profit could be sheltered from higher-rate tax is detailed in Chapter 5.)

National Savings

As the 36th issue National Savings certificate provides fixed tax-return of 8.5 per cent, this appears to be slightly better than the education trust. A husband and wife can each invest £10,000 in these certificates and a further £10,000 each into index-linked certificates which may also provide a greater return. Again, these may be attractive if the school fees do not need to be paid for the next five years, or at least the fees can initially be met from a building society deposit while the balance is invested in this manner to provide a larger lump sum to supplement the deposit account after five years.

Fixed-interest stocks

We looked at gilts, guaranteed bonds and zero coupon stocks in Chapter 5. Any of these might be appropriate but, again, you should compare the yields with those of the education trusts.

Ten-year endowment policies

The ten-year endowment policy also has the attraction of a tax-free return after at least 7.5 years of its term. Normally it is better to keep the policy going for ten years to get the best return. As with the single premium bond, the basic rate of tax has effectively been paid by the life company when providing the returns to policyholders.

These policies provide a good way of meeting future school fees but they are long-term plans and often the money is required well before the end of the ten-year period.

Baby bonds

The 'Baby Bond' introduced by the Chancellor in the 1991 budget, is proving popular among many parents and grandparents. Only available from friendly societies, it is a tax-efficient way to provide for children. By making regular savings or a lump sum investment on behalf of a child, your money grows into a tax-free sum. You decide when you want the child to receive the money – perhaps on an 18th or 21st birthday, or to pay school fees.

You can pay into the savings plan for a minimum of ten years, making annual or monthly contributions. Savings levels are just £18 a month or £200 a year; or if you prefer you can make a lump sum investment. Once you have taken out a Baby Bond, you can sit back and leave your money to grow tax-free until the maturity date.

TAX POSITION OF CHILD

It is important to consider whether you can take advantage of the tax position of your children. A minor child has a single person's allowance so that over £3,000 of income can be received each year tax-free. However, if the capital has been provided to the child by the parents, the income will be assessable on the parents until the child reaches 18. As mentioned earlier in this book, it is possible for a 'bare trust' to be created so that the income accumulates within the trust, but normally if the income is required for expenditure on the child, an assessment will be raised upon the parent at his or her top marginal rate. If the money has been gifted by the grandparents this problem will not arise and this is therefore a good way of ensuring that income is obtained without any tax being payable. In addition, each child has a separate capital gains tax exemption of £5,800 a year and this may be very valuable if the unit trusts are in the child's name as it is unlikely that any gain would be subject to tax.

DIRECT PAYMENT TO SCHOOL

A number of schools give a discount if you pay the fees in advance before the child commences his or her education at the school. It may be worth approaching the school directly to consider the discount which may be obtained. However, care needs to be taken – check the implications for if the child does not eventually go to the designated school.

You should start school fees planning as early as possible. Compare the likely net returns from the available investments against the benefit of a direct payment to an education trust or to the school. Education trusts are popular, but you may find that by carefully structuring your investments a better return can be obtained with alternative plans. One criticism of the school fees education trust is that, in some instances, the capital is tied up for a long time.

If a parent is the investor and retains the right to recover part of the fund, then this may form part of his or her estate for inheritance tax purposes. If the investment is not made by the parents it will be treated as a lifetime transfer each time the fees are paid and any residual value of the trusts will normally form part of the estate for inheritance tax purposes. If the right is waived then the transfer into trust will be treated as a lifetime gift and the funds will normally be held outside the estate for inheritance tax purposes.

11

UK TAX PLANNING

Personal financial planning means making the best use of financial resources in order to produce the maximum financial security for yourself and your family in the most tax-efficient way. Tax-efficiency (ie choosing and structuring transactions in such a way as to incur the least tax liability) is central to all personal financial planning. In this book so far, we have borne this in mind and considered the tax aspects of products and situations, as they are met in practice, and not in isolation.

Before we consider situations where the tax planning is a little more complicated, however, let's look at the main techniques for sheltering income and capital gains arising in the UK from the respective taxes, as a background to the discussion of the family company, employee benefits and estate planning later in the book.

INCOME TAX PLANNING

Income tax deductions

As we have seen, the most tax-efficient long-term investment is the pension scheme as tax relief is obtained on the contribution made, the fund rolls up tax-free and part of the fund can be taken as tax-free cash.

Business Expansion Scheme investments also provide tax relief until the scheme ends in December 1993 on the investment and there is no capital gains tax to pay on the sale of BES shares. However, any income generated by the BES company will be taxable in the normal way. (This arrangement is covered in Chapter 5.)

The other property-based tax shelter is building in an enterprise zone. You can either invest directly in a property in an enterprise zone or acquire units in a trust which acquires buildings in enterprise zones. **Chart 11.1** illustrates the benefit of this form of investment.

Chart 11.1	
	£000
EZD investment	120
Loan, say	(80)
Cash injection funded by tax relief	40
Income @, say, 8%	10
Interest at, say, 12%	(10)

It is possible to acquire units in an enterprise zone trust with 100 per cent of loan finance although the income is likely to be less than the interest payable. If you want to match the income with the interest, you could use the tax repayment from the investment to reduce the loan so that, on a long-term basis, the loan would be around two-thirds of the purchase price and the income would cover the interest. It is hoped that in future years, there will be an upward-only rental review.

The normal commercial considerations relating to property investments apply. You need to be sure that the purchase price reflects the true value of the property. In many cases, the purchase price is inflated due to the tax relief which you receive so that if you sold the building tomorrow, you would be unlikely to obtain the same price for it. Timing is important: if you invest in a zone at the right time, you can do well. Clearly, professional advice should be taken before any such investment is made. It is also important to ensure that the tenant is sound.

Tax-free income and growth

While the above investments provide income tax relief on the amount paid, there are other investments which do not provide the same measure of relief but provide an increase in your fund without income tax being payable. TESSAs produce tax-free income over a five-year period and PEPs also enable dividends to be received tax-free and gains made without a capital gains tax charge. There are a number of National Savings issues which provide tax-free growth and these investments are explained in Chapter 5.

Chapter 7 describes annuities, part of which may be treated as capital and therefore not taxable. For those wishing to give up their capital in exchange for a regular payment for the rest of their lives, annuities can be a tax-efficient way of improving net spendable income.

Investing for capital growth

For those paying income tax at the higher rate, it is more attractive to invest in capital-growth assets, especially if the capital gains tax indexation allowance reduces the effective tax charge. Also, single premium investment bonds shelter the higher rate of tax on any growth in the fund until the bond is cashed. Ten-year with-profit maximum investment plans also provide an income tax shelter in that the fund effectively suffers a tax rate approximately in line with the basic rate of tax and no higher tax charge is incurred if the plan is held for at least seven and a half years.

Other assets, such as works of art, antiques, gold coins and stamps, produce no income but you will need to be professionally advised on the appropriate time to acquire such assets. Investment properties can be structured for capital growth and Chapter 5 illustrates how you could borrow part of the purchase price so that the interest is covered by the rent and no taxable income arises. Equities, unit trusts and commodities could be acquired for capital growth rather than income.

It is more attractive to seek capital growth when tax rates are high. When the top rate of tax was 60 per cent people were less interested in receiving income and more interested in capital growth. Gilts are also more popular as the gain is tax-free.

Maximizing allowances and reliefs

It is common sense to make maximum use of the tax allowances and reliefs – not all of them can be carried over into future years if not used in the current year.

The personal allowance (£3,295 in 1991/2 and £3,445 for 1992/3), to which every taxpayer is entitled regardless of his or her circumstances, is a case in point. Whereas those in work or receiving substantial investment income will have no difficulty here, there will be many non-working spouses whose taxable income will fall short of £3,445. In years before 1990/91, this did not matter where a wife was not working as a wife's investment income was taxed on her husband, but with independent taxation this is no longer the case. A wife, or any other taxpayer, who receives, say, only £2,500 of income in 1991/2, will 'waste' £795 of her personal allowance. This translates into £198.75 of lost tax relief at the basic rate. Some asset-shifting or portfolio rearrangement to provide higher-yielding investments may solve the problem. With the ending of composite rate tax in April 1991, however, the problem of non-reclaimable tax deductions from bank and building society interest has disappeared.

The self-employed or those in business partnerships will sometimes incur losses, particularly during a recession or in the first few years of business. Even if the accounts show a profit, once they have been adjusted for tax purposes, the profit may be converted into a tax loss (where, for example, there has been a heavy equipment purchase). It is important to make use of such a loss in the most tax-efficient way. Detailed discussion of this is beyond the scope of this book, but readers should be aware that a tax loss can be used to get a repayment of income tax for the current or previous year, or be carried forward to reduce the tax payable in future profitable years. From 1991/2 tax losses can also be used to get repayment of capital gains tax, provided that they are first fully applied against taxable income. In the first four years of a business, a loss can be carried back to the three years before the business was set up, to get tax repayment of, say, PAYE paid on employment income in those years. However, this may involve wastage of personal allowances. Professional advice should be taken.

Income shifting

We have briefly covered income shifting between husband and wife in the context of independent taxation (which will be considered in more detail later in this chapter) and **Chart 11.2** illustrates the potential savings.

In the case study in **Chart 11.2**, by transferring the deposits from husband to wife, there is a significant tax saving of almost £5,000 in 1991/2. This is because the personal allowance of the wife is now being fully used so that income of £3,295 is not being taxed rather than being taxed on the husband at 40 per cent. In addition, most of the investment income is being taxed at 25 per cent on the wife rather than at 40 per cent on the husband.

There is little to be gained by parents shifting income to their minor, unmarried children, unless the income from funds provided by any one parent is no more than £100 in any tax year. Accordingly, modest sums of up to approximately £1,000 (assuming a ten per cent gross rate of return) can be given by a parent to a minor child in a tax-effective way. The resulting income can be treated as the child's for tax purposes, and, provided the child's total taxable income is no more than the personal allowance for that year, the child will be able to get a repayment of any tax deducted from the income (eg by a bank or building society). On the other hand, where the income is more than £100, the entire amount will be treated as the income of the parent who provided the funds, and taxed accordingly.

Income-skipping across a generation is possible, however, without any restriction on income received. If a grandparent, aunt, brother or any other relative gives funds to a minor child, the income is the child's for all tax purposes and there is no assessment on the donor. Gifts of capital have capital gains tax and inheritance tax implications, however (see Chapter 15).

Deeds of covenant in favour of children aged 18 and over used to be a widespread way of supplementing students' income. The parent who covenanted a gross amount of £2,000, for example, would actually pay £1,500 and the student could, provided his or her taxable income (which does not include the student grant, which is tax free) did not go over the level of the personal allowance, reclaim the remaining £500 from the Inland Revenue. This still works if the date of the covenant was before 15 March 1988 but new covenants after that date are no longer tax-effective.

Nowadays, very little tax relief is available to payers of maintenance. Anyone paying alimony or maintenance under a court order or separation agreement made after 14 March 1988 qualifies for a maximum deduction of £1,720 only – which translates to £688 of tax at the 40 per cent higher rate. No relief is due for payments made directly to the children. Maintenance payments under agreements or orders going back to earlier days are still

Chart 11.2

	£	£
Taxable earned income of husband	40,000	
Building society deposit interest		
£270,000 say, 10%	27,000	
	67,000	
Tax thereon in 1991/2		
£23,700 at 25% £5,925		
£43,300 at 40% £17,320		
£67,000 23,245		23,245

Transfer of deposits to wife

	Husband	Wife	
	£	£	
Earnings	40,000		
Taxable investment income			
(27,000 – 3,295)		23,705	
Tax £23,700 @ 25%	5,925	5,925	
Balance taxed at 40%	6,520	2	
	12,445	5,927	18,372
Saving			£4,873

relievable in full (but at no more than the 1988/9 level) although now paid gross.

The alternative is to give the former spouse a capital settlement. Any gift of capital on a divorce or separation is exempt from inheritance tax but there is, of course, no income tax relief.

As far as the spouse receiving maintenance is concerned, the fact that the payer is receiving limited relief is good news, as it means that the maintained party is completely exempt from income tax on the amount received (under post-14 March 1988 orders). By contrast, payments made under pre-15 March 1988 orders, for which the payer does still qualify for relief, are taxable in the hands of the maintained party although she (or he) may claim a deduction of up to £1,720 provided by the statute.

Charitable giving

Anyone contemplating donations to charity beyond loose change has every opportunity to make them in a tax-efficient manner, benefitting both the charity and themselves. (See chapter 16 for details.)

INDEPENDENT TAXATION OF HUSBAND AND WIFE

According to the latest information, there are still many taxpayers – married women with a modest amount of investment income in particular – who are not claiming the tax rebates to which they are now entitled, or are not making full use of the planning opportunities independent taxation offers, as illustrated in **Chart 11.2**.

The previous system

Independent taxation was introduced beginning with the tax year 1990/91. Before that time, a married woman's income (and capital gains) was deemed to be her husband's. The husband was assessed on the couple's joint income and was solely responsible for the payment of tax on both incomes. Tax returns were sent to the husband only and he was responsible for supplying details of both his own and his wife's income, gains and expenditure. What is more, the wife was not even entitled to her own personal allowance. The so-called wife's earned income relief could be used (by the husband) only to reduce taxation on the wife's earned income, not on her investment income. It is no exaggeration to say that for income tax purposes, married women were effectively non-persons.

There were two sets of exceptions under which married women could claim some responsibility for their own tax affairs. Under one system, called 'separate taxation', a married woman could choose to receive separate returns and separate assessments in respect of her own income. However, this option did not alter the total tax bill: this was still calculated on the basis of a single, joint liability; all that happened was that personal allowances, etc were split arithmetically in a complicated way between husband and wife to achieve the appropriate split of their joint bill. Because of its complexity and zero end result, this option was chosen by few taxpayers – no more than 10,000 at any one time.

The second option, 'separate taxation of wife's earnings' or 'the wife's earnings election', did alter the total tax payable by a couple. Provided both husband and wife agreed, the wife was treated as if she were a single woman as far as her earned income was concerned. This meant her earnings were taxed separately at her own rates, regardless of her husband's taxable income. However, because the husband had to lose the married man's allowance, this option would actually increase the couple's total tax bill unless their joint income and the wife's earnings were sufficiently high (a minimum of £30,510 and £7,025, respectively, in 1989/90). Even under the election, however, a wife's investment income, no matter how large or small, remained assessable on her husband.

The new system

Independent taxation sweeps away most of these unfairnesses. For the first time in the history of income tax, a married woman is treated as a taxpayer in her own right with her own personal allowance to be used against all her income, whether earned or from investments. Her income is not aggregated with her husband's in any circumstances. A married man no longer receives a married man's allowance but a (single) personal allowance, like his wife. However, to compensate for the loss of the married man's allowance, a married man now receives an additional allowance called the 'married couple's allowance'. Despite its name, it is given to the husband only but, if his taxable income in any tax year is too small to make use of the allowance, he can, if he wishes, transfer the unused part of the allowance to his wife. The wife cannot insist on a transfer nor can she refuse (although there are few circumstances where she might wish to do so).

The married couple's allowance is a modest £1,720. It was originally fixed at the difference between the single person's and the married man's allowance under the old system, so as to compensate exactly for the removal of the married man's allowance.

The 1992 Budget proposes that from 6 April 1993 married couples may choose to allocate the married couple's allowance to one for the other or split the allowance. The wife will have the right to claim half the allowance.

Quite apart from those instances where husbands have few or no earnings of their own, transfers might arise in tax years where a loss from a business reduces the husband's taxable income to a low or zero figure. Older taxpayers receive higher allowances (known as age allowances) and the equivalent of the married couple's allowance for older taxpayers is transferable under the same rules.

Advantages of the new system: non-earning wives

There are two obvious advantages of the new system. First, married women with little or no earnings but a modest amount of investment income can now reduce or eliminate their liability to tax – something they could not do before as their investment income was aggregated with their husband's income and no separate allowance was available. As a result of this, together with the change in the way tax on bank and building society interest is deducted, married women in this position can now claim repayments of tax on their income from savings.

The position in **Chart 11.3** would have been no different had Mrs Ticklerton received £1,200 in dividends from UK companies instead of bank or building society interest. The £400 tax credit attached to the dividends would be repayable by the Inland Revenue.

Recent surveys indicate that there are still many thousands of married women who do not know that they are now in a position to reclaim tax in this way.

Chart 11.3

Mrs Ticklerton stays at home to look after two young children. She has no earnings but receives £1,200 a year in bank and building society interest after tax deduction. In 1991/2, she can claim a tax repayment of £400 as follows:

	£
Bank and building society interest received	1,200
Tax deducted from that interest	
£1,200 × 25/75	400
'Gross income' received	1,600
Personal allowance	3,295
Taxable income	nil
Tax repayable	£400

Advantages of independent taxation: high-earning couples

The second major advance conferred by independent taxation is on those couples who would previously have saved tax by making a wife's earnings election, or those whose income would have fallen just short of making the election worthwhile. In effect, the election is now mandatory for all married couples but there is no loss of allowances for the husband, since he receives the married couple's allowance regardless of his wife's income.

To compare this with the situation had independent taxation not been introduced, let us suppose that the single personal allowance would have been £3,295, the same as the personal allowance in 1991/2. With incomes like these, a wife's earnings election would almost certainly have been made. **Chart 11.5** shows how the figures would have looked.

Mr and Mrs Ullswater are £1,228 better off under independent taxation by simply 'doing nothing'. Planning, however, could lead to greater savings.

Chart 11.4

Mr and Mrs Ullswater are directors of their design company. In 1991/2, he draws a salary of £25,000 and she draws a salary of £20,000 (after deducting contributions to their company pension scheme). Mr Ullswater has a share portfolio and receives £4,800 (tax credit £1,600) in dividends from UK companies whereas Mrs Ullswater has savings with banks and building societies. Her net income from these investments is £2,700 (tax deducted £900). Their tax liability is as follows:

Mr Ullswater	£	Mrs Ullswater	£
Salary	25,000	Salary	20,000
Dividends and tax credits	6,400	Interest (gross)	3,600
	31,400		23,600
Personal allowance	(3,295)	Personal allowance	(3,295)
Married couple's allowance	(1,720)		
Taxable income	£26,385	Taxable income	£20,305
Income tax:			
£23,700 @ 25%	5,925	£20,305 @ 25%	5,076
£2,685 @ 40%	1,074		
Tax payable	£6,999	Tax payable	£5,076
Total joint tax bill	£12,075		

Chart 11.5

Mr Ullswater	£	Mrs Ullswater	£
Salary	25,000	Salary	20,000
Interest (gross)	6,400		
Dividends and tax credits	3,600		
	35,000		
Personal allowance		Personal allowance	
(single)	(3,295)	(single)	(3,295)
Taxable income	£31,705	Taxable income	£16,705
Income tax:			
£23,700 @ 25%	5,925	£16,705 @ 25%	4,176
£8,005 @ 40%	3,202		
	£9,127		£4,176
Total joint tax bill		£13,303	
Saving from independent taxation		£1,228	

Chart 11.2 shows the tax savings which can be achieved by income shifting. If we go back to **Chart 11.4**, we see that £2,685 of Mr Ullswater's income is taxed at 40 per cent, whereas Mrs Ullswater could receive a further £3,395 of taxable income before she would have to start paying tax at 40 per cent. If Mr Ullswater were to transfer the whole of his 'surplus' income of £2,685 to his wife, both of them would stay within the basic rate and so save another £2,685 × 15 per cent – £402.75 of tax. In their case, this could easily be done by one of them transferring shares generating £2,685 (gross).

Suppose that Mr Ullswater transfers a parcel of shares to his wife so that his dividend income falls from £4,800 (net) to £2,786 (net: tax credit £929) and Mrs Ullswater receives £2,014 (tax credit £671). **Chart 11.6** shows what their tax position for 1991/2 would now be.

A transfer of assets between husband and wife is free of capital gains tax – the transferee takes over the asset at a cost equal to the transferor's indexed base cost. Put simply, if an asset cost the husband (or wife) £500 and the indexation factor is £100 at the time of the transfer, the wife (or husband) takes over the asset at a base cost of £600.

For income tax purposes, it is important to remember that the gift of the asset must be unconditional and irrevocable and the title to the asset must pass as well as the right to income. If these conditions are not observed, the income is treated as remaining in the hands of the transferor for all income tax purposes.

As with all tax planning, non-tax considerations must be taken into account. There may be very good reasons why one spouse does not wish, or is unable, to transfer assets to his or her partner, and other tax-planning strategies must then be adopted.

Chart 11.6

Mr Ullswater	£	Mrs Ullswater	£
Salary	25,000	Salary	20,000
Dividends and		Dividends and	
tax credits	3,715	tax credits	2,685
		Interest (gross)	3,600
	28,715		26,285
Personal allowance	(3,295)	Personal allowance	(3,295)
Married couple's allowance	(1,720)		
Taxable income	£23,700	Taxable income	£22,990
Income tax:			
£23,700 @ 25%	5,925	£22,990 @ 25%	5,747
Total joint tax bill		£11,672	
Saving over earlier scenario		£403	

Transferring assets to make use of the personal allowance

An asset transfer from one spouse to another should also be considered where one spouse (usually the wife) has very little or no income. In such a situation, the wife's personal allowance (representing a potential tax repayment of £823.75 at the basic rate in 1991/2 and £861.25 for 1992/3) is effectively going to waste while the husband is needlessly paying tax at 25 per cent, or even higher, on his income. Also, use of the new 20 per cent tax band for income up to £2,000 as proposed in the 1992 Budget could save a further £100 per annum. If some assets were transferred to the wife, the husband's tax bill would fall whereas the wife would have zero liability on the same income; where it was paid under deduction of tax (eg bank and building society interest, government securities or company loan stock) or with a tax credit (UK company dividends) she could claim a tax repayment.

The maximum tax a couple could save in this way in 1991/2 would have been by transferring the full £3,295 of income to a wife who previously had taxable income of zero by a husband on whom the income would all have

---

Chart 11.7

	£	£
Taxable income of Mr Vickers in 1991/2	26,000	
Tax payable		6,845
Transfer of assets worth £30,000 producing		
10% income to wife		
Revised taxable income of Mr Vickers	23,000	
Tax thereon		5,750
Income of wife	3,000	
Personal allowance	(3,295)	
Tax due		nil
Saving		£1,095

---

been taxed at 40 per cent. The saving would then be £3,295 × 40 per cent – £1,318.

INDEPENDENT TAXATION AND CAPITAL GAINS

Independent taxation has also changed the way married couples are treated for capital gains tax purposes. The changes are twofold – husbands and wives are now each entitled to an annual exemption (£5,800 in 1992/3), whereas previously they had to share one annual exemption between them, but losses by one spouse can no longer be claimed by the other.

Although a husband and wife are now treated as separate taxpayers, there has been no change in the rule that transfers of assets between husband and wife are free of capital gains tax. Clearly, if the assets that a couple want to sell are going to realize a gain of, say, £11,600, and are in the name of one spouse only, the capital gains tax payable may be as much as £5,800 × 40 per cent – £2,320. If some of the assets are transferred to the other partner, however, and both realize a gain of £5,800, the tax payable is nil.

Care must be taken here. The partner transferring the assets must on no account make it a condition of the transfer that they be sold, for example. The partner receiving the assets must be at full liberty to do what he or she wants with the assets. The transfer should not take place immediately before the sale.

A transfer of assets is also the way to overcome the bar on using your wife's or husband's losses. If a husband's gains, for example, stand at £11,600 and the wife has assets that would realize a loss of £6,000 on sale, a transfer of assets to the husband before sale could bring the husband's net gains for the year to below the annual exemption and so free them of tax. Of course, the transfer should only be made where the wife/husband does not have a superior need for the assets or the loss herself/himself. And, as we have said before, a transfer of assets should only be made if other non-tax considerations allow it. Future plans and requirements must not be lost sight of and this should all be done as part of a coordinated financial planning strategy.

INDEPENDENT TAXATION AND INHERITANCE TAX

Any transfer of assets undertaken for income tax or capital gains tax planning reasons alters the balance of both the transferor's and the transferee's estates and, as a consequence, their inheritance tax profile. This emphasizes the need to always bear in mind the overall effect of a planning exercise – dealing with one tax can lead to problems with other taxes.

Inheritance tax is considered in detail in Chapter 15, but it should be said here that independent taxation has had no effect on inheritance tax rules. Husbands and wives have always been considered as separate taxpayers for inheritance (and before it, capital transfer) tax purposes.

CAPITAL GAINS TAX PLANNING

As with income tax, an important part of capital gains tax planning lies in making full use of the available exemptions and reliefs. For those in business, retirement relief is particularly valuable and can completely exempt as much as £375,000 of capital gains.

The annual exemption

The most important exemption available to all taxpayers is the annual exemption, the level of which, currently to be £5,800, is indexed (although the government can, and does, override the indexation from time to time). Thus, if a person makes £3,000 of net gains in 1992/3, no capital gains tax is payable, as the gains fall fully within the exemption. If, on the other hand, a person makes £7,000 of net gains, capital gains tax is payable by him/her on only £1,200 (£7,000–5,800).

Husbands and wives are each entitled to their own annual exemption, so a married couple could make £11,600 of gains in 1992/3 free of tax.

The rules also help with capital losses brought forward from previous years so that the annual exemption is not wasted. However, unlike the annual exemption for inheritance tax, the capital gains tax annual exemption cannot be carried forward. The person who makes £3,000 of net gains in 1992/3 has not used £2,800 of his annual exemption. This amount is lost and cannot be carried forward to add to next year's exemption. The current year's losses must be used in full in netting off against the current year's gains.

Bed and breakfasting

One of the commonest techniques of capital gains tax planning is 'bed and breakfasting' – selling shares and then buying them back (or more properly, buying an identical number of the same shares) shortly afterwards. This is done both to realize a gain or a loss without permanently disposing of an asset and to establish a new base cost.

For example, if you have shares standing at a gain near the end of the tax year and net gains to date are well below your annual exemption, those shares could be bed and breakfasted without a tax penalty, at a cost of the broker's fee (inclusive of VAT) and 0.5 per cent stamp duty. Provided the gain realized still falls within your annual exemption, no capital gains tax will be payable and a new, higher base cost of the shares is established for future disposals.

Similarly, if net gains to date are above the annual exemption, and some shares are standing at a loss, some of the loss-bearing shares could be bed and breakfasted, bringing net gains down below the annual exemption. Of course, if a loss is realized, the new base cost of the shares is lower than the original. As always, a balance must be found between the advantages of the immediate transaction and your long-term aims.

Chart 11.8

	£	£
Year 1		
Proceeds from sale of 7,800 shares, say	7,800	
Base cost, say	2,000	
Gain		5,800
Annual exemption		(5,800)
Year 2		
Proceeds from sale of 15,000 shares, say	15,600	
Base cost of original holding	(2,000)	
Base cost of new holding	(7,800)	
	5,800	
Annual exemption	(5,800)	

Bed and breakfasting techniques could equally be used for straightforward disposals. Full use of the annual exemption and strategic loss-realization can as well be made by permanently disposing of the appropriate assets (which need not then be limited to tangible assets in which a ready market for repurchase of an equivalent holding exists). With a permanent disposal, however, it is even more important to decide whether selling an asset at a loss now is preferable to keeping it in the expectation or hope that it will appreciate in value.

Retirement relief

Retirement relief is very valuable for the self-employed. Although it is available only to those aged 55 or over (unless retiring because of ill health), the relief does not actually depend on retirement (except in the special ill health case). Any individual who otherwise qualifies will receive the relief whenever he or she disposes of a shareholding in the family company or of a part of his/her unincorporated business. It is even available in certain circumstances on the sale of an asset used in such a business.

The detailed rules are complicated but the essentials are as follows:

- Except in the case of ill health, you must be 55 or over

- You must be disposing (by sale or gift) of all or part of your interest in a business (if you are a sole trader or partner) or of shares in your family company (a company is an individual's family company where he or she holds at least 25 per cent of the shares or he/she and his/her family hold more than 50 per cent)

- You must have owned that interest or held those shares for at least one year ending with the disposal. Maximum relief is obtained after ten years of ownership

- In the case of shares in a family company, you must have been a full-time working director and the company must be a 'trading company' or the holding company of a 'trading group'

- In the case of ill health, you need not be 55 but there must be medical evidence to prove that the state of your health makes you permanently incapable of the sort of work from which you are retiring.

The first £150,000 of a qualifying gain is completely exempt, together with one half of the next £450,000. Clearly, since only part of a business needs to be sold to attract retirement relief, it is possible to qualify for the relief on several disposals in relation to the same business, but any previous relief is taken into account so that it is never possible to get more than the maximum, ie £375,000.

This maximum is available only where you have owned the business or the shares for at least ten years. In some circumstances, it is possible to add on periods of ownership of other businesses, as long as you have owned the interest or shares in the current business for a continuous period of at least one year ending with the disposal. Where the period, as made up in this way, is still less than ten years, the maximum exemption is reduced in proportion. So, where the period of ownership is nine years, nine-tenths of the maximum relief is available; for eight years, eight-tenths etc.

In the case of shares in a family company, the relief is additionally restricted if the company has assets in its balance sheet which are chargeable to capital gains tax but are not used directly in the business (eg investment property or portfolio shareholdings). For this reason, it is useful to realize such investments and convert them into cash used for trading purposes before any disposal of shares.

Because a husband and wife both qualify for retirement relief separately they could double the amount of relief otherwise available if both spouses are full-time working directors.

Chart 11.9

Mr Black makes a gain of £235,000 on selling his business, which he set up 7.5 years ago. He qualifies for retirement relief. The exemption is calculated as follows:

£150,000 × 75% × 100%	£112,500
£122,500 × 50%	£61,250
Exempt gain	£173,750
Gain chargeable to tax	£61,250

How to use capital losses

Realizing a loss for capital gains tax purposes when you dispose of an asset is by no means unusual, especially since what would otherwise be a gain on paper can be transformed into a loss by the indexation allowance, which is linked to the RPI.

It is worth discussing briefly how best to use these losses, although the room for manoeuvre is in fact quite limited.

In the first place, there is no choice. Any losses realized in one tax year must first be aggregated with any gains of that year to produce a net total of taxable gains, even if this is less than the annual exemption (currently to be £5,800). What if there is an overall net loss?

Unlike income tax losses from a business, a net capital gains tax loss cannot be carried back to previous years, except on death. It must be carried forward to future years. Nor can the net loss of a husband be set against net gains of his wife, or vice versa (this could be done until the introduction of independent taxation in 1990/91).

Once a net loss has been brought forward from a previous year, its treatment is a little more generous. First, losses can be carried forward indefinitely, so there is no need for rules to determine to which year a brought-forward loss belongs. Second, once the current year's losses have been used to reduce the current year's gains and there is still a positive balance of net gains, losses brought forward may be used to reduce the net gains still further, but only to the extent necessary to bring the reduced total to the value of the annual exemption. This ensures that, unlike the current year's losses, losses brought forward are not used needlessly.

Chart 11.10

	£000
Proceeds 1991/2	100
Base cost	(80)
	20
Indexational allowance since 1982, say, 70%	(56)
Capital loss	36

Chart 11.11

Thomas has made net gains of £9,350 in the tax year 1991/2. He has losses brought forward of £5,600. His capital gains tax liability for 1991/2 is as follows:

	£
Net gains for year	9,350
Losses brought forward (part)	3,850
	5,500
Annual exemption	5,500
Gains chargeable to tax	nil
Losses brought forward to 1991/2	5,600
Losses used in 1991/2	3,850
Losses carried forward to 1992/3	£1,750

We have already seen how assets standing at a loss can, where necessary, be realized (bed and breakfasted) to bring net gains for the year down to the level of the annual exemption.

It should be noted that where gains from the sale of an asset are exempt from capital gains tax (government securities and certain company bonds, for example), any losses are not allowable – that is, they cannot be used to reduce gains and are effectively ignored for all tax purposes. The same goes for the first disposal of any BES shares. However, BES shares may qualify for a special relief for losses on shares in unquoted trading companies. This type of loss is remarkable in capital gains tax terms in that it is one of the few examples where a capital gains tax loss can be used to reduce taxable income for *income tax* purposes. The rules are complicated so professional advice is necesssary.

12

INTERNATIONAL TAX PLANNING

RESIDENCE – WHAT DOES IT MEAN?

The UK tax system, as it applies to foreign income and foreign nationals, is based on the concept of residence, like that of most other nations (but not all – US citizens, for example, remain subject to US income tax wherever they may be living). However, there is also a related, but separate, concept of *domicile*, which is of importance for income tax and capital gains tax, and the deciding factor for inheritance tax. Briefly, UK income tax is chargeable on:

- the worldwide income of UK residents and
- the UK income of non-UK residents.

UK capital gains tax is chargeable on the worldwide gains of UK residents but non-UK residents are exempt from capital gains unless they carry on a business here.

As you might expect, however, things are a little more complicated than this. Although residence, for example, is central to determining the tax charge, there is actually no definition of the concept in tax legislation and there is a further concept, not defined either, of 'ordinary residence', to consider.

Very broadly, residence, ordinary residence and domicile can be thought of as the same idea, associated with increasing long-term behaviour. Thus, residence is a purely physical concept, changing from year to year; ordinary residence involves habit and can only be determined for each year by looking at a number of years together; domicile is associated with an individual's permanent intention to settle and goes beyond the grave!

(Further details of residence are set out in Appendix 9; of domicile in Appendix 10.)

DOMICILE

At the time of writing, there are proposals to change the position regarding domicile. It is proposed that there will no longer be a domicile of *origin* so that, for example, if a woman was born in Egypt but has been living in the UK for some years, she may have contended that she has retained the domicile of origin and has not acquired a domicile of choice in the UK. If the domicile of origin is abolished, this will mean that she is more likely to be treated as being domiciled in the UK unless she can show that she is not likely to stay in the UK long-term. It is therefore more likely that people who have been treated as non-domiciled in the UK but have been living here for many years, may find that the Inland Revenue will review their domicile position and this could lead to a change in their domicile status for UK tax purposes. Advice on this matter should be urgently sought.

Domicile can play a very important role in income tax and capital gains tax as an individual who is UK-resident but not domiciled in the UK is only taxed on foreign income that arises after he or she becomes resident if it is remitted here; and all individuals who are resident but not domiciled in the UK pay no capital gains tax on disposals of assets situated abroad unless the proceeds are remitted here.

Domicile is also a key factor in determining liability to inheritance tax. A person domiciled in the UK is liable to inheritance tax in respect of his or her worldwide estate whereas a person domiciled elsewhere is liable only on the estate or assets located in the UK. A person is deemed to be domiciled in the UK if he or she has been resident in this country for 17 of the last 20 years.

RESIDENCE AND DOMICILE – THE EFFECT ON UK TAX LIABILITY

The parts played by residence ('R'), ordinary residence ('OR') and domicile ('D') in determining liability to UK income tax, capital gains tax and inheritance tax are summarized in **Chart 12.1**.

TAX PLANNING FOR A NON-DOMICILED PERSON

If you are non-domiciled, then by transferring capital abroad, you could defer a significant income tax charge.

If a non-domiciled person retains cash deposits in the UK, then the income will normally be subject to UK income tax, assuming that that person is resident in the UK. **Chart 12.2** shows that £8,000 of tax would be paid leaving £12,000 to be used for spending purposes. However, if a non-domiciled person transfers the deposit to, say, a Jersey bank deposit account, the income can then be credited to a separate account. So long as any withdrawals to the UK are made from the capital account (Account No. 1 in **Chart 12.2**) no tax will be payable. This is because the income has not been remitted.

It is important to separate capital from income. If only one account is held and all the interest is credited to that account, the Inland Revenue will treat any withdrawals to the UK as remittances of income. However, if separate accounts are set up with income retained in a separate account, then the tax deferral of £8,000 a year as shown in **Chart 12.2** can be achieved until the capital account is exhausted. It is even possible to continue the tax deferral thereafter by careful planning.

If a non-domiciled but UK-resident person has UK assets, the sale of those assets could give rise to a capital gains tax charge. It is possible to convert those UK assets into non-UK assets by, for example, the use of bearer shares or certain other techniques involving trusts. The sale of a non-UK asset owned by an offshore trust may not give rise to a capital gains tax charge.

For inheritance tax purposes, there will be no charge on non-UK assets. Again, by converting UK assets into overseas assets, UK inheritance tax savings could be made. It may be appropriate to transfer those assets into a

Chart 12.1

Tax	R & OR & D R or OR & D	D but not R	R & OR but not D	Neither D, R or OR
Income tax (1)	worldwide income	UK source income only	UK income and foreign income remitted	UK source only
Capital gains tax	gains on worldwide assets	UK situated assets of UK business only	UK gains and foreign gains remitted	UK situated assets of UK business only
Inheritance tax	worldwide estate	worldwide estate	UK estate only	UK estate only

Note: (1) The income tax rules are more complicated than shown here. Individuals who are resident but not ordinarily resident may qualify for beneficial treatment.

```
                    Chart 12.2  Non-domiciled person

                                           £000        £000
  UK deposit amount                         200

  Interest at, say, 10%                       20
  Tax at, say, 40%                            (8)         8
  Income used for spending                    12

  Transfer of UK deposit abroad
  Jersey deposit account (Account No 1)      200
  Interest retained abroad (Account No 2)     20
  Transfer to UK from Account No 1            12
  Tax due                                                NIL
  Tax deferred                                             8
```

non–UK trust so as to protect the position if you are shortly likely to be deemed domiciled (ie because you will have lived in the UK for 17 of the last 20 years). You will need to carefully consider the capital gains tax ramifications of such action and professional advice should be taken before any planning arrangement is effected. However, the savings can be substantial.

OFFSHORE TRUSTS

Before 18 March 1991, the use of offshore trusts (or UK trusts which subsequently became offshore trusts) could mean significant tax savings for people who are UK-resident and domiciled. Many UK residents are not willing to export themselves but may be willing to export their trust while they remain in the UK. However, the new legislation has restricted the use of offshore trusts for this purpose.

For non-UK domiciled individuals and non-residents, offshore trusts may still be very attractive. Many people who are coming to the UK may be advised to set up a trust before setting foot in the UK. This is so that future income, capital gains and inheritance tax may be deferred or avoided. Again professional advice should be taken. Too often, planning is undertaken when in the UK – by which time it may be too late.

Before 18 March 1991, many UK residents and domiciled individuals transferred assets into an overseas trust in which their children are the beneficiaries. While this is no longer tax-efficient, it may be appropriate for a

UK individual to set up an offshore trust for the benefit of, for example, minor grandchildren.

If you have set up an offshore trust under the pre-March 1991 system, you will need to be careful about any payments out of that trust. If the trust has been set up for your benefit so that you are the life tenant, any income is likely to be taxable upon you as if you had received it personally. For that reason, you may wish to withdraw the income from the trust and spend it in the UK. If capital gains have been made by the offshore trust these gains may be tax-deferred under the old legislation, so you will suffer a capital gains tax charge if a capital payment is received by you from the trust. Capital payments can arise if the offshore trust acquires a home for your benefit – unless you pay a market rent to the trust for the use of the home, but this would be taxable on the settlor. This is not usually advisable.

In addition, there is now a 'parking charge'. This is similar to an interest charge in that if you receive a capital payment after 5 April 1992 in respect of a pre-March 1991 trust, the Inland Revenue can increase the tax charge by ten per cent a year for up to six years. You will need to consider this carefully if you plan to take any large capital sums out of the trust in the future. However, your offshore trust can reinvest in capital assets and defer capital gains on future disposals.

BEARER SHARES

Not very common in the UK, these are shares in which ownership passes simply by transfer and does not depend on an entry in a register of shareholders. The share certificate itself is proof of title, rather like a £5 note (where the Bank of England promises to pay the bearer the sum of £5).

The usefulness of bearer shares is that for tax purposes, they are regarded as situated where the share certificate is situated (ie with its owner), whereas non-bearer shares are situated where the share register is kept, ie in the country where the company has its registered office.

Bearer shares held outside the UK are non-UK property, even if they represent the share capital of a UK-resident company. They will be exempt from inheritance tax if comprised in a non-domiciled individual's offshore trust and their sale by a non-UK domiciliary will be free from capital gains tax as long as the proceeds are not remitted to the UK.

Bearer shares can be used to relocate UK business assets out of the UK and so out of the inheritance tax and capital gains tax net. Suppose a non-UK domiciliary owns a UK-resident company. Bearer shares with full voting rights and control can be created and transferred into the hands of the overseas trustees of an offshore trust set up by the non-UK domiciliary. What was previously a UK-situated asset, subject to inheritance tax and capital gains tax, thus becomes a foreign asset, which can be gifted or sold without incurring a liability to either tax.

INHERITANCE TAX PLANNING

As we have seen, a liability to inheritance tax is determined by domicile and not residence. From the inheritance tax point of view alone, therefore, there is no advantage to be gained for a UK-domiciled individual from placing or acquiring assets abroad. The same goes for establishing an offshore trust. Overseas property that is part of an offshore trust created by a UK-domiciled individual and to which a UK-domiciled individual is beneficially entitled is as much a part of his or her estate as UK-situated property in a UK-resident trust.

However, if an overseas trust is created by an individual who is not UK-domiciled at that time, any overseas property of that trust is exempt from inheritance tax, whatever the domicile or residence status of the beneficiaries. This is especially important if you are likely to become UK-domiciled for inheritance tax purposes because, for example, you have lived in the UK for 16 of the last 17 years. The UK property of an offshore trust is not exempt, whether the trust was set up by a foreign domiciliary or a UK domiciliary. However, a non-UK company owning a UK property may avoid the UK inheritance tax charge but there may be other UK tax implications to consider such as income tax and capital gains tax if the property is your home, so this plan of action may be unwise.

An individual who has been resident in the UK for 17 of the last 20 years is deemed to be domiciled here for inheritance tax purposes, regardless of his or her actual domicile. It would therefore be helpful for a non-domiciled individual who is approaching 17 years' residence here to set up an offshore trust to shelter his/her foreign property from inheritance tax.

EMIGRATION

Many UK residents may now be searching for ways in which they can defer or avoid UK capital gains tax on the sale of, for example, their family business. In the past, the use of UK and offshore trusts have provided the answer, but this route is no longer available.

It may be possible to transfer shares to an offshore company within an appropriate tax jurisdiction. However, the Inland Revenue is likely to challenge the residence of the company. Simply setting up a company outside the UK does not necessarily mean that it will not be taxed as a UK-resident company. If board meetings are held in the UK, even informal ones, and the company is effectively run from the UK, then it is likely to be held to be resident in this country. However, if you travel abroad and transact business outside the UK, it may be possible to set up a non-UK company to hold the shares in your UK trading company.

Some people have avoided paying capital gains tax by emigrating before they sell their UK assets. If you are not resident nor ordinarily resident in the UK when you sell, for example, shares in your trading company, then no capital gains tax will be payable. You may wish to incorporate an unincorporated business prior to emigrating. Of course, you would need to consider the country of residence when the sale is made: if you emigrate to America, you may avoid UK capital gains tax but pay tax on the gain in America. Therefore you will need to emigrate to a country with an appropriate tax system.

It is not an easy matter to become non-resident and not ordinarily resident in the UK. It is normally advisable to remain outside the UK throughout the entire year in which you dispose of your shares. For example, assuming that you are not working abroad full-time and have no available accommodation if you leave the UK in March 1993, you should not set foot in the UK during 1993/4 when the gain is made. You should not return to the UK for much more than a few weeks in the following tax year and your return trips to the UK should not be more than a month or two in the following tax year. Therefore, you should primarily remain outside the UK for three tax years before contemplating a return to the UK. Different and more beneficial rules may apply if you are working abroad full time.

The Inland Revenue is likely to look closely at your return trips. If you leave the UK for one complete tax year but then return for, say, 300 days in the following tax year, the Inland Revenue may not accept that you have become not ordinarily resident in the UK.

You should also have sold or let UK property. If you return to your home and stay there for *one day* during the year, you can still be held to be UK-resident!

In many cases emotional and family ties make emigration an unworkable solution. While the tax involved may be substantial, you may be miserable living abroad, away from your family and friends.

Strangely, while UK income tax rates have been relatively low, there has been an advantage in structuring a sale of shares in a manner which attracts income tax rather than capital gains tax. The tax charge can effectively be reduced to 20 per cent as shown by **Chart 12.3**.

In the case study in **Chart 12.3**, if the shares have a base cost of £100,000, a sale of £750,000 would attract capital gains tax of £260,000, leaving net proceeds of £490,000.

If, instead, a dividend of £750,000 net of basic-rate tax is received, the company would need to pay ACT (Advance Corporation Tax) of £250,000

	£000	£000
Chart 12.3		
Sale of shares	750	750
Base cost, say	(100)	
Capital gains	650	
Capital gains tax at, say, 40% (ignoring annual exemption)		260
		490
Dividend	750	750
ACT payable by company	250	
	1,000	
Higher-rate tax @ 15%		(150)
		600
Benefit		110

but it may be able to set this payment against its mainstream liability for that year and possibly set the payment against the corporation tax which has been paid in the last six years. Therefore, the payment of ACT may be a cash flow problem only. The ACT payment would need to be made 14 days after the normal quarter date and it may take nine months to a year to recover the tax. However, you would be deemed to have received a gross dividend of £1m and based upon a higher-rate income tax charge of 15 per cent, your net receipt would be £600,000, a benefit of £110,000.

You could structure the sale so that you take a large dividend from the company to reduce the effective tax rate to 20 per cent (as the tax charge in **Chart 12.3** of £150,000 on a net dividend of £750,000 represents an effective rate of 20 per cent). The balance of the proceeds could then be taken as capital so that you could take advantage of the base cost of the shares, the indexation allowance, retirement relief, annual exemptions, etc.

The position could be improved further if some of the shares were held by a UK life interest trust. If the shares were to be acquired under certain circumstances the receipt by the trust would be capital under trust law and it might be possible to avoid the higher-rate tax charge. However, at the time of writing, a consultative document has been published on the taxation of trusts and it is likely that legislation will be introduced to charge such payments to the higher rate of income tax. Indeed, under current legislation, it is possible that a capital loss could be created by this buy-back arrangement.

If you are contemplating a sale of your company, there are many other matters which would need to be considered in advance of the sale, such as the possible use of a pension scheme.

The matters covered in this chapter are very complicated and professional advice should be taken at all times.

13

THE PRIVATE COMPANY

A number of issues apply to private companies which do not necessarily relate to large quoted companies. Many of the private companies in the UK are family controlled in that over 50 per cent of their shares are held by members of one or possibly two families. Family issues can often have a significant impact upon the way in which private companies are run. (The different strengths and weaknesses of family firms are fully described in *The Stoy Hayward Guide To The Family Business*.) Family businesses often display a number of good characteristics, including the following:

- Commitment
- Knowledge
- Flexibility of time, work, money
- Long-range thinking
- A stable culture
- Speedy decision-making
- Reliability and pride

Unfortunately, they also have certain pitfalls:

- Rigidity
- Business challenges, eg modernizing outdated skills, managing transition and raising capital
- Succession
- Emotional issues
- Leadership and legitimacy

Chart 13.1 is the family tree of the Brown family. You can see that the founder of the Brown family business was John. He arranged for certain shares to be held by Juliette, his sister, as her husband was originally in the business but died some years ago.

The business is now being carried on by Gordon. Gordon is divorced from Mary and is now living with his second wife, Lisa. You will see that there are three children from the marriage of Gordon and Mary and both Andrew and Robin are in the business but Susan, his daughter, and her husband Charles are not involved in the business.

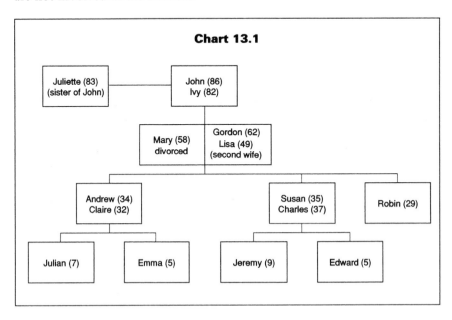

Chart 13.1

Gordon is the driving force behind the company which he controls, and minority shareholding interests are held by his mother, father and aunt, as follows:

Shareholding in Brown Ltd	Ordinary £1 shares
John	8
Ivy	8
Juliette	8
Gordon	76
	100

It is important that the Brown family establishes what each members wants to do regarding the company. For example, Gordon may wish to pass the business down to his two sons but his wife may be more interested in selling the company. Indeed, a sale may be worthy of consideration because if the family could obtain, say, £1m after tax, this could ensure that all the family were well-protected. Gordon could retire, but what would become of his two sons? They may be at different stages of their business development. In this case the older son has taken the lead and may be the ultimate successor while Robin may still need to prove himself.

COMPANY VALUATION

It is easy to value the shares of a quoted company. You simply check the share price in the *Financial Times* and apply it to the number of shares held. However, shares in a private company are much more difficult to value. You will often find two different parties coming out with two or even more values for the same shareholding. **Chart 13.2** is a highly simplified valuation.

It is normal to value a controlling interest on an assets basis although many trading companies tend to be valued on an earnings basis. Certainly if you are valuing a minority shareholding interest, then the earnings basis may be more relevant. If the company has been paying dividends, then the dividends basis of valuation may be used. However, for illustrative purposes, you will see that if the maintainable post-tax profit is £200,000 and if an appropriate price/earnings ratio is 8, in respect of a company in the same sector, then the value of the company would be £1.6m. If the net assets are £1.2m and goodwill is taken as twice the post-tax profit, then the asset value gives the same result. In many cases the asset and earnings bases provide very different values and it is then important to establish the more appropriate basis to be used in respect of the company and shareholding to be valued.

VALUATION OF SHAREHOLDINGS

Having established that Gordon wishes to seek a successor for the family

Chart 13.2 *Valuation of Brown Ltd*	
	£000
Maintainable profit	300
Less Corporation tax at, say, 33%	(100)
	200
Value on earnings basis	
Price/earnings ratio of, say, 8	1,600
Value on assets basis	
Net assets, say	1,200
Add Goodwill, say, twice post-tax profits	400
	1,600

business, it is necessary to value the individual shareholdings.

Chart 13.3 *Valuation of shareholdings*

	Holding %	Value of company £000	Discount £	Discounted value £000	Inheritance tax relief %	Inheritance tax value £000
John	(8)	128	(50)	64	(30)	45
Ivy	(8)	128	(50)	64	(30)	45
Juliete	(8)	128	(50)	64	(30)	45
Gordon	(76)	1,216	(15)	1,034	(50)	517
	(100)	1,600				

You can see from **Chart 13.3** that John, Ivy and Juliette each hold eight per cent of the shares of the company. On an arithmetical basis this would provide a value of £128,000. However, it would be normal to discount that shareholding by around 50 per cent as they each hold a small minority shareholding interest and cannot have a significant influence in the direction of the company. For example, if Gordon was to pay a significant bonus to himself and his other working directors, this could reduce the profitability of the company. Gordon could also decide on the dividend policy and whether the company should be sold at some time in the future. Although minorities have certain rights, they are clearly in a poor negotiating position and so a larger discount would normally be applied to these holdings. Therefore the discounted value could be £64,000 and if you assume that inheritance tax business property relief is received at 30 per cent of the value, then the value for inheritance tax purposes is £45,000.

Gordon's 76 per cent shareholding interest would be arithmetically valued at £1.216m. The discount applied to his holding would be much less as he controls the company and the discounted value could be just over £1m. He could get 50 per cent business property relief (assuming the company does not contain any investments and is a trading company). Therefore, for inheritance tax purposes, his shares could be valued at £517,000. The 1992 Budget proposals increase inheritance tax relief to 100 per cent for Gordon and 50 per cent for the other family members.

OUTSIDE SHAREHOLDERS

Shares are often held by non-working members of the family. Often, these shareholders wish to retain the shares for emotional purposes but if no

167

dividends are being paid, they are little more than paper in practical terms, though they still attract inheritance tax.

It may be more appropriate for all concerned for the minority shareholders to be bought out, giving them cash which can more usefully be used to produce income during their lives, and so that their holding does not create difficulties if the company becomes more profitable. For example, if Andrew and Robin are to take over the company and make it more profitable, they may be upset to know that part of the increase in value of the company will be going to members of the family who have not contributed to that growth.

In this case study, it has been decided that the grandparents and aunt should be bought out. It is quite likely that neither Gordon nor his sons would not have the capital to buy out the shares so the shares may need to be bought out by the company.

The shares can be acquired using an Inland Revenue approved arrangement so long as certain conditions are met. This will mean that the purchase is subject to capital gains tax and there are no further tax implications on the company. However, it will be necessary to show that the purchase is required for the benefit of the trade and tax clearances may be submitted to the Inland Revenue for confirmation that they are satisfied that the purchases are being carried out for *bona fide* trading purposes. If the purchase is merely to put cash into the hands of the grandparents, this will not be sufficient. However, grandfather is still working for the company, and he may have different views on trading matters. This could be a stumbling block and it may be better to buy in the shares and remove the grandfather as a director if this is having a bad effect on the trading of the company. **Chart 13.4** shows the taxation ramifications based upon higher–rate income tax.

You can see from **Chart 13.4** that the base cost and indexation represents 30 per cent of the value of the shares, so that there will be a gain of £45,000 which, after taking account of the annual exemption, produces a taxable gain of £40,000. If John is paying tax at the higher rate of 40 per cent, then tax of £16,000 will be payable. Of course part of the gain may be taxed at the basic rate thereby giving rise to a lower tax charge and, in many cases, the base cost will be greater.

The alternative method of buying the shares is under an unapproved method if it has, or can create, sufficient reserves. If certain of the relevant conditions are not satisfied, then the purchase of shares will be treated like a dividend. Therefore the payment of £64,000 will be treated as a net dividend and the company will need to pay ACT of £21,000. It may be able to set this against its mainstream liability for the current year and possibly carry back the payment for the previous six years, but there would be a cashflow disadvantage to this in that the ACT is payable and the relief is obtained at a later date. However, the total tax charge may be reduced as John will pay

---

Chart 13.4 *Share purchase: John*

Approved route

Value of shares	64	
Base cost and indexation allowance (say, 30%)	(19)	
	45	
Annual capital gains tax exemption	(5)	
Taxable gain	40	
Capital gains tax, say, 40%		16

Unapproved Route

Distribution	64	
ACT	21	
Gross distribution	85	
Tax at 15%		13

Ivy and Juliette as above

Note: this assumes no retirement relief

---

only the higher rate of tax on the gross equivalent distribution. In the previous chapter we examined how the buy-back could be carried out using trusts and further reduce the tax payable.

RETIREMENT OF GORDON

It is necessary at this point to examine the pension scheme. In some cases, it has been necessary for companies to top up the pension scheme over a period until it will provide a level of income which, together with cash received from the company on retirement, will provide financial security.

The cash sum payable by the company on retirement may arise through the purchase of Gordon's shares. Gordon and his sons may have different views on the future of the company. The father (who has been in control of the company for many years) may be more cautious, while the children have a different approach.

If it is appropriate for the shares to be bought by the company using the approved method, then the tax charge can be reduced. You will see from **Chart 13.5** that Gordon is happy to gift 36 per cent of his shares in the company and hold 40 per cent so that he still retains more shares than his sons. It is necessary to consider the inheritance tax implications of this gift,

and to do this we must value the shareholding both before and after the gift –
the difference is the value transferred.

		Chart 13.5 *Gordon*				
		Arithmetic value £000	Discount %	Value for inheritance tax £000	Business property relief £000	Net transfer £000
Current holding	76%	1,216	(15)	1,034	(517)	517
Retained holding	40%	640	(30)	448	(224)	224
Gift	36%					293

This case study assumes that the minority interest shares have not yet been
acquired but that Gordon is happy to gift part of his shareholding. He
currently holds 76 per cent of the company's shares and the discounted value
is just over £1m. If he reduces his holding to 40 per cent, he will no longer
control the company and a larger discount may be appropriate. Assuming a
discount of 30 per cent, his shareholding would be valued at £448,000. The
gift should attract business property relief so the gift for inheritance tax
would be just under £300,000. If the Budget proposals are enacted, 100 per
cent relief may be available to Gordon for the gift so that the gift would be
fully exempt.

It is necessary to consider whether Gordon is happy to gift the shares
directly to the sons, especially if they have not yet proven themselves in the
business. He may also wish to effectively control the voting rights of the
shares while ensuring that they are passed outside his estate and into the
estates of his sons by using a trust.

An alternative course of action would be to set up a grandchildren's trust
and start to skip a generation by passing shares in trust for the youngest
children. However, these are still very young and Gordon may feel that most
of the shares should be passed down to his children.

CURRENT FINANCIAL POSITION

Chart 13.6 shows the current financial position of Gordon and his wife.

Chart 13.6 *Current position*	
	£000
House	250
Cash deposits	50
Shares in family company	1,034
	1,334
Business property relief	(517)
	817
Nil rate band (as per 1992 Budget proposal)	(150)
Taxable estate	667
Inheritance tax at 40%	267

The Browns live in a home worth £250,000 and the mortgage has been fully repaid. They have some cash deposits but the bulk of their wealth is tied up in the family company. Prior to any gifts, there is likely to be inheritance tax of around £267,000 after taking account of 50 per cent business property relief and a nil rate band (on the assumption that the wills of Gordon and Lisa leave everything to each other). If the Budget proposals are enacted, the charge falls to only £60,000 due to full business property relief.

At this point, it is worthwhile considering Gordon's marital position. He is divorced from his first wife and his current wife Lisa is much younger than him and may not necessarily get on well with his children. If he were to die suddenly, there is the possibility of his wife remarrying, so if he passes wealth into his wife's hands it may not find its way to his children. For this reason, it may be advisable for him to rewrite his will so that his assets are left in trust for his wife so that she gets income during her lifetime with the capital then passing to his children on her death.

PURCHASE OF GORDON'S SHARES

It is now assumed that Gordon made the gifts some years ago and some of the shares have been transferred out of the trust to his sons. Also the shares of the minority interest shareholders have been acquired. Gordon now wishes to retire and would prefer to receive cash for his shares so that he can leave his sons to run the business without any interference from him.

Chart 13.7 below again looks at the different ways in which the shares could be bought in by the company.

Chart 13.7 *Sale of retained holding*		
Approved route	*£000*	*£000*
Value of shares purchased	448	
Base cost and indexation allowance at, say, 30%	(134)	
	314	
Retirement relief	(150)	
	164	
Tax at 20% (ignoring annual exemption)		33
Unapproved purchase		
Distribution	448	
ACT	149	
Gross distribution	597	
Higher rate at 15%		90

The alternatives in **Chart 13.7** are not the only ones but you will see that the approved purchase may be more attractive as retirement relief may be available if Gordon has been a full-time working director for over ten years and meets the other qualifying conditions. **Chart 13.8** shows how Gordon's financial position has changed.

Chart 13.8 *Revised position*		
	£000	*£000*
House		250
Cash deposits	50	
Share sale	448	
Less capital gains tax	(33)	
		465
		715
Nil rate band for John and Lisa as per Budget		
1992		(300)
Taxable estate		415
Inheritance tax at 40%		166

Gordon's estate now has cash instead of shares in the trading company. Gordon should be able to receive around £46,000 of interest each year from the cash deposits, assuming that interest rates are ten per cent, and if he has a reasonable company pension, he may be financially secure. **Chart 13.9** is a summary of the share transactions.

	Total	John	Ivy	Juliette	Gordon	Trust for Andrew/Robin
Chart 13.9 *Revised share structure*						
Originally	100	8	8	8	76	
Gift	–				(36)	36
Share purchase	(64)	(8)	(8)	(8)	(40)	
	36	Nil	Nil	Nil	Nil	36

Gordon originally gifted 36 shares into the trust for his two sons, and this brought his shareholding to 40 shares. The purchase of the shares held by John, Ivy, Juliette and himself reduced the number of shares in the company to 36. However, these will now all be held by the trust for Andrew and Robin so that he will have achieved the succession of the business to them and will have arranged for the minority shareholders to be removed. Although the inheritance tax charge will increase (as the company shares are replaced by cash, attracting no business property relief). Gordon's financial position is improved and he has achieved the main aims.

FAMILY FAIRNESS

One of the difficulties with this type of arrangement is that the needs of family members may be different. For example, Andrew and Robin may wish to take over the company while Susan may have no interest in it. It is often unhealthy for shares to be passed to non-working members of the family as this can cause friction in the future. For example, if Robin and Andrew are working full-time for the company and have the same number of shares as their sister, who has little involvement in the business, they may not understand why they are working partly for her benefit. The actions taken in this case ensure that Susan's financial needs are satisfied by her receiving other assets from the estate.

You can see from **Chart 13.10** that we have approximately equalized the value transferred. It may not always be possible to do this and it may have to be accepted that more value may be transferred to the sons if they are working full time for the business. However, it is possible that cash could be transferred at an earlier date to Susan to partly compensate her. If she has to

Chart 13.10	
Value to be transferred	*£000*
Value of Brown Ltd after cash purchase, say	1,000
Trust for Andrew	500
Trust for Robert	500
Balance of estate for Susan (715-166)	549

wait until Lisa's death to receive the capital then she may be disadvantaged and it may be necessary for a small shareholding interest to be held for the benefit of herself and her family. Alternatively, the share structure could be changed so that there are non–voting, but dividend–producing, shares for Susan.

This case study has concentrated on succession, but there are other matters, covered in this book, which would be relevant. For example, keyman insurance and inheritance tax protection insurance may be relevant; and pensions could play a very large part of the financial strategy.

There is no blueprint for these cases. Almost every case is different and it is necessary to tailor the financial plan to the needs of individual directors and shareholders.

14

EMPLOYEE BENEFITS

Over the past decade great changes have taken place in the field of employee benefits. The Government has introduced a number of incentives for companies to widen share-ownership by introducing share-ownership schemes. Profit Related Pay (PRP) has also enjoyed substantial tax advantages so that companies can use PRP to reward employees during prosperous periods while cutting back on salary costs during a recession hence minimizing the need to lay-off so many staff. During the 1970s and 1980s the company car was very much part of the ethos of employee benefits in the UK but it has been taxed more and more heavily over the last few years so that, in some cases, it is now better for the car to be owned by the employee. The ever-changing financial and taxation climate means it is important for company employees to get independent financial advice. As a result, financial clinics for employees have become very popular in recent years.

SHARE OPTION ARRANGEMENTS

Share options have traditionally been a very good staff incentive and are often considered to be *the* executive perk. Unfortunately, in recent years many share options have become worthless due to falling share prices. However, we will eventually move out of the recession and both profitability and company values should increase, hence now may be a very good time to set up a share option arrangement, while share prices are relatively low.

A share option works as follows. The employee is granted an option by his or her employer to purchase a fixed number of shares at a fixed price at some pre-determined date in the future. The option price is calculated by reference to market value at the date the option is first granted. For example, if the option price is £1 and if trading conditions have subsequently improved so that the company's share price is £3, the employee can exercise the option (that is buy the shares at the option price of £1) and either hold the shares or sell them and realize a capital profit of £2 per share.

The various tax-favoured share schemes have been very successful but, not surprisingly, by far the most popular has been the discretionary (otherwise known as executive) share option scheme introduced by the Finance Act 1984. Under this scheme, there is no income tax charge on the profit made by the employee provided various conditions are met. In particular, the option should not be exercised within three years of the date of granting or of an earlier exercise.

There is, however, the possibility of a charge to capital gains tax on the eventual disposal of the shares although, after taking account of the annual exemption, it is possible that they can be sold over a period of time with little capital gains tax being payable. The benefits of selling shares over a period of time are illustrated in **Chart 14.1**.

By spreading the sale of the shares over two tax years, a saving of £1,400 has been achieved. It may also be possible to transfer shares to a spouse so as to use his or her annual exemption.

EMPLOYEE SHARE OWNERSHIP PLANS

Employee share ownership plans (ESOPs) have grown significantly in recent years. They were originally devised in the United States and have been extremely popular there. They have been used as an alternative to flotation. The steps involved are as follows:

1. The ESOP borrows from the bank.
2. The ESOP purchases shares in the company.

Chart 14.1 *Share option – 5,000 shares*

	£	£
Option price	5,000	
Sale price in 1991/2	15,000	
Gain	10,000	
Annual exemption	(5,800)	
	4,500	
Capital gains tax at, say, 40%		1,400
Sale of 2500 shares in one tax year: gain	5,000	
exemption	(5,800)	
Sale of 2500 shares in next tax year – as above		
Tax		Nil
Tax saving		£1,400

---

3. The company makes a tax-deductible contribution to an employee share scheme.
4. The employee share scheme uses the funds in buying shares from the ESOP.
5. The ESOP repays its bank loan out of the sale proceeds.
6. The shares held by the employee share scheme are distributed to employees.

One of the benefits of ESOPs is that shares can often be acquired at a low price for subsequent disposal to employees over a period of time. Thus, all employees may be able to benefit from the initial low price even if it was either inappropriate or difficult for them to do so at the time they came to acquire the shares. In addition, it is possible for the shareholder selling shares to a qualifying employee share ownership trust (ESOT) to defer the capital gains tax liability by reinvesting the proceeds in any replacement taxable asset.

PROFIT-RELATED PAY

The Government has been increasingly concerned at the way salary payments are regarded by the employer as a fixed overhead rather than a variable cost. Thus if the economy suffers a downturn, companies will be forced to either make employees redundant or go into liquidation. In order to mitigate the impact of the recession on unemployment and business failure, the Government introduced tax-free profit-related pay (PRP) in order to encourage salaries to vary in line with company profitability. This enables employees to enjoy the company's boom times but may lead to a reduction in wage costs during bad times without the need to make employees redundant.

The Government has been anxious to see PRP used more widely and the Inland Revenue's PRP office has gained something of a reputation for being 'user friendly' in order to encourage companies to establish PRP schemes. The tax-free PRP can now be as much as 20 per cent of total pay or £4,000, whichever is lower. As many employees pay the higher rate of tax, an annual saving of £1,600 could be achieved based upon 40 per cent tax rates. Most bonus schemes can now be converted to tax-free PRPs with little difficulty.

THE COMPANY CAR

It is often said that the car is one of the most expensive assets acquired by an individual, second only to the home. However, in corporate Britain, only a minority of British executives own the car they drive. Historically, this has been due to the tax–effectiveness of owning a car through a company.

The car is the most visible of all fringe benefits and much of its popularity lies in the fact that it is a potent status symbol. Indeed, it used to be said that the only other country which placed a greater emphasis on the car as a status symbol was Russia where, if you drove a large black limousine in the centre of the road, everyone knew exactly who you were.

The current recession has hit employees very hard. Those who have kept their jobs have found inflation exceeding their salary rises. If asked whether they wish to continue to drive the top–of–the–range company car or have additional cash and drive a smaller car, many might opt for the smaller car.

Due to the increasing tax charge on the company car, it is now advisable, in some cases, for an employee to finance the car personally (funded out of mileage allowance payments and/or increased salary) rather than for the company to provide the car as a perk. **Chart 14.2** illustrates the point.

CAFETERIA APPROACH

Many more companies are today using a 'cafeteria' approach to benefits, whereby they provide a range of benefits from which employees can choose. Some people may prefer a more expensive car while others may prefer a cheaper car and more cash, for example. There are a number of perks which can be provided. For example:

- Company car
- Additional holidays
- Use of company assets
- Luncheon facilities
- Medical insurance
- Cheap loans

Chart 14.2 *Facts as set out in Appendix 11*

	£
Cost to company of running car	6,893
Cost to employee	1,024
Company cost paid to employee as extra salary	
Net saving to employee	1,008

- Season ticket loan

- Nursery facilities

- Mortgage assistance

- Financial planning counselling

The 'shopping basket' approach has become more popular recently, especially with the company car coming under increasing scrutiny. Companies are now taking a fresh look at the provision of benefits and many feel that it is more meaningful for an individual to choose his or her benefits from a menu rather than to impose a set package. It is also possible for the company to tailor the cost to suit its own requirements. For example, it could introduce the cafeteria approach on a points system and weight the points according to the benefits the employer would prefer to provide.

The amount of flexibility in the scheme can be restricted by having some benefits pre-allocated. For example, an employer may choose to set a minimum (but not a maximum) level of pension contribution. By contrast, he or she may wish to select a maximum (but not minimum) level of company car. With holidays, however, he or she may wish to set both a minimum and a maximum level of days leave that can be taken in any year. (An illustration of the flexible benefits approach is set out in Appendix 12.)

COUNSELLING OF DIRECTORS AND EMPLOYEES

This book has identified a number of areas where financial planning is essential. It has also shown how difficult it is for a busy executive to plan his or her own financial affairs. In some cases, you will not have the expertise to do so and even if you do, you may not have the time.

The provision of financial advice to employees is very important. You may value your director or employee and provide them with a medical check-up every year or two. Why not provide them with a financial check-up every couple of years?

Some companies have approached financial counselling on the basis that they will provide the cost of the initial meeting, for example, £90. This will provide the executive with an hour's consultation together with follow-up notes of the meeting. There is often a requirement for more detailed advice and some companies have felt that the employee should then pay for that separately. Other companies have agreed to provide certain staff with advice costing up to, say, £400, which could include the follow-up letter or a report.

The cost of follow-up work very much depends upon the matters which have been identified at the initial meeting and it is reasonably easy for the consultant to then quote a fixed fee for the follow-up work. This is on the basis that a fee-based organization would be used rather than a commission-based organization which would not charge but then retain all the commission. This matter is discussed in more detail later in this book. In many cases, the cost of the exercise will be relatively small and may be outweighed by a commission rebate or the financial benefits identified by the consultant.

PENSIONS – THE MOST TAX-EFFICIENT PERK

In many cases, the pension will be the most tax-efficient perk. (Chapter 6 identifies the tax-efficiency of this arrangement and the need for a good pension upon retirement.) Part of the financial counselling meeting may be taken up with explaining the likely pension which will be produced at retirement and whether the funding rate is appropriate. As we have seen, if you do not fund your pension scheme at the appropriate level, you may be in for a real shock when you retire.

15

ESTATE PLANNING

Estate (or inheritance tax) planning forms one of the key elements of any financial planning strategy. Many people find it very difficult to approach the subject dispassionately as it means facing up to one's own mortality. It is important to not only take advantage of all the available estate-planning techniques but also to ensure that you are adequately provided for during the rest of your life. There is nothing worse than giving too much wealth away to your children and then finding that you are reliant upon them for your future needs. However, if you retain too much wealth within your estate, a large part of your funds will go the Inland Revenue rather than to your beneficiaries.

THE HISTORICAL POSITION

Death duties and taxes on gifts have been charged for most of this century. Estate duty was introduced by the Liberal Government in 1894 and continued virtually unmodified for 80 years until 1974, when it was replaced by capital transfer tax which was both a death duty and a cumulative tax on lifetime gifts, with the tax rates rising steeply to a maximum rate of 75 per cent. Even though the rate of tax on lifetime gifts was one half of the rate at death, it meant that any significant gifts would be charged to tax whereas under estate duty, it was possible to avoid a gift by planning in advance.

The Conservative Government has significantly reduced the impact of the tax. In March 1986, it was changed to inheritance tax so that again it was possible to make a significant gift and avoid the tax if the donor survived for seven years from the date of the gift. At that time, the 'gift with reservation' rules (which applied under the old estate duty law) were revived.

THE POLITICAL CLIMATE

In the 1992 Budget, the Conservative administration proposes to increase the nil rate band to £150,000. More significantly to many business people, they propose to introduce a new 100 per cent relief for:

- interests in unincorporated businesses

- holdings above 25 per cent without control in unquoted or USM companies

- owner-occupied farmland and farm tenancies.

The relief is to be 50 per cent for:

- holdings of 25 per cent or less without control in unquoted or USM companies

- controlling holdings in fully quoted companies

- certain assets owned by partners and used in their partnership or owned by controlling shareholders and used in their company

- interests of landlords in let farmlands.

These changes will be very helpful for many private businesses. While the inheritance tax threshold of £150,000 is low enough to catch many estates, it is proposed that this threshold will be increased in the next few years and may possibly double.

The Labour Party introduced capital transfer tax and are unhappy with the existing inheritance tax regime. Inheritance tax has been referred to as a 'voluntary' tax as large gifts can be made without a charge so long as the donor survives for seven years. Significant planning can be undertaken under inheritance tax. The new 100 per cent business property relief means that family companies can be passed on to the next generation during lifetime or on death without the imposition of tax. However, if you are considering selling your business in the future you should consider gifting now with the benefit of business property relief before you convert your shares into cash which does not attract the relief.

A donee–based tax already operates in Ireland, France and some other countries. Under the March 1992 Budget proposals, if a person leaves an estate of £300,000 to his or her three children, then tax of £60,000 will be payable as shown by **Chart 15.1**.

You can see from **Chart 15.1** that the same tax charge would arise if the estate is left to three children or one child only. However if the exemption is, say, £100,000 under a new donee–based tax, then there may be no tax payable by the recipient.

PRACTICAL CONSIDERATIONS

The principle behind making lifetime gifts is to take advantage of exemptions so as to transfer wealth free, or practically free, of tax during one's lifetime, thereby reducing the inheritance tax payable on death. Of course, not everyone is either able or willing to pass on wealth during their lifetime. Many are not able to make significant lifetime gifts without seriously affecting their own standard of living.

Even if you have sufficient funds, you may not wish to give away any of your assets during your lifetime. Whereas the potential for inheritance tax savings may be enormous under the current system, there is a variety of reasons why you may be unwilling to make the necessary gifts. You may simply be unsure to whom to make the gift and in what amounts to transfer the assets. It could also be that family circumstances make gifting unwise or

---

Chart 15.1

	£000	
Estate	300	
Inheritance tax exemption	(150)	
Taxable estate	150	
Inheritance tax @ 40%		60
Receipt by each of 3 children	100	
Inheritance tax payable @ nil rate band, say	(100)	
Inheritance tax due		NIL

problematic. Relationships with spouses and children may fluctuate.

Many people prefer not to transfer assets directly to minor children. A child's character may change dramatically during adolescence and by receiving funds at an early age he or she may become less motivated to establish a career. All this does not mean that estate-planning is of no interest or that lifetime gifts are out of the question, but rather that care must be taken. A significant amount of tax may be saved by ensuring a tax-efficient distribution of assets on death. It must be stressed that this always involves making a will – leaving your estate to be split according to the intestacy rules is neither sensible nor efficient. It is a common fallacy, for example, to believe that if you die without making a will, your assets pass automatically to your spouse.

At the beginning of this book, we discussed the need to consider your current capital income and inheritance tax position. The same applies to an estate-planning exercise: you need to determine whether you have net surplus income and whether there are any assets which could be gifted at this time. **Chart 15.2** begins our case study.

Having examined the capital position, it is necessary to consider how the estate would be left by Alan and Betty Bradford. It is understood that they wish to leave all their assets to each other with the balance going to their two children. Therefore no inheritance tax will be payable on the first death but the tax will be payable on the second death.

You will see from **Chart 15.3** that it has been assumed that Alan Bradford dies first and leaves all his assets to his wife so that a tax charge of £284,000 will arise on her death. This represents 33 per cent of the estate and the family may well consider that too much is going to the Inland Revenue. We have ignored the business property relief of 50 per cent (or possibly 100 per cent if the 1992 Budget proposals are enacted) in respect of the family company shares as it has been assumed that the shares would be sold by Betty Bradford before her death. If full business property relief is available, the tax charge falls to £132,000.

If we assume that Betty Bradford is now a widow and has sold the company and liquidated all her assets other than the family home, then her net spendable income would be as set out in **Chart 15.4**.

You will see that Mrs Bradford has deposits of around £640,000 together with an index-linked pension from her late husband's company of £20,000 a year. This provides her with net income after tax of £55,000. If we assume that her expenditure is £25,000 a year, then there is a large surplus of income.

Although the pension is index-linked the deposit interest will not be so Mrs Bradford needs to be wary of giving away too much during her lifetime.

She could, however, make gifts out of capital or income and look at all available estate-planning techniques to mitigate the inheritance tax charge.

Chart 15.2   *Mr & Mrs A Bradford: capital statement as at 1.1.92*

	Assets and liabilities at current values	
	Mr Bradford	*Mrs Bradford*
	£000	*£000*
Home		
Current valuation	110	110
Less mortgage	(30)	(30)
	80	80
Unquoted shares		
Family trading company	260	120
Investments		
Bank and building society deposits	30	5
Quoted shares	15	10
Gilts, bonds etc	10	30
	395	245
Tax and other liabilities	(15)	–
	380	245
Life policies: sum assured	125	
Pension scheme: likely lump sum	50	

THE BASIC RULES

The charge on death

The inheritance tax charge on death is based on the value of the deceased's estate. Assets passing to the spouse or, for example, to charities and political parties, are left out of account and there are various reliefs for business property, agricultural property, etc.

The tax is charged at two rates on everything that remains. The first £140,000 (£150,000 if the March 1992 Budget proposals are enacted) is charged at 0 per cent and the remainder at a flat rate of 40 per cent. The amount charged at 0 per cent (called the nil rate band) is subject to indexation each year, although the government is, of course, free to override the indexed figure and substitute a lower or higher value as it chooses. The value of the nil

Chart 15.3 *Mr & Mrs Bradford: inheritance tax payable*

	£000
Net assets Mr Bradford	380
Net assets Mrs Bradford	245
	625
Add mortgage redemption proceeds	60
Other life policies	125
Tax-free lump sum from pension	50
	860
Inheritance tax payable:	
£150,000 @ 0% (as per 1992 Budget proposal)	
£710,000 @ 40%	284
860,000	576
Effective rate of inheritance tax	33%

rate band for 1991/2 was £140,000. Inheritance tax has long-term ramifications. Taking advantage of the current flexible tax regime is advisable as the rules are likely to become more restrictive on any future change of government.

Because we do not know what rates a Labour administration would opt for (even if it kept to a donor-based tax), we cannot quote any comparative figures in the following examples, but for the sake of illustration, **Chart 15.5** shows the inheritance tax currently chargeable on estates of various sizes following the 1992 Budget proposals to increase the nil rate band to £150,000

Chart 15.4

	£000	£000
Total estate	860	
Less value of home	(220)	
Deposits		640
Interest @, say, 10%		64
Pension, say		20
		84
Tax thereon		(29)
		55
Expenditure		(25)
Surplus		30

Chart 15.5 Inheritance tax payable on estates of various sizes		
Size of estate	Inheritance tax currently payable	Inheritance tax payable on the progressive scale
£	£	£
100,000	nil	nil
125,000	nil	2,500
150,000	nil	5,000
200,000	20,000	15,000
250,000	40,000	30,000
300,000	60,000	45,000
350,000	80,000	65,000
400,000	100,000	85,000
500,000	140,000	135,000
750,000	240,000	285,000
1,000,000	340,000	435,000
1,500,000	540,000	735,000
3,000,000	1,140,000	1,635,000

and the inheritance tax that would be payable following a future change of government on an estate of the same size if the charging structure was as follows: £100,000 @ 0 per cent; next £50,000 @ ten per cent; next £50,000 @ 20 per cent; next £100,000 @ 30 per cent; next £100,000 @ 40 per cent; next £100,000 @ 50 per cent and the remainder (above £500,000) at 60 per cent (referred to in the table as the 'progressive scale').

The charge on lifetime gifts

Most outright gifts to individuals and trusts other than discretionary trusts are exempt if the donor survives seven years. This category of gifts is called 'potentially exempt transfers' (PETs). Gifts to an 'accumulation and maintenance trust' are also PETs.

Gifts to charities and political parties are absolutely exempt ie they are exempt whether or not the donor survives seven years. Other gifts (a gift into an ordinary discretionary trust, for example) are chargeable to inheritance tax at the lifetime rate, which is half the death rate. The tax is charged not on the value of the gift alone but on the total of chargeable gifts made in the last seven years.

Gifts made within seven years of death

If, having made a PET, a donor dies before seven years have elapsed, the transfer becomes chargeable. The rate of tax is the death rate, but the tax calculated in this way is reduced by a percentage depending on the number of years that have elapsed since the PET was made, though no reduction is made if death occurs less than three years after the PET is made.

Although the rate of tax used is the death rate, it is applied to the value of the PET at the time it was made, not to the value of the assets on death. There is one exception – if the value of those assets has actually fallen in the interim, the market value at death can be used instead of the original value.

Not only must PETs be brought into charge at death: where chargeable gifts were made in the seven years before death, tax will have been paid at the lifetime rate. The tax on these gifts must now be recomputed at the rates and nil rate bands, etc applicable in the year of death and any additional tax arising will be a debt on the estate.

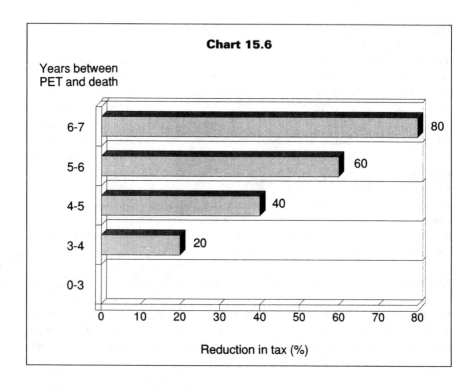

Treatment of debts

Normally, any outstanding debts at the time of death can be deducted in computing the value of the estate. However, to prevent abuse, these debts must have been incurred for full consideration and in good faith and the funds must have been applied for the deceased's own benefit. Thus a mortgage on the deceased's own house would be deductible but a mortgage on a house bought for one of the deceased's children would not be.

Basic exemptions and reliefs

Gifts or transfers to a spouse are completely exempt, whether during lifetime or on death. Thus, a gift to a spouse, even if made within seven years of death, will neither give rise to inheritance tax itself nor affect the inheritance tax payable on death. An estate left entirely to a spouse escapes inheritance tax altogether, although, as we have seen, it can merely result in a greater inheritance tax bill on the death of the spouse. If an asset is left to a spouse, the capital gains tax base cost is revised to the probate value. The asset can then be given away by the spouse as a PET, without a capital gains tax charge.

The nil rate band

It is important to remember that the nil rate band is 'born again' at the end of every seven-year period. That is, once seven years elapse after a gift (or any other chargeable transfer) has been made, the gift falls out of the reckoning. This means that an individual may make gifts up to the value of the nil rate band then in force every seven years without incurring any inheritance tax liability at all. Since husbands and wives have always been taxed independently as far as inheritance tax and capital transfer tax are concerned, a husband and wife can each give up to the basic rate band every seven years. At the present value of the band (£150,000 in the 1992 Budget proposals), this means estate of up to £600,000 can be given away tax-free just over every seven years. If the assets being given away are, for example, family company shares qualifying for 100 per cent business property relief, the tax-free value is limitless.

The annual exemption

The first £3,000 of chargeable transfers (events giving rise to an inheritance tax charge) by any individual in a tax year are exempt. If the full £3,000 is not used, the balance may be carried forward for one year only. The annual exemption applies to lifetime transfers only.

Small gifts exemption

Gifts of £250 or less to any one individual in any tax year are exempt. There is no limit to the number of individuals who may be the beneficiaries. Thus, gifts of £200 to ten individuals in a single tax year will all be exempt under this rule.

Charities and political parties

Gifts to either registered charities or 'qualifying' political parties are exempt, in life and on death. Political parties qualify if, at the last general election, they secured at least two MPs or 150,000 votes.

Gifts 'in contemplation of marriage'

Gifts made on the occasion of a marriage have a special exemption. These exemptions are: £5,000 from each parent; £2,500 from each grandparent; and £1,000 from anyone else.

Gifts for maintenance of a family

These include transfers of assets made for the maintenance of the other party as part of a separation or divorce settlement and gifts for the maintenance, etc of children and dependent relatives.

Normal expenditure out of income

This is a useful exemption for gifts that can be shown as affordable out of the individual's normal income without a significant effect on his or her standard of living, and that are made on a regular basis. It is most commonly used in personal financial planning to exempt the payment of premiums on a life policy that has been assigned to children.

Business property relief

Where a chargeable transfer is made containing assets comprising 'business property', the value of those assets is reduced for inheritance tax purposes by either 50 per cent or 30 per cent, as shown by **Chart 15.7**. The rates in accordance with the 1992 Budget proposals mentioned earlier in this chapter are shown in brackets.

Chart 15.7

Nature of asset	Relief (Post-Budget)
A business or an interest in a business	50% (100%)
Shares in a trading company giving over 25% control to the donor and his spouse	50% (100%)
Shares in a trading company giving no more than 25% control to the donor and spouse	30% (50%)
Land, buildings, machinery or plant used in a business carried on by the donor in partnership or by his company	30% (50%)

Agricultural property relief

This is a similar relief applying to 'agricultural property', which is, broadly, agricultural land (including farm buildings) or shares and securities in a company owning agricultural land etc, provided the shares and securities are part of a controlling holding (taking a husband's or wife's interest into account). The relief is 30 per cent (50 per cent under the 1992 Budget proposals) unless the transfer is of property of which the donor has vacant possession (and certain minimum occupation requirements are satisfied), in which case it is 50 per cent (100 per cent under the 1992 Budget proposals). Like business property relief, it works by reducing the value for inheritance tax purposes of the assets transferred.

Gifts with reservation

Essentially, where a gift is not an outright gift but the donor reserves some continuing use or benefit for him or her self from the asset concerned, it is not exempt from inheritance tax. There is no tax to pay at the time (if the gift would otherwise be a PET) but when the donor dies, the asset is counted as still forming part of his or her estate, as if it had not been given away at all.

A gift which is not a PET (eg a gift into a discretionary trust) may also be a gift with reservation (where, for example, the donor or his or her spouse is included in the class of beneficiaries or potential beneficiaries), so that tax can be paid at the time of the gift and again on death.

If the reservation (the donor's continuing benefit) lapses more than seven years before death, there is no charge on death.

The most commonly quoted example of a gift with reservation is where a parent passes ownership of his or her house to a child but reserves the legal right to continue to live there until his or her death.

THE FAMILY HOME

Of all your assets, your family home is the one you are least likely to want to give away, for obvious reasons. There is also the problem of the gifts with reservation rules. Giving away ownership of your house while retaining a legally enforceable right to continue to live in it and have use of the contents could prove expensive in terms of inheritance tax on death and would, in fact, negate the whole tax–planning idea behind the gift in the first place.

There are various ways round this problem, which we shall now consider.

Outright gift

You could make an outright gift of the home and rely on an unwritten and informal arrangement with the new owner to allow for continued residence. Few people are prepared to do this, however, in case relationships go awry. With the loss of capital gains dependent relative exemption, the sale proceeds would also be subject to capital gains tax. The Inland Revenue would still attempt to invoke the gifts with reservation rules.

Payment of a full rent

The gifts with reservation rules do not bite if the donor pays a full market rent for living in the house as furnished accommodation once ownership has passed to the donee – this solution is not very popular either. The donor would have to fund the rent (at its full market value) out of after-tax income and it would be taxable in the hands of the donee. Capital gains tax would also be payable in this instance on any sale of the home by the donee. Even so, overall savings could be made, although these will accrue to the donee at the donor's expense.

The means of avoiding the gifts with reservation rules illustrated by **Chart 15.8** is not popular because of the income tax implications.

Change in circumstances

If, after the donor has gifted the house, his circumstances change in a way that was then unforeseeable and he needs to occupy the house because he is no longer able to maintain himself (whether through old age or otherwise), the gifts with reservation rules do not apply, provided, additionally, that the donee is a relative of the donor and his/her allowing the donor to live in the house represents a reasonable provision for his care and maintenance.

This is clearly of use where circumstances genuinely result in the donee needing to care for the elderly donor, but, by its very nature, it is not a planning tool.

Gift of a share in the house

A partial solution to the house problem is to give a share in the house, rather than the entire title, to say, the children, and for all the joint owners, including the parents, to live in the property. Correspondence with the Inland Revenue indicates that provided the parents (donors) continue to pay their share of the running costs and the children (donees) live in the house

---

Chart 15.8

Dennis, a widower, makes a gift of his house, worth £200,000 to his daughter and agrees to pay her a full market rent (say, £16,000 a year) in order to avoid the gifts with reservation rules. He dies nine years later, when the house is worth £250,000.

	£	£
Saving by daughter		
9 years' rent	144,000	
Less tax @ 40%	57,600	
		86,400
Inheritance tax saving:		
250,000 @, say, 40%		100,000
Capital gains tax on eventual sale, say,		(10,000)
		176,400
Cost to Dennis		
9 years' rent		144,000
Net saving		32,400

Notes: (1) In practice, the income tax payable by Dennis's daughter would be less than £57,600, as she could set-off running expenses, etc, against the rent.
(2) The base cost of the house for capital gains tax purposes would be £200,000. The resulting gain would be reduced by indexation and for any time Dennis's daughter actually spent living in it as her main residence following Dennis's death.
(3) Dennis would have no capital gains tax to pay on the gift of the house, as it has always been his only or main residence.

---

together with the parents, the gifts with reservation rules should not apply, even if the share given away is disproportionately large.

This is obviously a good solution where the children (or other donees) are still living at home, but if they have moved away and established homes of their own they may well be unwilling to give up their independence and commitments. Unless they live in the house, however, the solution does not work.

If this arrangement does commend itself, and husband and wife are already joint owners, they could give up to £300,000 of the value of the home immediately, free of inheritance tax (provided no other chargeable gifts had been made in the preceding seven years) and capital gains tax. Even if the inheritance tax nil rate band has been wholly or partly used up, the gift of the share would be a PET, so no tax would be payable, however great the value transferred, provided the parents survived seven years. Term assurance may be requested on the gift in the event of an early death.

Carving out an interest

A 'carve out' is an old estate duty device which should succeed for inheritance tax as long as all steps are carried out in the correct sequence.

The idea behind it is first to create a lease (carving out an interest from the existing freehold) to enable the parents/donors to continue to have a legal right to occupy the property, and then to transfer the freehold interest to the children/donees. Estate duty case law, confirmed by the Inland Revenue to be valid for inheritance tax, provides that there is no gifts with reservation problem as there is no gift of the retained interest (the lease), only of the freehold, now subject to the lease. There are several points to remember:

- If you own a freehold, you cannot grant a lease in favour of yourself. The lease has to be granted to a nominee (your solicitor can advise)

- It is most important to carry out the operations in the right order. The lease must be granted first – if it is granted at the same time as or after the gift of the freehold, the carve out does not work

- The lease must be for a fixed term and not for life

- There will be no capital gains tax on the grant of the lease or the gift of the freehold (provided always that the property is the donor's only or main residence). Capital gains tax will, however, be payable by the donees when they eventually sell the home, with a reduction for any period they spend living in it as their principal residence. Since their ownership is subject to a lease, the base value of their interest will be low and this will result in a greater capital gains tax bill than might otherwise be the case

- The value of the freehold will fall out of the donor's estate at death but the lease will form part of the estate and inheritance tax will be payable accordingly

- The grant of the lease and the subsequent gift of the freehold must on the face of it be independent transactions. If they are too blatantly associated or contain unusual terms, the Inland Revenue may try to invoke both specific and general anti-avoidance provisions. This is a complex area and professional advice is strongly recommended.

The possible financial saving on a carve out is shown in the example in **Chart 15.9**.

This is a complicated arrangement and clearly professional advice should be taken. If you are effecting a carve-out arrangement in respect of your home, you must accept that capital gains tax is likely to be payable when the house is sold by your beneficiary.

Also, if you sell the house during your lifetime, part of the value will be attributed to the lease and part to the freehold reversion. The proceeds relating to the freehold reversion will be outside your control, although it is possible to transfer the freehold reversion to a trust for the benefit of, say, your children with you as a trustee. Although you may have some form of effective control over the assets of the trust, this is not foolproof and therefore part of the proceeds may not be available to be reinvested in your new home. You will receive the proceeds from the sale of your lease which you can then reinvest but you must be sure that this is adequate.

There could be an income tax charge on the sale of the lease and it may be appropriate to surrender the lease at that time to avoid the charge.

The above plan is more attractive for a second home, especially if there is no capital gains tax payable upon the gift of the freehold reversion. This is because there is no effective capital gains tax downside as capital gains tax would be payable in any event upon the sale of the second home. However the basic capital gains tax disadvantage in any inheritance tax plan is that all assets are revalued at death so that if the assets are retained in the estate, inheritance tax will be payable, but the rebasing provisions will significantly reduce capital gains tax at that time.

Transferring the home into a trust

A less complicated alternative to the carve out is for the donor to create an 'interest in possession' trust in favour of his or her spouse and to give the freehold to the trust. The trustees should have wide powers of appointment over a class of beneficiaries which includes the donor as well as his/her

---

Chart 15.9

Alan owns a house worth £230,000. He grants a 25-year lease of the house to a nominee for himself and then makes a gift of the freehold (reversion) to his son. He dies 18 years later, when the house is worth £275,000, the value of the lease is £90,000 and the value of the freehold reversion £165,000.

Inheritance tax saved on death:	
£275,000 × 40%	£110,000
Inheritance tax payable on lease:	
£90,000 × 40%	£36,000
Saving	£74,000

Note: it is assumed that Alan has other assets in his estate that absorb the nil rate band. The saving is, of course, the difference between the value of the house with vacant possesion, which falls out of the estate, and the value of the lease, which remains in the estate. The longer the donor survives after creating the lease, the less time it has to run and the smaller its value.

---

spouse. After a year or so, the trustees could revoke the greater part of the spouse's interest, say 80 per cent, over to the intended 'donees'. The donor and spouse would continue living in the home for the rest of their lives and the inheritance tax payable on death would be limited to the value of the 20 per cent interest in income.

A gift from an interest in possession trust is a PET for inheritance tax purposes, so that death within seven years may incur a charge.

Selling the home: a simple tax-saving arrangement

A couple wishing to sell their home and, perhaps, move to a smaller residence, could save eventual inheritance tax by the simple expedient of making a gift of the cash proceeds to their children. The children would then use the cash to buy a new home for their parents. Since it is the cash that is the subject of the gift, there is no gift with reservation.

The gift of the cash should not be conditional on the purchase, otherwise the Inland Revenue might be able to invoke the inheritance tax avoidance rules. Indeed it is likely that this arrangement will be challenged by the Inland Revenue. As before, when the childen come to sell the house, there will be an element of capital gains tax to pay for the period of their parents' occupation.

Joint ownership by husband and wife

Where husband and wife own a home jointly, they do so under one of two different forms of legal ownership.

If, for example, both husband and wife sign the purchase deed jointly (they will usually also have a single mortgage loan, in the name of both of them), both own the whole of the interest in the house and when one of them dies without having disposed of the interest, that interest lapses and the surviving spouse is left in sole ownership of the whole.

The second form of ownership is as 'tenants in common'. This means that husband and wife each own a separate half share in the house (as might have happened, say, if they had bought into the house when still single); in such situations, they are likely to have separate loans, in their name only. During lifetime, both husband and wife in this situation are free to dispose of their half share only. That share does not lapse on death but forms part of the estate of the deceased spouse. Unless he or she has made other arrangements in the will, that share will be dealt with under the intestacy rules. Joint tenancy is less flexible than a tenancy in common and most planning arrangements, including those already discussed, assume a tenancy in common exists. If it does not, this can usually be effected without any tax penalty.

GIVING

Methods of giving

Essentially, assets can be passed either by way of an outright gift to an individual or they can be placed in a trust.

Whereas making an outright gift is straightforward and usually involves little cost or administration (but remember that capital gains tax may now be payable on many occasions), and is often the most tax-efficient way, there are situations in which the most suitable method would be to set up a trust.

Usually, the most powerful motive for using a trust arrangement is unwillingness to surrender all control of the asset, especially if it consists of family company shares. Additionally, donors may think it unwise to give considerable wealth with no strings attached to younger members of the family or others.

As already described, the way round this problem is to create a trust to administer the assets and appoint oneself as a trustee but care will need to be taken in this regard to avoid invoking the gifts with reservation rules. It is worth noting that the inheritance tax consequences depend on whether the trust is an 'interest in possession' trust or a discretionary trust.

The assets to be gifted

The choice of which assets to hand over depends to a large extent on the results of the income statements considered earlier in this chapter. Where there is a comfortable surplus of income over expenditure, income-producing assets (such as quoted company shares, cash deposits, let property etc) can be given away; in the case of a couple where one partner is paying tax at 40 per cent and the other is not, it makes sense for the partner with the higher tax bill to give away his or her assets, as this will reduce the tax liability by 15 per cent more.

Where, on the other hand, there is only a modest surplus of income over expenditure, or indeed a deficit, non-income-producing assets should be chosen, such as works of art, private company shares (assuming dividends are not regularly paid), unlet property, life policies etc.

Appreciating assets

Assets appreciate (or depreciate) at different rates. Fast-growing assets are, of course, welcome, but the longer they remain in the estate the greater the eventual inheritance tax liability will be. That is why, unless they are essential for some other purpose (providing a nest egg on retirement, for example), they are a good subject for lifetime gifts. The earlier they are given away, the smaller the possible inheritance tax liability (on an early death, if they are the subject of a PET) or actual inheritance tax liability (where they are put into a discretionary trust, for example).

An investment property, especially if it has sitting tenants, should not be overlooked. A property subject to a tenancy will be worth much less than one with vacant possession, so the actual or potential inheritance tax liability on a gift of a tenanted property will be correspondingly less. The capital gains tax implications of the gift should be carefully borne in mind.

It is often advisable to pass family company shares to family members, whether under trust or otherwise, at the outset of the venture, when their value will be low. As the company prospers, the shares will appreciate in value out of the donor's estate.

Skipping a generation

When parents are thinking of making gifts of assets to children, the possibility of skipping a generation should not be overlooked. In the case of older parents, the children will quite often have built up a sizeable estate themselves. Where income-producing assets are concerned, they may not need the extra income and whatever assets are involved, a gift from the parents may ease the parents' inheritance tax position but add to the children's own inheritance tax problems.

Where possible, gifts directly to grandchildren should be considered in these circumstances. Remember that the income tax rule that taxes parents on their minor children's income from funds provided by the parents (where this income is more than £100 a year) does not apply to funds from grandparents – or any other relatives for that matter. So, if a grandchild under 18 receives a gift producing income of £1,000 a year from a grandparent, the child will be able to claim a repayment of tax, provided his or her total income does not exceed the personal allowance (£3,295 in 1991/2). This can produce considerable savings.

TRUSTS

A trust is a way of ensuring that assets and the income they produce are held or paid out, as the case may be, for the benefit of a person without that person having control over them. Or, put another way, a trust is a device by which an individual may relinquish the ownership of an asset without necessarily losing control.

The person who sets up a trust is known as the *settlor*. The trust is administered by *trustees*, of whom the settlor can be one but professional advice should be sought on this matter. The person(s) for whose benefit the trust is set up are known as the beneficiaries. There is nothing to stop the settlor from making him or her self a beneficiary, although the tax consequences are usually unfavourable.

The income of a trust can be paid to, or accumulated on behalf of, one set of persons while the underlying capital ultimately accrues to a different person(s). A common will trust (a trust set up by an individual's will) leaves assets on trust for children (the remaindermen) but the income from those assets to the widow for her life (the widow in these circumstances is known as the life tenant). NB: Different terms are used in Scotland.

The rules of the trust are contained in the trust deed, which is a legal document. Although trusts can exist without there being a trust document, there are no circumstances within the scope of this book where that could be recommended.

Over the years, several different types of trust have evolved to suit different circumstances and requirements.

Chart 15.10

Gregory gives £15,000 of 7.5% Treasury stock to his grandson. Gregory has an estate of over £500,000 and an annual income well in excess of the basic-rate band. The grandson has no other income.

	£	£
Inheritance tax saving by Gregory:		
£15,000 @ 40%	6,000	
Net annual income loss:		
£15,000 × 7.5% × 60%		(675)
Income received by grandson:		
£15,000 × 7.5% × 75%	844	
Income tax reclaimed:		
£15,000 × 7.5% × 25%	281	1,125
Income tax benefit		450

With a top tax rate of 60 per cent for both income tax and inheritance tax (likely on any future change of government), the figures look even better:

	£	£
Inheritance tax saving by Gregory:		
£15,000 @ 60%	9,000	
Net annual income loss:		
£15,000 × 7.5% × 40%		(450)
Annual income received by grandson:		
£15,000 × 7.5% × 75%	844	
Income tax reclaimed:		
£15,000 × 7.5% × 25%	281	
		1,125
Income tax benefit		675

Bare trusts

A bare trust is little more than an outright gift where the trustee holds the assets in name only. The beneficiary has an absolute and unconditional right to both capital and income. A bare trust is often made in favour of a young person under 18, in which case it can be a useful tax-saving device.

We have already mentioned the tax rule under which the income of a child under 18 from funds originating from a parent is taxed on the parent, unless the income is less than £100 a year. If the funds are given to the child in the form of a bare trust, this tax rule does not apply provided the income is accumulated until the child reaches the age of majority. In this case, the income of a parental bare trust in favour of a child is treated as the child's and not the parent's.

This quirk is unlikely to survive long. The 1991 consultative paper on the taxation of trusts recommends that the income be taxed on the parent whether or not it is accumulated.

Interest in possession trust

The interest in possession trust has been very popular in recent years. The beneficiaries must have a right to the income from the outset but the trustees will be able to control the investment of the trust's assets. It is possible to structure the trust so that the beneficiaries receive the income but do not receive the capital until, say, age 70 – or earlier at the trustee's discretion. This effectively enables the trustees to transfer capital out of the trust in accordance with their wishes. Therefore if a father wishes to effectively transfer assets to a child age 25 but retain control of those assets during the rest of his life, the interest in possession trust may be appropriate. If the father is, say, aged 55 and the assets can pass to the child at age 70 or earlier at the trustee's discretion, then the father can leave the assets in the trust for the next 45 years until he is age 100 (if he ever reaches that age) or arrange for the assets to be passed out of the trust to the child during his lifetime.

These trusts are also useful for passing assets to a newly-married child so that they can be protected in case the child becomes divorced. If they had been gifted directly to the child, then the other party to the marriage may have found it easier to enjoy those assets. This trust may also be appropriate if the settlor has children from a previous marriage. The fund may provide income for the second wife but ensure that it passes to the settlor's children on the spouse's death.

Discretionary trust

In a discretionary trust, the settlor specifies the person or class of persons who are to be the beneficiaries (eg all his grandchildren, born or yet to be born) but the trustees have complete discretion as to which particular beneficiary will benefit and when any payments of income or capital are to be made. Income may be, and often is, accumulated whereas in an interest in possession trust, the income must be allocated to the income beneficiaries.

While it is flexible and can avoid capital gains tax holdover relief problems, the transfer is chargeable and will need to be covered by the nil rate band to avoid a tax liability. Also action will be required within ten years (possibly by resettling the assets of the trust) to avoid a ten-yearly tax charge.

Chart 15.11

Mr Horncastle wishes to set up a trust in favour of his grandchildren with assets worth £130,000. He has made no other gifts in the last seven years. The net capital gain on the assets after indexation is £50,000 and Mr Horncastle's top rate of income tax is 40%

	£
Gift into interest in possession trust:	
Inheritance tax liability (assuming he survives seven years)	Nil
Capital gains tax liability (£50,000 – £5,800) @ 40%	17,680
	17,680
Gift into discretionary trust:	
Inheritance tax liability: £130,000 @ 0%	Nil
Capital gains tax liability: (assuming holdover election)	Nil
	Nil

Notes: (1) Some assets qualify for capital gains tax holdover relief whatever the circumstances of the gift. Thus if the assets were shares in a family company, for example, holdover relief would be available on the gift into the interest in possession trust also.

(2) Holdover does not get rid of the capital gains tax liability but effectively defers it and passes the burden to the trustees. If or when the trustees dispose of any of the assets, their capital gain will be increased by the appropriate amount of Mr Horncastle's liability that was held over.

Accumulation and maintenance trust

An accumulation and maintenance trust is a special form of discretionary trust, with important tax privileges. Five important rules must be observed:

1. At least one beneficiary must become absolutely entitled to an interest in the income of the trust by the time he or she reaches 25. However, capital can be held in the trust for many years, as with the interest in possession trust.

2. No interest in possession (ie an immediate right to income or capital) may exist before that time.

3.   The income must before that time be accumulated or applied for the benefit, education or maintenance of a beneficiary.

4.   The beneficiaries must either all be grandchildren of a common grandparent or children, widows or widowers of those grandchildren who died before they became entitled to benefit.

5.   At least one beneficiary must be living at the time the trust is created.

The tax treatment in respect of trusts is covered in Appendix 13.

That is not the end of the story, however. Further charges to inheritance tax will occur whenever there is a distribution of capital out of a discretionary trust, and on every tenth anniversary of its creation.

These charges are based in the first instance upon the inheritance tax liability of the settlor at the time the trust was created. If the trust was created by a transfer under the nil rate band and no further transfers in or out are made, it is consequently possible to break the trust before the first tenth anniversary without incurring any inheritance tax at all, even if the underlying assets have appreciated in the meantime.

These rules do not apply to accumulation and maintenance trusts.

Professional advice

Trusts are complex legal structures and to make sure that the result is exactly what you want and that maximum tax-efficiency is achieved, professional advice is absolutely essential.

WILLS

Some people have an almost supernatural dread of making a will, and many others show a great reluctance to come to a decision about how they would like their possessions to be divided after they die, yet not making a will can lead to a great deal of avoidable difficulties and hardships.

There is also a commonly held belief that in the case of intestacy (dying without a valid will), all one's assets simply pass to a wife or husband. This is not true – certainly, legal provision is made for a surviving spouse (and in Scotland for children) but the amount of this provision is small (only £75,000 for a spouse where there are children) and part of the remainder of the estate is then placed in trust for children, parents, siblings etc.

Quite apart from the fact that this distribution is hardly ever how the intestate would have wished to arrange things, and can involve needless delay and effort at a time of distress, it often results in a far greater tax bill than is necessary.

Had Mr Ilford in **Chart 15.12** made a will and the assets been distributed as he wished, the inheritance tax payable would have been zero (the £150,000 bequeathed to his children being covered exactly by the nil rate band).

Chart 15.12

Mr Ilford has an estate of £600,000. He wishes £150,000 to go to his children, the remainder to his wife. However, he dies without making a will. The intestacy rules work as follows:

	£	£
To widow absolutely		75,000
Interest in possession trust:		
income to wife, capital on her death to children		262,500
In trust for children		262,500
	£600,000	
Inheritance tax payable on £262,500:		
£150,000 @ 0%		
£112,500 @ 40%		45,000
£262,500		

The moral is to draw up a will *now* with proper professional advice (relying on do-it-yourself wills is just leaving hostages to fortune) and have it reviewed regularly, not just to make sure that changes in tax and general law have been taken into account but also to adapt it where necessary to altered circumstances and relationships and to changes in the size and nature of your estate.

Putting things right: deeds of variation

If, for whatever reason, a will does not reflect the wishes of the deceased when he or she died (or even if it does), if the beneficiaries agree amongst themselves that they would like the assets distributed in another, possibly more tax-efficient, way this can be done without incurring additional tax penalties.

This second bite at the cherry is known as a 'deed of variation' or 'deed of family arrangement'. Provided all the beneficiaries named in the will put their names to the document and it is filed no later than two years after the death, the assets will be distributed as required by the deed. What is more, for tax purposes, this new distribution will be treated as if it had been contained in the will.

This gives the executors and beneficiaries the chance to make use of reliefs and exemptions that may have been overlooked. Of course, if the estate has already been distributed according to the original will, it is too late to reverse this with a deed of variation, and if a single beneficiary objects, the others cannot proceed with the deed. It is also important to remember that the special tax treatment only applies if it is specially claimed, and this must be done no more than six months after making the deed.

There does not have to be a will at all for there to be a deed of variation, so a deed can also be used to avoid the intestacy rules. In this case the beneficiaries whose unanimous agreement is necessary are those who would otherwise inherit under the intestacy rules.

An obvious use of a deed of variation would be to alter a will under which everything was left to the surviving spouse. This is tax-efficient in the short term, since no inheritance tax is payable, and may save tax in the long term if the will is varied so as to use the nil rate band to pass assets to children and grandchildren at this stage, rather than by a subsequent gift or bequest by the surviving spouse. This is especially important where the spouse is of an advanced age or in ill health, so that there is an increased likelihood that a lifetime gift by him or her would fall to be taxed on death within seven years.

Chart 15.13

	£000	£000
Estate left to widow		400
Widow's assets		200
		600
Inheritance tax on widow's death (according to		
1992 Budget proposals)		180
Deed of variation		
Assets passed to children	150	
Taxable estate on widow's death	450	
Inheritance tax thereon		120
Inheritance tax savings		60

The discretionary will

Another way of allowing maximum flexibility in the distribution of an estate without entering into a deed of variation is to write a so-called 'discretionary will'. Under this arrangement, the person making the will (the testator) indicates (possibly by a separate letter of wishes) how he or she would like the estate to be distributed but leaves the personal representatives absolute discretion to override the provisions in the will and redistribute the assets as they see fit among the named beneficiaries. Usually, the widow or widower is named as one of the personal representatives so that he or she can have a say in the distribution.

Again, as long as the distribution takes place within two years of the testator's death, it is treated for tax purposes as if it had been contained in the will.

Deeds of variation and discretionary wills: a health warning

Those thinking of making a discretionary will or of leaving beneficiaries to rely on a deed of variation should be aware that the use of these two devices may have a limited future. It was only at the last moment that the Government was persuaded to omit from the 1989 Finance Bill measures that would have virtually eliminated their use for tax-planning purposes. In doing so, ministers emphasized that they would keep the situation under review. While there appear to be no plans at present to reintroduce anti-avoidance measures in this area, future moves in this direction should not be ruled out.

Retirement relief is also very valuable. It now applies to a sale or gift of shares in a family company (or for whole or part of the business) by an individual who is 55 years of age (or younger if he or she has retired because of ill health). The rules broadly require that the business or shares must have been held by the donor for a complete year before the gift. If the various conditions have been fulfilled during the previous ten years, the first £150,000 of gains will be exempt and any gain between £150,000 and £600,000 will be taxed at half the income tax rate applicable. The conditions are somewhat complex and professional advice should be taken to ensure that relief is obtained.

THE NEED FOR INSURANCE

There are two methods of dealing with the potential inheritance tax charge. The first is to maximize lifetime gifts and to use the available reliefs and exemptions. However, although this planning will reduce the tax charge it is unlikely to be fully mitigated, as part of the estate may comprise the home and funds which are required to meet future living expenses. The second approach, therefore, is based upon the acceptance of an ultimate tax charge and uses life assurance as a way of providing funds for the beneficiaries so that they can meet the tax liability. A combination of both methods will often be used in an effective estate plan. (The various forms of non-state pension are discussed in Chapter 6). Death in service benefits are normally included in the scheme and this is where inheritance tax may be mitigated.

The pension scheme will normally permit benefits which arise from death while still a director or employee of the company. On death in service, the benefit will pass to the trustees who will exercise their discretion as to who should receive the payment. The director will normally provide a letter of wishes indicating who should benefit. This is not a legally binding document but if the trustees of the scheme are, for example, his co-directors, it would be unusual for them not to follow these wishes. Similar arrangements apply for personal pension plans, where life cover can be obtained and benefits can be paid directly to or in trust for the beneficiaries without an inheritance tax charge. For details of how to insure against death duties, see Chapter 8.

16

CHARITABLE GIVING

Charitable giving goes back to biblical times and many people allocate part of their annual income each year to charity. However, too often the tax benefits to both the charity and the donors are overlooked. Charities themselves have long been exempt to a large extent from income or capital taxes and it is about time that they became exempt from VAT. Donations to charity have enjoyed tax-privileged status but, particularly in the last few years, there has been a marked increase both in the tax benefits available and in the tax-exempt ways of giving.

A word of warning, however. Tax exemption is given only to charities recognized by law as such. What is or is not a charity in law is a complicated question, with the main body of law on this subject going back to the 16th Century. It is beyond the scope of this book to discuss this question but the matters covered in Appendix 14 should be borne in mind.

Chart 16.1 shows the tax benefits which apply at various levels to different types of giving.

GIFT AID

Individuals

From 1 October 1990, if you wish to make a 'one-off' donation to charity and not, at the same time, commit yourself to making a similar donation next year, you may still qualify for tax relief at 40 per cent. This relief was introduced in the Finance Act 1990 and is known as Gift Aid.

The gift must not be less than £600 (£400 from 1 July 1992 according to Budget proposals) when aggregated with other donations during a tax year. These limits are net of the basic rate of tax.

In **Chart 16.2**, the donation has cost Mr White £1,600, and provided the charity with £2,667, a 67% uplift! The reasons for the tax benefits are as follows:

- The contribution is deemed to be paid after deduction of basic rate tax, which is currently at the rate of 25 per cent. As the charity does not pay tax, a refund can be claimed from the Inland Revenue

- The donor can obtain tax relief at the higher rate of 40 per cent (less the basic rate of tax already deducted) for the grossed-up donation. In 1992/3 you are a higher-rate taxpayer if your taxable income exceeds £23,700.

Chart 16.1

Specific limit	Method of donation	Comment
Income tax and corporation tax		
Over £600 (£400 from 1 July 1992 according to Budget proposals)	Gift Aid and payroll giving	Considerable tax benefits to charity and donor
Under £600	Covenanted donation	Considerable tax benefits to charity and donor
3% of dividends	Gift by certain companies	Full tax deduction for payment
Capital gains tax		
None	Simple gift	Can avoid 40% capital gains tax
Inheritance tax		
None	Lifetime gift or bequest in will	Can avoid 40% inheritance tax
Other matters		
None	Interest-free loan	Avoidance of tax on income
None	Family charitable trust	To benefit from the tax benefits referred to above

---

Chart 16.2

Mr White, a 40% taxpayer, made a £2,000 one-off donation to charity by Gift Aid on 31 October 1991. The effects of making the gift were as follows:

	Received by charity £	Cost to Mr White £
Net gift	2,000	2,000
Basic-rate tax reclaimed	667	
Higher-rate tax relief obtained		(400)
Total received by charity	£2,667	
Cost to Mr White		£1,600

You must complete a simple certificate, normally provided by the charity, stating that you have deducted the basic rate of tax in respect of each donation. This certificate can be completed if you pay tax (of only £667 in the illustration in **Chart 16.2**). **Chart 16.3** shows the significant tax breaks at various levels of donation. The £400 relief is reliant upon the 1992 Budget proposals being enacted. The 60 per cent limit is not relevant now that the Conservatives have been re-elected.

Chart 16.3

Net payment under Gift Aid £	Tax rebate to charity £	Total received by charity £	Further tax relief to a 40% higher-rate payer £	Net cost to donor £	Further relief to a 60% higher-rate taxpayer £
400	133	533	80	320	107
600	200	800	120	480	160
750	250	1,000	150	600	200
1,000	333	1,333	200	800	267
2,500	833	3,333	500	2,000	667
5,000	1,667	6,667	1,000	4,000	1,333
10,000	3,333	13,333	2,000	8,000	2,667

Companies

It may be more convenient for a company director to donate to the charity through his or her company rather than from personal funds. Under the individual donation illustrated in **Chart 16.2**, Mr White would not need to pay over the basic rate of tax. However if his company makes a donation, that company pays over the basic rate of tax via form CT61 but then obtains corporation tax relief at the top marginal rate. The tax relief receivable depends upon the rate of tax payable by the company. **Chart 16.4** shows how tax benefits could uplift the donation by 60 per cent.

In **Chart 16.4**, the donation has cost the company £6,250 to provide the charity with £10,000, a 60 per cent uplift!

There are rules which prevent tax relief if the donor receives a benefit of more than £250 or 2.5 per cent of the value of the gift from the charity over the tax year. The payment must be an outright gift and not returnable in any way. Gifts can be repeated or 'one off'. When Gift Aid was first introduced, there was a maximum of £5,000,000 per tax year per individual, but this limit was removed from 19 March 1991. The only limit now is the size of the donor's taxable income.

Tax relief under Gift Aid works by assuming that each donation is made after the deduction of basic-rate tax and applying the appropriate gross deduction from the donor's taxable income. As with covenants, however, the basic-rate tax deemed to have been deducted is added back to the taxpayer's liability, so that any shortfall must be met by the donor.

In **Chart 16.5**, the charity is still able to reclaim the full £400 from the Inland Revenue but Charles has to pay £100 of that sum to the Inland

---

Chart 16.4

Company A had taxable profits of £300,000 in the year to 31 March 1991 and paid corporation tax at 37.5% on the top slice of its profits. Mr White, who owns all the shares of the company, arranged for his company to donate £7,500 under the Gift Aid scheme on 31 March 1991.

	Received by charity £	Cost to company £
Net gift	7,500	7,500
Basic rate tax reclaimed/paid	2,500	2,500
Corporation tax relief		(3,750)
Total received by charity	£10,000	
Cost to company		£6,250

Chart 16.5

Charles made a single donation of £1,200 to his favourite charity under Gift Aid at the beginning of the tax year 1991/2. Because of loss claims, his taxable income after personal allowances for that tax year is only £1,200. His tax position was as follows:

	£
Income tax payable: £1,200 @ 25%	300.00
Basic-rate tax deemed deducted from donation: £1,200 × 25/75	400.00
Balance payable to Inland Revenue	£100.00

Revenue himself, as only £300 was 'covered' by his own liability. The donation has thus cost him £1,300 and not £1,200.

Where income is likely to fluctuate or a loss claim is a possibility, any Gift Aid donations should be deferred until it is clear exactly what the tax position is likely to be. This is an unusual situation in practice.

Note that Gift Aid only applies to donations each of which is at least £600 (£400 according to 1992 Budget proposals). Two donations of £300 each in the same tax year will not qualify, because both are below £600. A single donation of £600 will, however, qualify.

DEEDS OF COVENANT

Tax benefits

Before the introduction of Gift Aid, obtaining tax relief on giving required the completion of a deed of covenant. This method continues for donations of less than £600 (£400 from 1 July 1992, as per Budget proposals). The tax relief is spread over four years rather than being received in one year, so if you wish to donate, say, £700 to charity, it would be better to do so under the Gift Aid scheme.

There is now no limit to the amount of tax relief available to a donor in respect of a charitable covenant, so you could covenant all your taxable income. (Prior to the 1986 Finance Act, there was a £10,000 limit on the amount of higher-rate tax relief a donor could receive.)

REGULAR DONATIONS

You can donate to charity on a regular basis via a non-loan deed of covenant. As the covenant must exceed three years, most are written on a four-year basis and commit you to making the same payment each year for four years. If, after say two years, you feel that you can afford to increase your donation this can always be effected by a 'top-up' non-loan covenant or by making an additional 'one off' payment by way of a loan covenant.

LOAN COVENANT

An alternative to Gift Aid if you wish to make a one-off donation to charity is to donate by way of a loan covenant. The procedure for, say, £500 is as follows:

1. You sign a four-year covenant for £125 net pa.

2. You make a cash payment of £500 to charity of which £125 is treated as the first instalment of the covenant, and £375 is treated as an interest-

---

Chart 16.6

Mr Green, a 40% taxpayer, is willing to make a regular annual donation of £500 to charity by way of a deed of covenant.

Year	Payment by Mr Green	Tax rebate to charity	Toal receivable by charity	Tax Relief to Mr Green	Net cost for higher rate tax-payer
	£	£	£	£	£
1	500	167	667	100	400
2	500	167	667	100	400
3	500	167	667	100	400
4	500	167	667	100	400
	£2,000	£668	£2,668	£400	£1,600

Net receipt by charity £2,000 + 668 = 2,668

Net cost Mr Green £2,000 − 400 = 1,600

---

free loan.

3.   Each year thereafter, £125 of the loan is deemed to be used for payment of the covenant instalment then due.

In this way you are allowing the charity to have the use of your 'one off' donation 'up front', but for tax purposes the donation is treated as having been made over four years. The charity can reclaim tax on each instalment. For 1991/2, the amount reclaimable would be £41.67, for each of the years remaining it would depend on the basic rate of tax in each year.

The eventual cost (providing tax rates do not alter) to Mr Green will be £400, and the eventual amount received by the charity will be £667.

Although this method of making a donation will still give you the same amount of tax relief as making a one–off donation under Gift Aid, provided that tax rates do not alter, Gift Aid is more beneficial as you receive the whole amount of tax relief in the year in which you make the gift. However, if your gift is less than £600 (£400 in 1992 Budget proposals) then you will need to pay by deed of covenant rather than by Gift Aid.

Chart 16.7

Mr Green wishes to make a further £500 'one off' donation to charity and agrees to enter into a loan covenant. Charity receives £500 'up-front'. Further tax relief is received by the charity and Mr Green as follows:

		Loan covenant £	Tax rebate charity £	Tax relief Mr Green £
Year 1	Loan	500	–	–
	Covenant	(125)	42	25
2	Covenant	(125)	42	25
3	Covenant	(125)	42	25
4	Covenant	(125)	41	25
Total tax relief/rebate			167	100

DOCUMENTATION

The documentation for charitable giving is now relatively simple. The procedure requires that:

1. You complete the appropriate Deed of Covenant form which is normally available from the charity.

2. You sign the deed, where indicated, in the presence of a witness who should not be your husband or wife.

3. You return the Deed of Covenant to the charity with your first payment, or first payment plus loan.

Further details regarding the deed of covenant are set out in Appendix 15.

Payment should not be made prior to the date of the covenant as it will not attract tax relief. For covenants where the second and subsequent instalments are below £400 net pa, no further tax deduction certificates (R185) need to be signed by the donor. However, for all covenant instalments, do not forget to include the details on your annual tax return.

COMPANY DONATIONS

As mentioned earlier in this chapter, you may prefer to make your donation through your company. This can be an attractive means of charitable giving as it relieves you of the burden of payment which should attract corporation tax relief against taxable profits and provide a tax benefit to the charity.

If your company cannot donate to the charity through the Gift Aid scheme (for example, because the donation is too small) then the deed of covenant system can be used, as shown by **Chart 16.8**.

If your company makes a loss for tax purposes, the payment under a Deed of Covenant may not attract tax relief as it cannot be added to the tax loss which is carried forward. If you would like your company to donate to charity by Deed of Covenant, you should check the position with your professional advisors to ensure that no adverse tax implications arise.

The company covenant should be authorized by a board minute under company seal. The covenant form will need to be signed by the Company Secretary and a Director.

If your company is a non-close company (this includes most quoted companies), then three per cent of the dividend income can be paid to the charity by way of a single gift and qualify for tax relief. Again you should consult your professional advisor on this matter or speak to the relevant charity.

Chart 16.8

Mr White's company, X Ltd, wishes to donate £500 pa starting from 1 December 1991 to charity. The taxable profits of X Ltd for the year to 31 March 1992 are £100,000. X Ltd has no associated companies.

		£
X Ltd	Payment made to charity	500
	Income tax payable to Inland Revenue	167
	Gross payment by X Ltd	667
	Corporation tax relief (assuming 25% corporation tax rate)	(167)
	Net cost	500
Charity	Payment received from X Ltd	500
	Tax rebate	167
	Total receipt	667

Give as you earn

A company can arrange for its employees to donate to charity through the PAYE system. The Give As You Earn (GAYE) or 'payroll giving' scheme was introduced in 1987 to encourage regular donations to charity by employees (or ex-employees on the payroll, eg occupational pensioners) who did not wish to involve themselves with the legal formalities associated with deeds of covenant.

Under the scheme, the employer contracts with an agency charity to collect sums that have been deducted from the participating employees' salaries or pensions and hand them over to the agency charity, which is under an obligation to distribute them to the charities of the employees' choice.

It is important to remember that employers are under no obligation to operate a GAYE scheme and that the maximum any employee can donate in a tax year is £600. Subject to that, the employee may nominate any charity or charities he or she wishes.

Tax relief is provided because the donations are deducted from gross pay, in exactly the same way as company pension contributions, before applying PAYE. There is no question of deducting basic-rate tax and relief is thus obtained in full at the employee's top rate of tax. The maximum annual donation of £600 will thus cost a basic-rate taxpayer £450 and a 40 per cent taxpayer £360.

Capital gains tax

If you are about to sell shares in a company, thereby crystallizing a capital gains tax liability, and you also wish to donate money to the charity it is advisable to make a gift of some shares to the charity first so that the charity can sell them and realize the proceeds tax-free.

If by selling the shares or assets you realize a capital loss, it may be advantageous for you to sell the shares or assets yourself in order to obtain the benefit of any capital gains tax loss before gifting the proceeds to the charity. Before making such an arrangement, get professional advice.

Chart 16.9

Mr Black owns shares worth £100,000, and the capital gains tax liability thereon is, say, £20,000. He wishes to pay the benefit of the shares to charity.

If the shares are sold before the gift

	£000
Proceeds	100
Capital gains tax	(20)
Net receipt by charity	80

If the shares are gifted to the charity

Proceeds received by charity from the shares gifted by Mr Black (no tax payable)	100
Benefit (capital gains tax saving)	20

Inheritance tax

Inheritance tax is chargeable on estates on death and lifetime transfers. However, gifts to charity during lifetime or at death are completely free from inheritance tax and this is why you may want to include a bequest to a charity in your will so that the transfer goes to charity rather than partly to the Inland Revenue.

Gifts and bequests between husband and wife are exempt and this is why the tax charge is normally collected on the death of the surviving spouse. The tax rate is 40 per cent for chargeable estates in excess of £140,000 (£150,000 in 1992 Budget proposals).

Inheritance tax planning can also be undertaken within two years after the death of the donor by the beneficiaries becoming a party to a Deed of Variation and possibly passing more of the estate to the charity. Advice should be sought on this matter, as there may be changes to tax legislation affecting Deeds of Variation in the future.

Chart 16.10

Mr White had an estate worth £500,000. He died in January 1992 leaving £100,000 to charity in his will and the balance to his children.

If all the estate had been left to the children

		£000	£000
Estate			500
Inheritance tax on	£140,000 × 0%		
	360,000 × 40%	(144)	(144)
	500,000		
Net estate			356

As £100,000 was left to charity

Estate			500
Gift to charity			100
Inheritance tax on	£140,000 × 0%		400
	260,000 × 40%	(104)	(104)
	400,000		
Net estate to children			296
Net cost of gift of £100,000			60
Inheritance tax saving		40	

Charitable trusts

Tax relief is not, of course, limited to donations or covenanted payments to public charities. It is open to individuals or companies to set up their own private charitable trusts. Provided the objects of the trusts are genuinely charitable, the trust will be registered as a charity by the Charity Commissioners. The individual setting up the trust (the settlor) will usually be a trustee as well.

The trust itself will be exempt from income tax and capital gains tax. In common with all other charities, however, it cannot reclaim any VAT it may suffer and if it is conducting a business, it will have to register for VAT in the usual way if taxable turnover exceeds the registration threshold. There are, however, specific exemptions from VAT for certain equipment gifted to charity and for certain supplies by a charity. A charity's trading income, as opposed to its investment income, is not exempt from tax.

An outright gift into the trust is exempt from capital gains tax and inheritance tax and the transfer document (if there is one) is exempt from stamp duty. However, when an individual dies, any assets he or she has transferred into a charitable trust may be relevant when valuing his or her estate.

A common use of a private charitable trust in estate-planning is to gift shares in the family company to the trust, thus retaining control of the company (via family trustees) while reducing inheritance tax on the donor's estate. As a charitable trust, the trust will be able to claim a repayment of the tax credit attached to the dividends paid in respect of the shares, and hence indirectly the ACT paid by the company. The cost of operating a charitable trust should be considered before setting it up.

17

COMMISSIONS AND INDEPENDENT ADVICE

COMMISSION STRUCTURES

Many people are unaware of the charges and commissions incurred when they take out a financial product. This is hardly surprising as the financial services legislation still does not, in my view, provide the public with sufficient information.

To attract business, most insurance companies pay commission to intermediaries, so a company such as Scottish Widows pays a broker commission if a client takes out one of their policies. As the insurance company recognizes the need to take account of the cost of paying commissions, charges are made to the investment contract to take account of these payments. A few insurance companies, such as Equitable Life, do not pay commissions. However, they do have a direct sales force and charges will therefore be incurred by that company to cover the cost of that sales force, although these are unlikely to reduce investors' funds as much as the charges of other insurance companies who pay brokers commission.

Many financial products are structured as regular-premium arrangements. A regular-premium pension plan may continue for many years as may a life assurance contract. It is more valuable for an insurance company to sell a pension policy at, say, £2,000 a year which will continue for the next 25 years as £50,000 will be received over that period. If a single-premium policy of £2,500 is effected, then that may be the only money which the insurance company receives. To reflect the future commitment, commission is based upon the length of the term of the financial arrangement. The indemnity commission can be a substantial proportion of the first year's premium. **Chart 17.1** shows the high levels of commission which can be paid.

Chart 17.1 shows LAUTRO rates. Many intermediaries obtain an override to provide further commission of up to 30% of these rates. In addition to the indemnity premium commission, many contracts also provide ongoing annual commission at a significantly reduced level.

As you will see from **Chart 17.1**, the commission can be well over half the first year's premium. Often the payment is spread over two years or so of the contract but with over half the first year's premium being paid in commissions and reflected in the charges of the contract, you will see that if you only keep up the policy for a couple of years, you are likely to make a loss on the contract due to these charges. It is unlikely that you will even receive your money back, let alone any growth in the plan. As far as the introducer is concerned, there is normally an indemnity period so that if the contract terminates within the first four years, part of the commission can be clawed back. Therefore the introducer would need to reimburse the insurance company for part of the commission received.

At first glance it would be advisable to set up every contract on a single-premium basis but most policies are not sold in this manner. Over the term of the contract, single-premium commission can be greater than regular-premium commission. This is because the commission may be based upon, say, 2.5 per cent of the premium times the term, whereas the single-premium commission may be, say, four per cent a year. Therefore it will be paid at a higher rate each year and the total single-premium commission can eventually overtake the initial regular-premium commission. However, for most intermediaries, it will be more attractive to receive as much commission as early as possible.

I have come across many cases where a client was sold a policy by a pension salesman on an unreasonable basis. In one case, the client's company had made a very good profit and wanted to shelter some of the profit from tax. He was advised to arrange for his company to pay £50,000 into a pension

---

Chart 17.1

A 35-year-old man takes out policies for a term of, say, 25 years. Commission taken on an indemnity basis.

	Indemnity commission as a % of first year's premium %	Indemnity period in months
Personal pensions	50	27
Endowment policy	66	38
Term assurance	112	48
Whole of life range	80	38
Permanent health insurance	96	48

Source: Norwich Union, 6 December 1991

---

policy with an insurance company. He stressed at the initial meeting that he was unlikely to be able to commit his company to £50,000 a year and would normally wish to pay around £20,000.

He was told that he could reduce the premium in future years to £20,000 or less. While this was correct, it was by no means the entire story. What he was not told was that the charges were structured on the basis of an annual premium of £50,000 and over £25,000 of commission was paid.

Following a meeting with the relevant insurance company, it was agreed that the policy would be re-written so that regular-premium commission would be taken on the basis of £10,000 a year and single-premium commission would be taken on the balance of the premium for that year. Hence, the commission and charges fell by around £20,000.

This is not an uncommon story. Cases are often difficult to prove as very much depends upon the matters discussed at the meeting. Often notes are not taken so the unsuspecting client is not aware of the right questions to ask. This is a worrying feature of the way in which financial products are sold.

You will often not find out about the commission and charging structure until it is too late, getting an indication of the problem only when you wish to cash or transfer your policy some years later. For example, if you were to enter an employer's pension scheme (which is set up on a regular-premium basis), and then leave the scheme after three or four years, you may be disappointed with the transfer value. Again, this is because of the charges and commissions inherent in the contract. After four years, there will not have been enough time for the funds to grow in value or for additional contributions to have been received.

It is often very difficult to negotiate a reduction in initial charges. Normally the small print of the relevant policy document will provide comfort for the insurance company but not for you.

It is interesting to note that approximately 80 per cent of 25-year mortgage endowment policies do not run their full course, often because the policyholder moves house and sound advice is not received at the right time. In many cases, you should be advised to continue the policy rather than cash it and, as we saw in the chapter on investments, there is a very strong market for second-hand policies so that investors can pick up these investments after the charges have been levied.

The charging structure varies between companies. Some companies have a higher charging structure as greater commission is paid to the intermediaries to attract business. Certain companies' investment track records speak for themselves so there is less need to pay such high inducement payments but it is not always the case that the poorer performing company will pay the highest commission. **Chart 17.2** provides an indication of the charging structure of different companies.

	Reduction in yield
Chart 17.2 Reduction in yield	
Company name	at 7% growth pa 10 years
Abbey Life	2.98
Commercial Union	5.00
Equitable Life	1.50
Norwich Union	2.72
Standard Life	2.40
Swiss Pioneer Life	7.60
Zurich Life	3.30
Source: Money Management, April 1991	

COMMISSION-PAYING PRODUCTS

As we have seen, regular premium pension and life assurance contracts attract commission, as do many other forms of insurance such as permanent health, keyman, personal accident policies etc. Regular-premium endowment policies also incur charges on a regular-premium basis. Other investments are made on a single-premium basis and commission is provided. For example, a single premium with-profit bond would normally have a bid/offer spread of five per cent so that an initial investment of £100,000 would be reduced to £95,000 immediately after the investment is made. Commission of up to 5.2 per cent is paid to the introducer so that approximately £5,200 can be received.

In the investment section of this book, we have covered a number of different investment plans. Some of these are now listed in **Chart 17.3** below and you will see the level of commission which is normally paid to the introducer.

For the commission-based insurance salesperson, there is little financial reward in recommending a gilt or National Savings plan and little or no commission involved in suggesting that a client invests in stocks and shares.

There is a much larger payback for introducing a client to a single-premium bond or a regular-premium endowment or pension policy. There are many very reputable commission-based salespeople who always attempt to provide best advice. There are also many who leave a lot to be desired: this method of remuneration tends to bias the salesperson towards recommending a certain financial product.

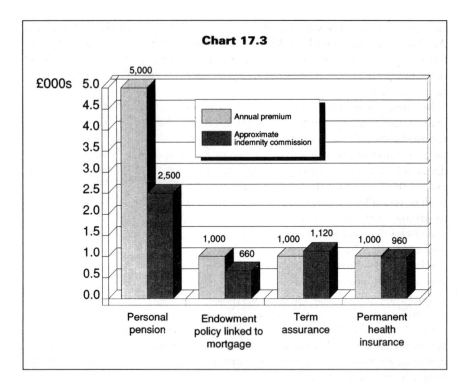

INTRODUCERS' REMUNERATION

So far I have concentrated on commission structures as the majority of financial planning consultants are remunerated on a commission basis. Therefore it is in their interest to sell a commission-based product so that there is a danger that they *sell*, rather than *advise*. In some cases, they may provide good advice only to find that the client has transacted the business elsewhere. Salespeople need to earn sufficient money from the clients who take up their recommendations to pay for the time spent on the other cases which produce no reward.

Happily, there is now a growing tendancy for advice to be provided on a fee basis. An initial meeting, at which the case can be discussed and initial proposals suggested, can cost anything between £50 and £220 depending upon the seniority of the consultant concerned and the time taken at the meeting. At the end of that meeting, the consultant will normally be aware of the further advice required and will communicate the initial proposals to the client.

The client will normally wish to see a written report so that he or she can consider the matter in detail and examine the way in which the proposals will change the financial position, in the same way as the case studies in this book. At that point, it should be possible to provide a fixed-fee quote for the follow-up report. This could cost anything from £200 to a couple of thousand pounds, depending upon the complexity of the case and the likely time required.

In most cases the cost would be below £1,000 unless the case is complicated. Most fee-based organizations rebate all the commission received although some retain some commission. At Stoy Hayward we work on a fee basis and rebate any commission received unless we are specifically directed by the client to charge differently. In many cases the commission can exceed the fee so that there is a net credit to the client. Existing clients may wish to retain the credit on the fees ledger. In some cases, it may be advisable to arrange with the insurance company for the excess commission to be waived so that additional units are acquired for the client. Alternatively, the commission could be repaid to the client.

Chart 17.4 is only an illustration: each case depends upon the time required and financial products needed.

There has been much discussion regarding the tax treatment of returned commission, and at the time of writing the position is still not completely clear. It is advisable to discuss any returned commission with your accountant to establish whether the commission would be taxable or whether it would restrict any tax relief on any pension or other financial product which had been effected.

I clearly favour a fee-based arrangement with total disclosure to the client of the fees and commission. Although improvements have been made under the Financial Services Act, with greater disclosure of charges, this still does not address the major concern that clients are not informed of the commission involved when taking out a financial product unless they know which questions to ask and constantly press the financial intermediary or insurance company for a complete answer. I suggest that you become fully aware of the fees and commission involved before taking out a policy – and get that information in writing.

Another problem is that many people are not willing to incur a fee for the required time involvement in providing best advice before taking out a policy. If financial advice is to be provided adequately it will often be necessary to spend a great deal of time on it. It is easy to come up with very quick recommendations without thinking through the taxation ramifications and the manner in which those recommendations will change your financial structure.

It is also important that you are fully aware of all the financial products available so that you can select the most appropriate plan.

However, until the public fully appreciates the commission involved, and also accepts that a *reasonable level of fee will need to be incurred for sound financial*

Chart 17.4

35-year-old man. Policies as in **Chart 17.3**. Commission on an
indemnity basis.

Time costs	£	£
Initial meeting	90	
Preparation of report	750	
Follow-up meeting	120	
Completion of documentation	250	
Total fee		1,210
Commission rebate		(5,240)
Credit		(4,030)

---

advice, I do not foresee any major changes in the way in which financial
products are sold.

TIED OR INDEPENDENT

Considering the levels of commission which can be earned, it is perhaps not
surprising that so many people are in the insurance and pensions business.
However, it is only the few who make a fortune from this business. Many
insurance brokers and salespeople struggle to earn a decent living, especially
during a recession when less money is available to be invested in financial
products, or where a company's profitability has suffered, leaving less money
for pension and insurance products.

Another disappointing feature of the financial service industry is how
relatively few independent organizations there are in comparison with tied
salespeople. For example, Standard Life has an excellent reputation for with-
profit and certain other contracts but it is not the best company for *all*
products. Its salesforce can only sell Standard Life products. Many building
societies and banks are now tied to one company.

It is quite often the case that companies specialize in a few products but are
uncompetitive in other sectors. Insurance companies can be very selective in
the way they produce statistics. For example, they can show that one of their
funds is a top performer, while they may have a range of investment funds,
some of which are performing badly.

To get the best return, you should choose the best company for each
product. The problem with going to a tied agent is that you may be
recommended a number of products by a company which may be the leader
in one sector but not in another. It is important that you seek fully

independent advice.

INDEPENDENT ADVICE

Independent advice can be obtained from certain specialist organizations. If you are to use a broker who will be working on either a commission or fee basis, then you should ensure that the broker is fully independent and can therefore recommend the best company for the right product. It is important that the adviser has sufficient knowledge of all aspects of the matters which need to be covered, including:

- All forms of investment

- Pensions

- Life assurance arrangements

- UK tax-planning (income, capital gains and inheritance tax)

- International tax (if necessary)

- Estate-planning and trust arrangements

The above list is not exhaustive but it is likely that many of the above matters will need to be considered. It is important that the initial adviser provides a comprehensive service, even if it is then necessary for certain matters to be concluded by other specialists. You need to be able to see the whole picture.

Advice can, of course, be obtained from your local bank manager, but you would need to ensure that their level of advice is sufficient in respect of the above matters. The banks have improved their technical support services and many now have both an independent and a tied arm. You should enquire into whether the advice will be fully independent. They tend to work on commission rather than a fee basis.

Life offices and banks are able to field very experienced specialists. Some are able to provide a good comprehensive service, with advice extending to tax, but you must make sure that the advice is independent.

Specialist brokers and accountants are more likely to provide you with sound advice, where, again, you have made sure that they are independent. One of the sad implications of the Financial Services Act 1986 is that it has tended to squeeze out some of the reputable smaller brokers who were able to give both an impartial and personal service. This has left the field open to large companies with their own salesforce. Even so, good brokers both large and small can still be found.

Consulting actuaries will often work on a fee basis but their advice is normally more limited towards pensions and certain investments, though they are starting to extend to tax and legal matters. A solicitor may be able to assist in the legal work connected with the implementation of a financial planning arrangement, though while some have broad experience and can provide an overall plan, many are limited in their breadth of experience on these matters.

This brings us to the chartered accountant. The last few years have seen a trend towards firms of accountants who have created a personal financial planning section which includes specialists from the pensions and life assurance industry. Those with a specialist team should be able to provide sound advice. Again, you should enquire as to whether they are likely to be commission or fee-based, and seek references.

Accountants are required to inform their clients of any commission received if they are registered through the Institute of Chartered Accountants. Some accountants have set up companies based on FIMBRA (Financial Intermediaries, Managers and Brokers Regulatory Association) so that there is no requirement to notify clients of commissions received but some may do so in any event. Some accountants retain commission while others operate on a fee basis and credit all commission against the time costs when rendering a bill – but do ask. The latter are more likely to provide impartial advice.

You should also enquire into the level of advice you will get. Some link directly with the relevant finance houses while others advise on the structure of the arrangement but link with a broker who will select the investment house.

On balance, certain brokers, accountants and some solicitors and banks are more likely to offer sound impartial advice.

Appendix 1

THE PROTECTION OF INVESTORS IN BUILDING SOCIETIES

*Extract from the Building Societies Association
Fact Sheet 9, October 1991*

'Building societies have an outstanding record for safety. Since the war, no ordinary investor in a building society which is a member of The Building Societies Association has lost any of his or her savings. On the few occasions when societies have run into financial difficulty other societies have always stepped in to ensure that savings are fully protected. The security which building societies offer rests on three separate factors –

1. *Prudential Requirements*

The law and regulations under which societies currently operate are such as to ensure that in the normal course of events it is unlikely that a building society could run into financial difficulty.

They require that at least 80% of a building society's total commercial assets (ie total assets less liquid and fixed assets) be in the form of loans for house purchase to individuals which are secured by first mortgage on land. In addition, before lending in this category, societies must first obtain a valuation of the property concerned and may not lend more than 100% of the value at any given time. Moreover, residential property has proved to be an extremely good investment. Losses as a result of bad debts are minimal. Indeed in recent years losses for the industry as a whole have been negligible; at the end of 1990 provisions for mortgage losses accounted for only 0.24% of mortgage assets of about £175,000 million.

Societies' liquid funds and the manner in which these funds can be invested are closely controlled by regulations made by the Building

Societies Commission, the government body responsible for the prudential supervision of societies. Broadly speaking, societies can invest their liquid funds only in authorised banks and government guaranteed securities. In practice, a high proportion of liquid funds are held on a fairly short term basis.

Societies are required to meet other strict requirements for the prudent operation of their business, including the maintenance of adequate reserves and comprehensive accounting records and internal control systems.

The combination of these prudential requirements is the main protection for investors in building societies.

2. *Monitoring of Building Society Activities*

The activities of building societies are monitored very closely by the relevant government department, the Building Societies Commission. Societies are required to complete detailed monthly, quarterly and annual returns on their activities and these enable any potential difficulties to be identified at an early stage.

3. *The Statutory Investor Protection Scheme*

The Building Societies Act 1986 provides a new legislative framework for building societies and includes provision for a statutory Investor Protection Scheme. This replaces the voluntary scheme set up by the BSA in April 1982 and covers all authorised building societies. The statutory scheme is along similar lines to that which exists for the banks, with two important differences –

Firstly, unlike the banks' scheme the building society Investor Protection Scheme does not have a permanent fund of money. The reason given for this by the Treasury Minister concerned is that "experience suggests that calls on the scheme are likely to be much less frequent than those on behalf of depositors with small licensed deposit takers under the Banking Act Scheme."

Secondly, the maximum level of protection is 90% of the total amount invested in building societies up to £20,000, irrespective of the number of accounts held. The comparable figure for banks is 75 per cent.

In the case of joint accounts, the protection applies to £20,000 per individual.

4. *Building Society Subsidiaries*

The statutory Investor Protection Scheme does not cover building society subsidiaries. Under section 22 of the Building Societies Act 1986, however, a society is under an obligation to meet the liabilities of its subsidiaries and associates.

Summary

The protection which an investor has is predominantly the management of the institution with which funds are placed, together with prudential supervision. The record of building societies for security stands by itself and is not dependent on formal schemes.'

Appendix 2

INVESTORS' PROTECTION SCHEME

LIST OF MEMBERS OF THE BSA

Alliance & Leicester
Barnsley
Bath Investment
Beverley
Bexhill-on-Sea
Birmingham Midshires
Bradford & Bingley
Bristol & West
Britannia
Buckinghamshire
Cambridge
Catholic
Chelsea
Cheltenham & Gloucester
Chesham
Cheshire
Cheshunt
Chorley & District
City & Metropolitan
Clay Cross Benefit
Coventry
Cumberland
Darlington
Derbyshire
Dudley
Dunfermline
Earl Shilton
Ecology
Furness
Gainsborough
Greenwich
Halifax
Hanley Economic

Loughborough
Manchester
Mansfield
Market Harborough
Marsden
Melton Mowbray
Mercantile
Mid-Sussex
Monmouthshire
National & Provincial
National Counties
Nationwide Anglia
Newbury
Newcastle
North of England
Northern Rock
Norwich & Peterborough
Nottingham
Nottingham Imperial
Penrith
Portman
Principality
Progressive
St Pancras
Saffron Walden Herts & Essex
Scarborough
Scottish
Shepshed
Skipton
Southdown
Stafford Railway
Staffordshire
Standard

Harpenden
Haywards Heath, The
Heart of England
Hinckley & Rugby
Holmesdale
Ilkeston Permanent
Ipswich
Kent Reliance
Lambeth
Lancastrian
Leeds & Holbeck
Leeds Permanent
Leek United
Londonderry Provident

Stroud & Swindon
Surrey
Swansea
Teachers'
Tipton & Coseley
Town & Country
Tynemouth
Universal
Vernon
West Bromwich
West Cumbria
Woolwich
Yorkshire

Appendix 3

CREDIT CARD CHARGES AND INTEREST

Credit Cards	Card	P.M.	APR	Fee
AA	Visa	2.195%	(29.7%)	£10
AIB (GB)	Visa	1.80%	(25.5%)	£8
AIB (GB) Direction	Visa	1.80%	(23.8%)	–
AIB (NI)	Visa	1.95%	(26.0%)	–
AIB (NI)	M'cd	1.75%	(23.1%)	–
American Express Optima	Amex	1.76%	(23.3%)	£10
B. of Cyprus (London) Ltd	Visa	1.50%	(19.6%)	–
Bank of Ireland	M'cd	1.955%	(26.15%)	–
Bank of Scotland	M'cd/Visa	1.90%	(28.4%)	£10
Barclays	M'cd/Visa	1.85%	(27.8%)	£8
Beneficial	Visa	2.05%	(27.6%)	–
Chase Manhattan	Visa	1.93%	(25.9%)	–
Clydesdale	M'cd	2.20%	(29.8%)	–
Co-operative	Visa	2.35%	(32.1%)	–
Co-operative Gold	Visa	2.00%	(26.8%)	–
Coutts	Visa	1.65%	(22.3%)	£15
CRS Ltd	Visa	1.85%	(24.6%)	–
First Direct	Visa	1.73%	(24.0%)	£10
Girobank	Visa	2.10%	(28.3%)	–
Girobank Gold	Visa	1.35%	(18.7%)	£36
Halifax B.S.	Visa	1.80%	(26.9%)	£10
Leeds Permanent B.S.	Visa	2.20%	(29.8%)	–
Lloyds	M'cd	1.90%	(26.8%)	£12
Lloyds Gold	M'cd	1.50%	(21.4%)	£40
Midland	M'cd/Visa	2.00%	(28.1%)	£10
National & Provincial B.S.	Visa	1.89/1.81%	(25.2/24.0%)★	–
Nat West	M'cd/Visa	1.90%	(26.8%)	£12
Nat West Primary	Visa	2.00%	(28.3%)	£6
Nat West Mastercard	M'cd	1.85%	(26.1%)	£12
Nat West Gold	Visa	1.60%	(22.7%)	£35
Northern (NI)	M'cd/Visa	2.20%	(29.8%)	–

Robert Fleming/S & P	M'cd/Visa	1.90%	(25.3%)	–
Robert Fleming/S & P	M'cd/Visa	1.69%	(23.7%)	£8
Royal Bank of Scotland	M'cd/Visa	2.00%	(26.8%)	–
Standard Chartered	Visa	2.20%	(29.8%)	–
Town & Country B.S.	Visa	1.98%	(26.5%)	–
TSB	M'cd/Visa	1.95%	(26.0%)	–
Ulster	Visa	2.20%	(29.8%)	–
Unity First	M'cd	2.07%	(27.8%)	–
Yorkshire Bank	Visa	1.95%	(26.0%)	–

* Interest variable – lower rate on higher-debit balances.

Store Cards

	Note	Payment by direct debit		Payment by other methods	
		P.M.	APR	P.M.	APR
Argos		2.65%	(36.8%)	2.95%	(41.7%)
Burton	(1)	2.25%	(30.6%)	2.45%	(33.7%)
C & A		2.40%	(32.9%)	2.50%	(34.4%)
Currys		2.65%	(36.8%)	2.95%	(41.7%)
Debenhams		2.25%	(30.6%)	2.45%	(33.7%)
Dixons		2.65%	(36.8%)	2.95%	(41.7%)
House of Fraser		–	–	2.50%	(34.4%)
John Lewis		–	–	1.80%	(23.8%)
Laura Ashley		2.25%	(30.6%)	2.45%	(33.7%)
Littlewoods		2.37%	(32.4%)	2.75%	(38.4%)
M.F.I.		2.40%	(32.9%)	2.40%	(32.9%)
Marks & Spencer	(3)	2.00%	(26.8%)	2.20%	(29.8%)
Next		2.60%	(36.0%)	2.60%	(36.0%)
Sears Selfridges		2.00%	(26.8%)	2.20%	(29.8%)
Storecard	(2)	2.50%	(34.4%)	2.50%	(34.4%)

(1) Also includes Principles, Top Shop, Top Man, Evans & Dorothy Perkins.
(2) Includes BHS, Habitat, Heals, Richards & Mothercare
(3) Interest charged from date of purchase if A/C not cleared in full

Appendix 4

SUMMARY OF PENSION CHANGES

Date	Event
17 April 1987	Finance Act 1987 introduced a number of changes including: – The salary that could be used to determine the level of tax-free cash was capped at £100,000 – the maximum accrual rate for pension changed to $\frac{1}{30}$th – the basis of accelerated accrual for maximum tax-free cash changed
26 October 1987	Free Standing Additional Voluntary Contributions became available
November 1987	Joint Office Memo 91 – base contribution for determining spreading of special contributions to company pension schemes increased to £20,000
6th April 1988	– Tax charge on repayment of personal contributions for occupational pension schemes increased to 20% – vesting period reduced to 2 years with no age constraint – Contracting out permitted using the Rebate of National Insurance contributions – 2% incentive for contracting out commences – revaluation rate of GMP changes from 8.5% to 7.5% for early leavers Income and Corporation Taxes Act 1988 – codification of Retirement Annuity legislation in Sections 618 to 629 – codification of Personal Pension legislation in Sections 630 to 655 – codification of Retirement Benefit Schemes (Occupational Pensions) legislation in Sections 590 to 612 and schedules 22

and 23

30 June 1988 — Last day on which Retirement Annuities were available.

1 July 1988
- Personal Pension Schemes become available for the first time
- Contracting Out through Personal Pensions available for first time (deeming back provision allowed)

14 March 1989 — Finance Act 1989 introduced a number of changes including:
- introduction of a cap on the amount of salary that could be pensioned under an exempt approved scheme – started at £60,000 – operative immediately for new schemes
- new definition for calculating tax-free lump sum payable
- early retirement allowed from age 50 without restriction

31 May 1989 — Last date on which it was possible to enter an existing occupational pension scheme and not be 'capped'

21 July 1989 — Social Security Act 1989:
- equal treatment for men and women from 1 January 1993 except for: survivors' benefits
                     age at which schemes provide benefits
     NOTE: Barber v Guardian Royal Exchange has
ovverriden this and discrimination is not permissible

17 May 1990 — Judgement of European Court of Justice in case of Barber v GRE.(The Maastricht protocol restricts the implication of the judgment to service after 17 May 1990.)

27 June 1990 — Social Security Act 1990 introduced a number of changes including:
- revaluation of all service for early leavers, from final salary schemes
- inflation proofing of pensions in payment earned after A-Day, up to 5%, for final salary schemes
- utilization of scheme surpluses for inflation proofing pre A-Day pension
- Independent Trustees required for schemes being wound up
- liability of final salary schemes becomes a legal debt on company on wind up of scheme
- limit on the level of self investment for pension schemes

17 August 1990 — Social Security Act Commencement Order (No 1)

           – restriction on distribution of surpluses before inflation proofing of pension benefits

12 November 1990 Independent Trustee must be installed for final Salary Schemes when company is going into liquidation or administration

3 December 1990 Definition and control of amount of self-investment commences – this includes a pension scheme owning property which is leased back to company (transitional provisions apply for existing schemes)

1 January 1991 Revaluation of preserved pension for pre 1985 service comes into force for scheme members who leave after that date

28 February 1991 – Commutation of trivial pension limit raised to £260 pa

1 April 1991 – Pensions Ombudsman opens for business
– New system for automated approval of company pension schemes comes into force

31 July 1991 Last day for registration of existing pension arrangements

5 August 1991 New regulations on investments within small self administered schemes comes into force

1 October 1991 Memo 108
The Inland Revenue introduced some important technical changes to occupational pension schemes
– Provision of continuation life cover no longer available for post–89 scheme members
– Corporation Tax relief threshold for spreading increased to £25,000 (or the regular contribution level) from £20,000
– new spreading rules in force

9 March 1992 Self investment for self-administered schemes. For small self-administered and insured schemes – self investment 50 per cent of funds (except first two years which are limited to 25 per cent of fund).

5 April 1993 2% incentive for contracting out reduced to 1% only for personal pension scheme. No incentive for other schemes.
Rebates for contracted out schemes reduce – new level estimated at 4.8% of banded earnings

Future It is proposed that Final Salary schemes must provide inflation linking of pensions in payment up to 5%. This could increase the funding rate of some schemes by approximately 50%.

Appendix 5

PERSONAL PENSION ARRANGEMENTS 1991/2

Age at 6 April 1991	*Personal pension Scheme* %	*Retirement annuity policy*
Under 36	17.5	17.5
36–45	20.0	17.5
46–50	25.0	17.5
51–55	30.0	20.0
56–60	35.0	22.5
61–74	40.0	27.5
Income limit for pension purposes 1991/2	£71,400	No limit
1992/3	£75,000	No limit

Appendix 6

SUMMARY OF CERTAIN ANNUITY RATES

Basic assumed – pp £10,000, rates as at 20/02/92, payable (m) in advance, 5 year g'tee, escalation as indicated, pensions are p.a.

		Male		Female	
		Level	*5%*	*Level*	*5%*
Ages		*£ p.a.*	*£ p.a.*	*£ p.a.*	*£ p.a.*
1) Single Life					
70		1400.40	1065.60	1252.80	908.40
65		1267.20	918.00	1144.80	788.40
60		1165.20	805.20	1068.00	700.80
55		1086.00	716.40	1014.00	636.00
50		1027.20	648.00	976.80	588.00

2) Pension paid to member and on his/her death payable to the surviving spouse at a level of 100% of the pension at time of death.

Member 70 Spouse 65		1080.00	732.00	1098.00	756.00
65	65	1054.80	703.20	1054.80	703.20
65	60	1015.20	654.00	1028.40	672.00
60	60	998.40	634.80	998.40	634.80
60	55	973.20	598.80	980.40	610.80

3) Pension paid to member and on his/her death payable to the surviving spouse at a level of 50% of the pension at time of death.

Member 70 Spouse 65		1219.20	867.60	1170.00	825.60
65	65	1150.80	795.80	1098.00	744.00
65	60	1128.00	764.40	1083.60	726.00
60	60	1075.20	709.20	1032.00	666.00
60	55	1060.80	686.40	1022.40	652.80

Source: Standard Life, 20 February 1992

Appendix 7.1

NET INCOME

Year	Deposit interest @ 7.5% net of tax £	Expenditure increasing @ 5% £	Balance £
1	13,125	(13,000)	125
2	13,134	(13,650)	(516)
3	13,096	(14,333)	(1,237)
4	13,003	(15,049)	(2,046)
5	12,849	(15,801)	(2,952)
6	12,628	(16,591)	(3,963)
7	12,331	(17,422)	(5,091)
8	11,949	(18,292)	(6,343)
9	11,473	(19,207)	(7,734)
10	10,893	(20,167)	(9,274)
11	10,198	(14,117)	(3,919)
12	9,904	(14,823)	(4,919)
13	9,535	(15,564)	(6,029)
14	9,083	(16,343)	(7,260)
15	8,538	(17,159)	(8,621)
16	7,892	(18,018)	(10,126)
17	7,132	(18,918)	(11,786)
18	6,248	(19,865)	(13,617)
19	5,227	(20,857)	(15,630)
20	4,055	(21,901)	(17,846)

Appendix 7.2

NET INCOME

Year	Deposit interest @ 7.5% net of tax £	Annuity net of tax 100,000 @, say, 7% £	Expenditure increasing @ 5% £	Balance £
1	5,625	7,000	(13,000)	(375)
2	5,597	7,350	(13,650)	(703)
3	5,544	7,718	(14,333)	(1,071)
4	5,464	8,103	(15,049)	(1,482)
5	5,353	8.509	(15,802)	(1,940)
6	5,207	8,934	(16,592)	(2,451)
7	5,023	9,381	(17,421)	(3,017)
8	4,797	9,850	(18,293)	(3,646)
9	4,524	10,342	(19,207)	(4,341)
10	4,198	10,859	(20,166)	(5,109)
11	3,815	11,402	(14,117)	1,100
12	3,897	11,972	(14,823)	1,046
13	3,976	12,571	(15,564)	983
14	4,050	13,200	(16,343)	907
15	4,118	13,860	(17,160)	818
16	4,179	14,552	(18,017)	714
17	4,232	15,280	(18,918)	594
18	4,277	16,044	(19,864)	457
19	4,311	16,846	(20,857)	300
20	4,334	17,689	(21,901)	122

Appendix 8

WHOLE OF LIFE ASSURANCE

With-profit

The initial sum assured is increased by annual and terminal bonuses. The policy can normally be cashed after ten years and any profits will escape income tax, otherwise a higher-rate charge will arise subject to top-slicing relief.

Without-profit

The sum assured remains constant.

Low-cost

Combines a with-profit whole life policy with a decreasing term-assurance policy so that the sum assured will not increase as fast as the with-profit policy but the premiums should be cheaper.

Unit-linked

The sum assured is normally guaranteed for ten years and will thereafter reflect the value of the funds in which the premium is invested. The value of the policy will depend on the performance of the funds. There are various forms of unit-linked policies. Some have a minimum life cover and are more often in the form of a savings plan. Others produce a standard cover under which premiums should remain constant so long as the units appreciate at approximately 10.5 per cent pa. The maximum-cover policies have a guaranteed sum assured but the premiums may need to be increased periodically depending upon the performance of the fund.

Inflation-linked

The above policies can be inflation-proof if the premiums increase in line with the RPI so that the sum assured and likely surrender value will be accordingly increased.

Appendix 9

RESIDENCE

What is meant by the UK?

The UK is defined as England, Wales, Scotland, Northern Ireland and territorial waters. Special rules apply to North Sea workers. Neither the Channel Islands nor the Isle of Man are part of the UK for tax purposes.

Residence

The courts have ruled that 'residence' must have its natural meaning so it is largely but not exclusively a matter of physical presence. It can safely be said that someone who spends more than 182 days in the UK in any tax year is resident for that year, whatever other rules there may be. Note that resident status is determined by reference to a whole tax year, although in years of arrival or departure, individuals may be treated as becoming or ceasing to be resident, or ordinarily resident, from the day of arrival or departure.

Ordinary residence

Ordinary residence is more or less synonymous with habitual residence. A person may be resident without being ordinarily resident (eg where a person who normally lives abroad comes to the UK on holiday or for business reasons and spends more than 182 days in the UK in a particular tax year) or ordinarily resident without being resident (eg where a person who normally lives in the UK spends more than half the tax year on holiday abroad). Most people living in the UK will be resident and ordinarily resident.

People who are resident in the UK but not ordinarily resident may in certain cases enjoy a restricted liability to income tax. On the other hand, individuals who are not resident but are ordinarily resident in the UK are liable to capital gains tax as if they were resident.

Going abroad

A UK-resident and ordinarily resident person remains resident and ordinarily resident if he or she goes abroad for a period of 'occasional residence'. What is meant by occasional residence is not defined but absence for just over one whole tax year has been held to be sufficient to lose residence status, where accompanied by a distinct break in the pattern of life.

A person who goes abroad for an extended period, covering several tax years, but has accommodation available to him or her in the UK is still UK-resident for any year in which *he or she sets foot in the UK*, no matter for how short a period and is ordinarily resident if he or she visits the UK in most years. However, this rule does not apply to the majority of expatriates, who are people who have left the UK for full-time employment abroad.

Working abroad

A UK-resident person who leaves the UK for full-time employment abroad for a period that will extend to at least one full tax year is normally regarded as ceasing to be either resident or ordinarily resident from the day after departure provided that:

- all the duties of the employment are carried out abroad or any duties carried out in the UK can be regarded as incidental and

- visits back to the UK during the period abroad amount to no more than six months in any one tax year (the 183 day rule again) and to no more than three months per tax year on average.

Provided these conditions are observed, it does not matter whether the person has any accommodation available in the UK.

Although at first glance, it might appear tax-efficient to lose UK-residence status, this is not always the case. Many countries' income tax rates are higher than those of the UK. In the special case of those going to work abroad on short-term assignments, it pays to remain UK-resident while at the same time being predominantly away from the UK for a period of at least 365 days.

Dual residence

The fact that someone is resident in the UK under UK law does not exclude his or her being resident in another country, under that country's laws, at the same time. This is known as dual residence, since it is unlikely that more than two countries are involved at any one time. This could result in double taxation of the same income. Where the other country has a double tax treaty with the UK, however, the treaty will contain rules for deciding in which of the two countries the individual is resident for the purposes of the treaty.

Appendix 10

DOMICILE

The meaning of domicile

Unlike residence, which is a criterion used by most countries, domicile is a concept peculiar to the UK and to some other countries with legal systems stemming from our own. An individual has his or her domicile where he/she has permanent roots.

When we are born, we acquire a domicile of origin, which is the domicile of our parents. It is difficult to establish another domicile (a domicile of choice). To do so, a person must normally sever all important ties with his or her domicile of origin and prove the intention to settle permanently in another country – buying a burial plot in the new country is usually only one indication!

Having a home in another country, or even spending most of one's life there, is not enough. For example, a person with a UK domicile who has worked and lived abroad all his or her adult life, will retain his/her UK domicile if he/she has the intention of returning at one time or another and living the rest of his/her life in the UK.

Note that, strictly speaking, there is no such thing as domicile in the UK. Individuals can be domiciled in either England and Wales or in Scotland or Northern Ireland, but for tax purposes, there is no difference between the three and the phrase 'UK domicile' will be used as a convenient shorthand.

Appendix 11

COMPARATIVE COSTINGS FOR BUSINESS CAR USAGE FOR TAX YEAR 1991/2

CONTRACT HIRE REPORT FOR IVOR CONTRACT HIRE

Personal data

1.	Employee's name	Ivor Contract Hire
2.	Top rate of income tax applicable	25.00%
3.	Employee's company car	VW Golf GTI
4.	Engine capacity	1,796 cc
5.	Original cost when new	£12,500
6.	Age of car at next 5 April (in years)	1 year
7.	Average fuel consumption (mpg)	28
8.	Total annual mileage	16,666
9.	Business proportion of annual mileage	22.00%
10.	Usual price paid per gallon (inc. VAT)	£2.25

Company car

	Company car £	Personally leased car £
Employer's cost	6,893	6,893
Employee's cost	1,024	16

Appendix 12

FLEXIBLE BENEFITS

Name: Benefits Allowance: 4000
Job Title: Benefits Pre-Allocated: 1700
Salary: 20000   Flexible Benefits Points: 2300

Health Benefits	Period	Unit	Cost per Unit	Allocated	Minimum Choice	Maximum Choice	Your Selection
Annual Leave	Annual	per day	40	600	600	1200	
Pension	Annual	per £500	100	750	750	1500	
Death in Service	Annual	cover 1×sal	50	100	100	200	
Permanent Health	Annual	£2500	125	250	250	750	
Medical Expenses	Annual		200				
+ spouse			200		200	600	
+ child			200				
Medical Check	Annual	per visit	100		100	200	
Travel Benefits							
Car	3 Years	£10/month	30		450	900	
Season Ticket Loan	Annual	per £100	10		40	300	
Lifestyle Benefits							
Mortgage Assistance	Annual	per £1,000	75		375		
Childcare Provision	Annual	per £100	50		250		
School Fees	Annual	per £100	50		1200		
Financial Counselling	Annual	per visit	50		50	200	
Leisure Benefits							
Meal provision	Annual	day/week	50		50	250	
Corporate Membership	Annual	per £10	5				
Personal Development	Annual	per £10	5				
Clothes	Annual	per £10	5		50		
Dry Cleaning	Annual	per £10	5		50		
Use of company assets	Annual						
Share Benefits							
Share options		period of scheme					
						Total	

Appendix 13

THE TAX TREATMENT OF TRUSTS

One of the major problems now relates to the capital gains tax arising on a gift. While a gift of business property (including shares in private companies) can attract holdover relief, a gift of an investment property could give rise to a capital gains tax charge. It may be appropriate to gift the property to a discretionary trust so that the gain can be held over, but care needs to be taken here. The gift will be chargeable to inheritance tax but if it falls within the nil rate band this may not be a problem. The trust can then be broken within ten years to avoid any inheritance tax charge.

As no inheritance tax arises in respect of assets passing from the deceased to the surviving spouse, it may not be advisable to give assets pregnant with gains to a spouse during the donor's lifetime. This is because when the surviving spouse comes to sell the assets, his or her base cost for capital gains tax will be the original cost of the asset to the donor (it is as if the donor were making the disposal). As there is no capital gains tax on death, it is more efficient for the increase in value to take place tax-free in the deceased's estate. It is possible that a company may need to be restructured so as to avoid any investments when the gift is made. This is because the investments in a trading company can restrict holdover relief. This is a complex matter and much care needs to be taken.

Interest in possession trust

A gift of assets into an interest in possession trust for the benefit of children is a potentially exempt transfer so that no inheritance tax is payable unless the settlor/donor dies within seven years of the gift. The beneficiary who has the interest in possession is treated for inheritance tax purposes as if he or she were the unconditional owner of the underlying assets, so there is no charge to inheritance tax if the assets are distributed to him or her. However, it also means that the assets are regarded as part of his or her estate so that if he or she dies while still having the interest, the estate will bear an inheritance tax liability in respect of the trust assets, even if under the terms of the trust deed, they are to be distributed to other beneficiaries (the remaindermen).

The capital gains made by an interest in possession trust are currently taxed at a flat rate of 25 per cent.

A beneficiary who has an interest in possession can dispose of it like any other asset.

The trustees of an interest in possession trust pay income tax at the basic rate on the trust's income. However, the income is then taxed on the beneficiary so that higher-rate tax may then be payable. The beneficiary can use the income tax paid on his or her share of the income as tax credit, obtaining repayment where appropriate.

Discretionary trust

A gift into a discretionary trust is not potentially exempt and is a chargeable transfer subject to inheritance tax. As with other chargeable transfers, there will be no inheritance tax to pay if the value of the gift together with other chargeable transfers in the last seven years does not go over the donor's nil rate band.

For the very reason that a gift into a discretionary trust is immediately liable to inheritance tax (even if at the zero rate), holdover relief for capital gains tax is still available. For this reason, the discretionary trust has enjoyed a revival since capital gains tax holdover was restricted in 1989. No holdover is possible, for example, for a gift into an interest in possession trust.

The income of a discretionary trust suffers tax at 35 per cent (the basic rate plus an additional rate of ten per cent). Any beneficiary who receives an income distribution from the trust can treat the 35 per cent as a credit against his or her own liability and get a repayment where appropriate.

The capital gains of a discretionary trust are taxed at a flat rate of 35 per cent.

Accumulation and maintenance trust

A gift into an accumulation and maintenance trust is treated as if it were a gift into an interest in possession trust – ie it is potentially exempt. Neither is there a tenth anniversary charge or a charge on distributions of the trust capital to beneficiaries when they become absolutely entitled to it.

As with a gift to an interest in possession trust, no holdover relief is available to defer any capital gains tax payable on a gift into the trust unless it is a gift of a 'business asset' and the trust income is chargeable to 35 per cent income tax.

Given its dual status as a discretionary trust with an interest in possession trust inheritance tax treatment, the accumulation and maintenance trust is the most flexible vehicle for passing assets to children and grandchildren while retaining control over those assets. This is particularly attractive in the case of shares in a family company. The beneficiaries could be given an interest in income when they reached 25 but entitlement to the capital (the shares themselves) could be deferred until, say, the age of 40. By appointing him or herself as one of the trustees, the donor could retain control over company decisions, such as whether to pay a dividend, for example.

The 1991 consultative document on trust taxation

In March 1991, the Inland Revenue published a consultative document on changes in the taxation of UK-resident trusts – the result of a review initiated by the government in 1988. Together with changes in the offshore trust regime, these measures represent a fundamental upheaval of the way trusts are taxed and hence their use in personal financial planning.

Briefly, the consultative document includes proposals to:

- Replace the additional-rate charge on discretionary trusts with a general higher-rate charge (increasing the top tax rate from 35 per cent to 40 per cent) on the undistributed income of all trusts

- Give beneficiaries who receive discretionary distributions of income a tax credit at the basic rate only

- Tax trust gains at the trust's top rate of income tax (as is currently the rule with individuals) after allowing for a common basic-rate band for income and gains

- Adopt the capital gains definition of residence for income tax purposes also. This would have the effect of making many trusts currently offshore UK-resident, bringing them into the full UK tax net.

The government asked for responses to the document to be submitted by 30 September 1991. This suggested that, if there is widespread agreement (or at least, no widespread opposition), legislation may be introduced in the March 1992 Finance Act (election always permitting). However, the 1992 Budget did not include these proposals.

A review of all existing trust arrangements (both resident and offshore) should already have been undertaken to prepare for any likely changes, which ought not to be retrospective.

Appendix 14

CHARITABLE GIVING – POINTS TO WATCH

To qualify for tax exemption, a 'charity' must be registered as such with the Charity Commissioners for England and Wales. Scotland and Northern Ireland have their own charity law, although as far as tax is concerned, the law is uniform throughout the UK. It will have a registration number and is obliged to quote it on all its stationery, etc. Before making what you hope will be a tax-beneficial donation, check with the charity itself that it has charitable status.

Remember that the everyday understanding of the word 'charity' does not always translate directly into law. Several organizations that we might associate with charitable work in the ordinary sense of the word are denied charitable status in law because, for example, they may have partly political or quasi-political objectives. Conversely, certain bodies and institutions that members of the public would not normally associate with the word 'charity', eg leading public schools, have charitable status under law.

If the charity does not spend all of its income for charitable purposes, there may be a restriction of its own tax exemption and a 'clawback' of the tax relief given to the donor. This is an anti-avoidance measure and the vast majority of public and *bona fide* private charities should not be affected.

Appendix 15

DEEDS OF COVENANT

A deed of covenant is a legally-binding promise by a person or persons to make regular payments of money to another person(s) usually for nothing in return. It is a way of legally transferring income from the covenantor (the transferor) to the covenantee (the transferee).

The form a deed must take differs between the three legal jurisdictions in the UK, as follows:

- In *England and Wales*, a deed of covenant must be signed and witnessed by a single witness. There is no longer any need for it to be 'sealed and delivered', but it must be plain on the face of the document that it is a deed (heading it 'deed of covenant' will do)

- In *Scotland*, a deed must be witnessed by two witnesses unless it is typed or printed and the covenantor writes 'adopted as holograph' above his or her signature, in which case, no witness is necessary. Sealing by a physical person, as opposed to a company, has never been necessary in Scotland

- In *Northern Ireland*, a deed must be signed and witnessed by a single witness and 'sealed and delivered'.

There are further requirements a deed must meet before it is tax effective:

- It must be for nothing in return (a limited exception is available for charities like the National Trust, which give members free access to their property or some other benefit of little monetary value)

- It must be in favour of a charity (covenants made after 14 March 1988 in favour of individuals no longer attract tax relief)

- It must be capable of lasting for more than three years. This does not mean that it must last three years (eg if the covenantor dies after two years, this does not actually result in a clawback of relief), but it does mean that anything in the deed definitely limiting its duration to a shorter period will render it invalid for tax purposes

- The payments must be made out of income and cannot be instalments of capital.

It is important that no payment is made before the deed is completed as the tax relievable payments should be made within the term of the deed.

Some covenants are expressed in 'after tax' terms, so that the payment actually made by the covenantor remains fixed, whatever the basic rate of tax. A covenant to pay '£75 after deduction of the basic rate of income tax' would represent £100 of income to the charity and a £100 deduction from taxable income to the covenantor while the basic rate was 25 per cent, but if the basic rate were to be reduced to 20 per cent (which is still the current government's commitment), the equivalent gross amount would be:

$$£75 \times 100/(100 - 20) = £93.75$$

Some covenants contain an 'escape clause', under which the covenantor reserves the right to cease paying if certain contingencies happen (eg he or she decides not to renew membership of the particular charity concerned). Until 20 March 1990, the Inland Revenue accepted this type of terminable covenant as valid but it then announced, in statement of practice SP4/90, that it was to stop doing so on the grounds that the covenant was terminable at the covenantor's own volition, which made it invalid. However, the tax status of these covenants already in existence at that time was not being revoked. Anyone contemplating the inclusion of an escape clause in a new covenant should therefore take professional advice.

On the other hand, some covenantors want to protect themselves against falls in their income which would make the covenant commitment burdensome and do so by inserting a formula in the covenant linking payments to a certain level of their income. So, for example, they may promise to pay 'one quarter of my income before tax'. As long as the amount of the payment can be precisely determined, the Inland Revenue accepts this kind of covenant since the factors that determine the payment are largely outside the covenantor's control.

However, linking the covenanted payments to the dividends of a close company under the covenantor's control can cause complications, since it is within the covenantor's power to reduce or stop the payments altogether. In practice, provided the company is already an established one, the Inland Revenue usually has no objection, but setting up a new close company at the same time as executing a linked deed of covenant is not advisable.

The Inland Revenue has published model deeds of covenant for the three legal jurisdictions of the UK. Strictly speaking, a new deed of covenant must be drawn up by a solicitor and professional advice should be taken.

Appendix B

STOY HAYWARD

UNITED KINGDOM OFFICES

BELFAST
Franklin House
12 Brunswick Street
Belfast BT2 7GE
Tel: (0232) 439009
Fax: (0232) 439010
Contact: Frank McCartan

BIRMINGHAM
Waterloo House
20 Waterloo Street
Birmingham B2 5TF
Tel: (021) 643 4024
Fax: (021) 631 2400
Contact: Richard Thompson

BRISTOL
Oakfield House
Oakfield Grove
Clifton,Bristol BS8 2BN
Tel: (0272) 237000
Fax: (0272) 732741
Contact: Richard Mannion

GLASGOW
James Sellars House
144 West George Street
Glasgow G2 2HG
Tel: (041) 331 2811
Fax: (041) 332 6148
Contact: Gordon Armour

LEEDS
Century House
29 Clarendon Road
Leeds LS2 9PG
Tel: (0532) 341381
Fax: (0532) 425753
Contact: Elizabeth Lennox

LONDON
8 Baker Street
London W1M 1DA
Tel: (071) 486 5888
Fax: (071) 487 3686
Contact: Barry Stillerman

MANCHESTER
Peter House
St Peter's Square
Manchester M1 5BH
Tel: (061) 228 6791
Fax: (061) 228 1545
Contact: Stephen Halstead

NORWICH
Windsor Terrace
76-80 Thorpe Road
Norwich NR1 1BA
Tel: (0603) 620241
Fax: (0603) 630224
Contact: Murray Graham

NOTTINGHAM
Foxhall Lodge
Gregory Boulevard
Nottingham NG7 6LH
Tel: (0602) 626578
Fax: (0602) 691043
Contact: Kevin Derbyshire

PETERBOROUGH
Garrick House
76–80 High Street
Old Fletton
Peterborough PE2 8DR
Tel: (0733) 342444
Fax: (0733) 54704
Contact: Adrian Ansdell

SUNDERLAND
19 Borough Road
Sunderland SR1 1LA
Tel: (091) 565 0565
Fax: (091) 514 2083
Contact: Ian Rowan

Appendix C

STOY HAYWARD

INTERNATIONAL OFFICES

Stoy Hayward is the UK Member firm of Horwath International:

Andorra
Argentina
Australia
Austria

Belgium
Bermuda
Bhutan
Bolivia
Brazil

Canada
Cayman Islands
Channel Islands
Chile
China (People's Republic)
Cyprus

Denmark
Dominican Republic

Egypt
Ethiopia

Fiji
Finland
France

Germany
Greece
Guatemala

Haiti
Hong Kong
Hungary

India
Indonesia
Ireland
Israel
Italy

Jamaica
Japan

Kenya
Korea

Lebanon
Luxembourg

Malaysia
Malta
Mexico
Monaco
Morocco

Nepal
Netherlands
New Zealand
Nigeria
Norway

Pakistan
Panama
Paraguay
Philippines
Portugal
Puerto Rico

Saudi Arabia
Singapore
Spain
Sri Lanka
Sweden
Switzerland

Taiwan
Thailand
Turkey
Turks & Caicos Islands

United Arab Emirates
United Kingdom
United States of America

Zimbabwe

Appendix D

STOY HAYWARD

SERVICES OF THE FIRM

Accountancy & audit

Accounting Services
Company Secretarial
Computer Bureau
Family Business Unit
Specialist Audits
Statutory Audits

Financial advice

Corporate Disposals
Corporate Finance and Investigations
Entertainment Industry
Financial Planning
Mergers, Acquisitions and Flotations
Personal Financial and Pensions Planning
Raising Finance
Trust Management
Venture and Development Capital

Tax

Business Expansion Scheme
Corporate Taxation
International Tax Planning
Personal Taxation
Tax Investigations
UK Tax Planning
VAT and Customs Duty Planning

Corporate recovery & insolvency

Administrations

Bankruptcies
Corporate Recovery and Viability Studies
Investigations
Liquidations
Receiverships
Voluntary Arrangements

Consultancy services

Advanced Manufacturing
Business Location Services
Information Technology
Corporate Strategy
European Business Unit
Executive Search and Selection
Litigation Support
Feasibility Studies
Grants
Management Training
Marketing Studies
Organization Reviews
Project Management
Total Quality Management

STOY HAYWARD FRANCHISING SERVICES

Franchise feasibility and strategy
Management Recruitment
Market Studies
Computerization
Raising Finance
Project Management
Royalty and Performance Auditing

STOY BENEFIT CONSULTING LIMITED

Remuneration and Dividend Planning
Profit Related Pay
Pension Planning
Car benefits, and fringe benefits generally
Flexible Benefits
Employee and Executive Share Schemes
Employee Share Ownership Plans (ESOPs)

Phantom Share Schemes
Job Evaluation
Cash incentive schemes and deferred compensation plans
Personal Equity Plans, including single company plans (CoPEPs)

HORWATH CONSULTING

Specialist advice to the Hotel, Tourism & Leisure Industry
Market and Financial Feasibility Studies
Project Appraisal
Strategic Planning
National and Regional Tourism Planning
Marketing and Promotional Strategies
Financial Planning
Management Accounting, Control and Reporting Systems
Operational Reviews and Profit Improvement Studies
Manpower Planning and Training
Executive Selection
Planning Enquiries, Arbitration and Legal Support

Appendix E

STOY HAYWARD PUBLICATIONS

CLIENT SERVICE BROCHURES

Avoid Personal Bankruptcy – Act Now!
Business Information Services
Corporate Recovery & Insolvency Services
Litigation Support
Personal Financial Planning
Property & Economic Development Services
Services to the Franchisee
Services to the Property Industry
Stoy Hayward Review 1990–91
The Art of Consulting
The Franchise Opportunity
US Expatriate Services
Your Family Business – Planning for the Future

TECHNICAL PUBLICATIONS

	Price
Audit Guide (co-published with Butterworths)	£27.50
Business Expansion Scheme	
Business Tax Guide 1991/92 (co-published with Kogan Page)	£14.95
Commentary on the Budget (annual)	
Daily Telegraph Pensions Guide (co-published with Kogan Page)	£10.95
Effective Staff Incentives (co-published with Kogan Page)	£12.95
European Tax Data Card 1991/92	
Getting into Europe (co-published with Kogan Page)	£35.00
HAC Guide to Taxation of the Bloodstock Industry (co-published with Tattersalls)	£20.00
Horwath International Tax Planning Manual (published by CCH)	£250.00
How to Franchise Your Business (co-published with Franchise World)	£7.95
Inheritance Tax – a practical guide – 3rd Edition (co-published with Kogan Page)	£8.99
Model Financial Statements for Public and Private Companies	£29.95
Property Tax Planning Manual (co-published with Butterworths)	£24.95
Independent Taxation of Married Couples	

Tax Opportunities and Pitfalls 1991-92 (annual)
Tax Data Card 1991-92 (annual)
The Stoy Hayward Guide to Family Business (co-published with Kogan
    Page)   £12.95
The Stoy Hayward USM Yearbook 1990 (co-published with Macmillan)   £95.00
VAT & Property (co-published with Butterworths)   £35.00
Venture Capital 1992 (annual)

SURVEYS

A Study to Determine the Reasons for Failure of Small Businesses in
    the United Kingdom   £20.00
Goodbye GTi, Farewell Alloy Wheels   £75.00
Improving Property Accounts – Summary
                          Report   £40.00
IT Rulebook
Managing the Family Business in the UK – Summary
                          UK – Report   £25.00
Staying the Course – Survival Characteristics of the Family Owned
    Business   £35.00
The Effectiveness of Share Incentive Schemes (co-produced
    with BMSI) – Summary   £425.00
               – Report
The Essence of USM Success   £40.00

Newsletters

European Update (quarterly)
Family Business Newsletter
Personal Financial Planner (periodical)
Showcase (Employee Benefits Update) (periodical)
VAT News (Periodical)

HORWATH CONSULTING

Brochures

Franchising in the Economy 1991   £55.00
Horwath Consulting Statement of Experience:
    Tourism, Hotel, Leisure & Related Industries
Horwath Consulting/English Tourist Board Hotel
Occupancy Survey (monthly and annual)   £275.00
Shaping Europe's Hotel, Tourism & Leisure Industry
Shaping the Future of the Hotel, Tourism & Leisure Industry

Hotel Industry Studies

Annual Hotel Industry Studies for Individual Countries	POA
United Kingdom Hotel Industry (annual)	£40.00
Worldwide Hotel Industry study (annual)	£50.00

Technical Publications

An examination of Tourism Investment Incentives	£10.00
Guidelines to Hotel & Leisure Project Financing	
Horwath Book of Tourism (published by Macmillan)	£40.00
Hotel of the Future: Strategies and Action Plan	
(International Hotel Association) – Summary	£15.00
– Full Report	£250.00
Hotel Accounts and their audit (published by ICAEW)	£25.00
London's Tourist Accommodation in the 1990's – Summary	£15.00
– Full Report	£100.00
Tourism – A Portrait (published to mark the firm's silver jubilee)	£26.25
Uniform system of accounts for (published by AHMA) – Restaurants	£10.00
– Hotels	£16.00

Newsletters

Horwath Business Review (on the Hotel, Tourism & Leisure Industry) (quarterly)

Unless denoted otherwise all publications are available from
  Stoy Hayward, free of charge.

INDEX